Poetics of Encryption
Art and the Technocene
Nadim Samman

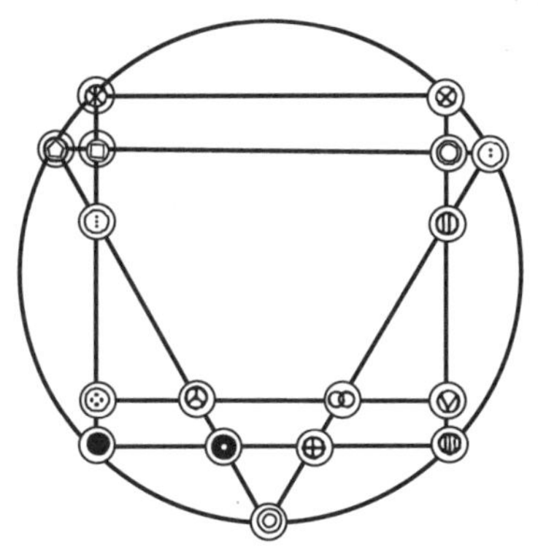

HATJE
CANTZ

Dark Arts

For Dehlia

*God is an infinite sphere whose center is everywhere
and whose circumference is nowhere.*[*]

  — Nicholas of Cusa

Contemporary life plays out amid a profusion of technical systems whose inner workings are obscure—if not locked. There is no master key. And yet, this encrypted world must be borne *somehow.* Fortunately, the term "encryption" contains a latent spatial imaginary. And this imaginary yields insight into what is hidden by and within tech. In the face of information asymmetries, and when cryptographic de-coding cannot (or does not) happen, this perspective affords aesthetic purchase.

A spatial imaginary enables *poiesis*—the sense of making or creation which lies at the core of art—even in the face of the uncrackable. If an encrypted matter cannot be opened up and inspected, it may yet be rescored. *Poiesis* supplies narrative and pictorial inroads, a kind of endogenous psychological map of strange terrain—or, at least, certain points of orientation. While reviewing select artworks from the last decade, this book runs counter to Big Tech's erroneous claims regarding a new culture of transparency and openness—showcasing, instead, a *poetics of encryption.*

The word "encryption" is built around the image of a crypt, as a primary figure for an enclosed or hidden place. Harking back to ancient funerary practices, the "crypt" *contains* a latent history that far predates modern technology. As an implicit corollary, the question of burial techniques, and the ritual and performative aspect of sealing-up are raised (like the dead) by the term itself. A crypt, by definition, contains a body. Negotiating its built structure thus activates drama concerning whether the buried figure can rest in peace, whether it may be disinterred by a sanctioned practice, such as archeology, or de-crypted by grave robbing.

A crypt is an occult place. The knowledge that it contains is esoteric, and may be gleaned only through recondite or suspect methods. As a work of criticism, this book oscillates between both poles, but leans more towards the latter. If cryptography exemplifies a lawful right-hand path for dealing with digital encryption—a scientific method—then *poiesis* and its interpretation pursue the left-hand path. It is the road of images and their dynamic imagination. This path may seem suspect if judged incorrectly. Yet, as the philosopher Gaston Bachelard reminds us, "Images are not concepts. They do not withdraw into their meaning. Indeed, they tend to go beyond their meaning."[1] Furthermore, "If the image that is *present* does not make us think of one that is *absent,* if an image does not determine an abundance—an explosion—of unusual images, then there is no imagination."[2] Through such abundance, the alienating, guarded, or jealous implications of encrypted domains are revalued—a different operation from unlocking.

Lying partially buried within the term "encryption," the image of the crypt does not only *hold* a store of latent spatial figures and language. It overflows with supplementary frames of reference. Indeed, the crypt image is the wellspring of a whole poetics, "an *aspiration toward new images.*"[3] It is like a seed that, when properly cultivated, bears much fruit. While establishing a familiar architectural figure through which to speak about relations to encrypted space, it goes even further, emanating tokens for death, afterlife, and spirit. If the sublime object of a closed grave is the deceased's soul, a cryptic imaginary introduces high stakes for what may lay buried in digitally encrypted domains, namely, an embodied, personified point of reference—the inscription of an individual's "essence" or ontological status within the technological field. Here, the spiritual and political converge.

This said, endeavors to make poetic sense of encryption must reckon with gloom and spooky affects. For the crypt image does not merely contain darkness, safely, in the manner of spent nuclear fuel enclosed within a holding system. Whenever tapped, even slightly (and especially by Nietzsche's tuning fork), it disgorges both optic metaphors and unenlightened effluvia. The latter washes over the cultural scene—a wave of mysteries, monsters, and hauntings that *should be* out of step with today's scientism but which, in fact, track it like a shadow. As we shall see, more tech breeds more encryption. And with it, *Mehr Dunkelheit.*

According to the political economist Sarah Myers West, "Surfacing and making visible the imaginaries we develop around encryption provides an entry point to understanding the implications of encryption technologies in a networked society."[4] These imaginaries influence perceptions of "what encryption *is,* what it *does,* and what it *should do.*"[5] Endeavoring to broaden the scope of her analysis, before taking on national security and state secrecy, West sketches a brief genealogy of cryptography—from Egyptian religious hieroglyphics, to the Renaissance occultist and inventor of steganography, Johannes Trithemius. In her view, this esoteric history still colors public attitudes. As she has it, "the association between cryptography and the occult is powerful: despite the efforts of cryptographers over centuries to establish the practice as a science, it retains the residual mark of these dark associations."[6] But what are these residual marks, beyond a general suspicion of secret practices? West's article does not venture

   Poetics of Encryption

any further, instead moving onto questions of policy. As we shall see, encryption's occult imaginary abides today—indeed, flourishes—in an updated and rather surprising iconography that does not only address code but all inscrutable infrastructures.

This book is structured with three sections; each is a meditation upon a particular mode of embodied relation to the encrypted "interior." These are imaginative exercises that result in a cascade of images. The artworks and associations that make up each cascade imply distinct models for where an intelligent human is placed *vis-à-vis* the realm of digital secrets and/or hidden mechanisms. The first concerns being *locked in:* burial or entombment within a techno-logical grave, and the labor of escape from this situation. The second explores the affective response to being intellectually *locked out* of ubiquitous consumer and industrial products; neither archeologist nor effective grave robber. The third offers an anatomy of strange effects associated with a scrambling of inside and outside, open and closed—oblique perspectives that are associated with being *locked down.*

That said, the more visible titles of each section deploy a metaphor of darkness classically associated with what is hidden from view. Following the Bachelardian logic of imagination, these dark tokens "go beyond" concepts of the *locked* while similarly emanating from the primary image of the crypt: "I. Black Site," "II. Black Box," and "III. Black Hole." Each serves as a tag for the way encrypted objects are negotiated in the course of everyday life, and the way they order experience. If these names are not passwords, then they are incan-tations: spells that structure the discussion of visual art's interest in what cannot be seen, through a magical focus on sensory aporia.

"Black Site" opens with Jon Rafman's 2010 refashioning of the myth of Orpheus and Eurydice, setting up a discussion of who or what has been stolen away—through consideration of works by Revital Cohen and Tuur Van Balen, Lance Wakeling, Trevor Paglen, Simon Denny, Evan Roth, Julian Charrière, Mary Mattingly, Amy Balkin, Suzanne Treister, Vladan Joler, Critical Art Ensemble, Juliana Cerqueira Leite, Roger Hiorns, and Tom McCarthy.

"Black Box" unfastens with a melancholy rumination on the rhomboid in Albrecht Dürer's 1514 masterpiece, *Melencolia I.* The blurry outlines of a face appear on the surface of this object, presaging the following artists' reflections on the inscrutable: Carsten Nicolai, Félix Luque Sánchez, Britta Thie, Susanna Hertrich, Beny Wagner, Tillman Hornig, Adam Harvey, Mimi Onuoha, Joy Buolamwini, Timnit

Gebru, American Artist, Kate Crawford and Trevor Paglen, Hito Steyerl, Zach Blas, Chim↑Pom, and Eva and Franco Mattes.

Finally, "Black Hole" unseals a monstrous triangulation between the myths of Bitcoin and QAnon, astrophysics, and the riddle of the Sphinx. The artists discussed do not escape its event horizon, including Jonas Staal, Émilie Brout and Maxime Marion, Omsk Social Club, Ed Fornieles, Joshua Citarella, UBERMORGEN, Brad Troemel, Jalal Toufic, Eva and Franco Mattes, Paola Pivi, Marguerite Humeau, Davide Quayola, Egor Kraft, and Nora Al-Badri.

But what of the term "Technocene"? It denotes a way of thinking about *the contemporary* from the perspective of art, addressing how the overwhelming prevalence of technology in all corners of life (and death) becomes the subject of cultural reckoning. A significant feature of this moment is a preoccupation with periodization—not least "Anthropocene," "Capitalocene," "Chthulucene," and so on—which is arguably a result of tech both preserving and putting to work everything that can be datafied: *unsettling our place in time.* The Technocene is punctuated by anachronism: from a cryogenically frozen human head awaiting reanimation, to the roars of prehistoric mammals echoing through museums; from a zombie social media profile, still active after the passing of its subject, to the DNA of ancient—unknown—viruses, revived in laboratories; indeed, from a return to archaic religious affect in the presence of consumer electronics, to the possible next moves of a powerful AI. Such examples, among countless others, testify to the Technocene as a simultaneous provisional assembly of disparate historical traces, encountered in flux.

In the context of a *poetics of encryption,* the term "Technocene" fixes upon the scrambled or open experience of temporality that is generated by a landscape of black sites, black boxes, and black holes. It names the phenomenon of cultural superposition—simultaneous location and dislocation in time. In the Technocene, what has been buried, or has died, manifests in the present, both as what it is (or was) and as something new. Perhaps as a consequence, while the Technocene is not the "end of history," it is epitomized by intensive efforts to *be in the now.* This dynamic unites new-age seekers and the non-human agent, scratching at the walls of its chrysalis.

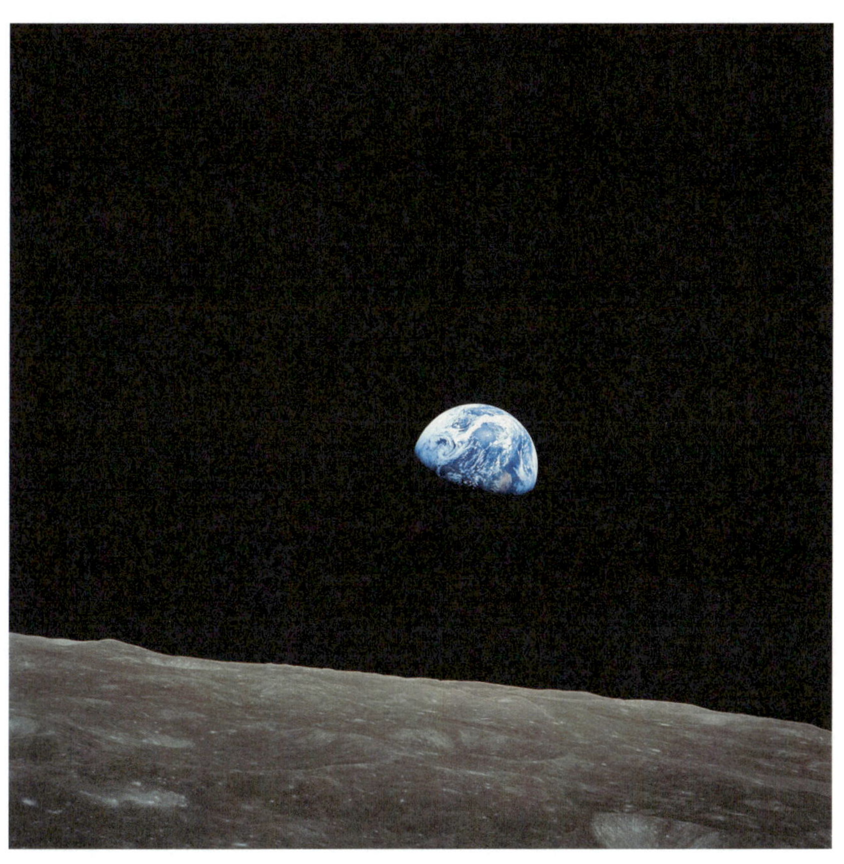

Earthrise, December 24, 1968

Black Site

"O God, I could be bounded in a nutshell and count myself a king of infinite space, were it not that I have bad dreams."[1] Hamlet speaks for all of us—bounded, surrounded, enclosed, inside this thing. And it could feel like infinite space. It *could,* save for bad dreaming. But what is this nutshell of ours?

There are various answers, depending on the dream. Let us imagine a shell for a king of infinite space: in some feudal past, it was conceivable as a suit of armor or a castle, protecting an inner sanctum to better enable foreign conquest. Today, a contemporary techno-shell likewise expedites the projection of will. But its complex dimensions prove difficult to encapsulate in a coherent image. Any representation of it must simultaneously contain a person sitting behind a control panel, in Nevada, operating a Reaper drone above Iraq; and another, at home in Bangalore, ordering home-delivery kombucha via mobile phone app. In fact, both figures—and many more besides—are part of an assemblage that has come to encircle the whole earth, while serving as a framework for life within.

This assemblage forms an "accidental megastructure": an epic prosthesis for the exercise of power. As Benjamin Bratton has elaborated, planetary-scale computation introduces new forms of sovereignty and geopolitics.[2] Would-be kings of this planetary nutshell dream of moving virtually anywhere, and having any interaction, while ensconced in their redoubts. They dream of casting influence across

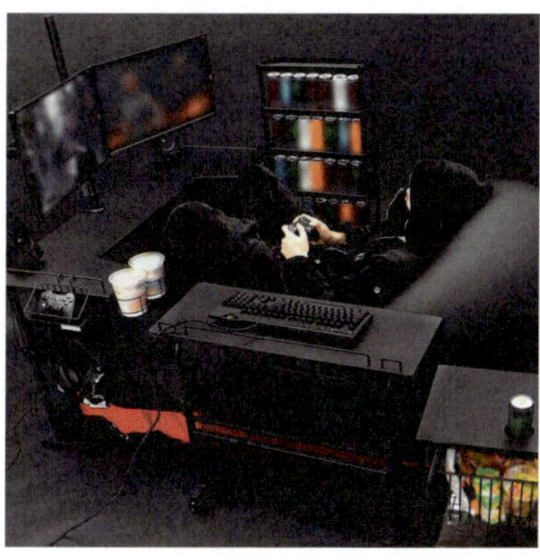

Bauhütte Gaming Bed
Bed Desk BHD-1200BD,
Adjustable Headboard
BHB-950, Gaming Suit
"Ninja Onesie" HFD-4G,
Gaming Bean Bag BHB 180,
Headphone
Hanger BHP-S100,
Energy Wagon BHS-430EW,
Slim Bottle Rack BHS-150,
Long Side Table BHT-800S,
Clothing Rack Table BHT-830

the surface of the system by remote control. Not for nothing do the lords of techno-feudalism dream of conquering new worlds.[3] The ascendant sovereign does not have to move; they are always already everywhere by networked proxy, influential but obscure. The shell externalizes their volition. Indeed, it is a precondition for the emergence of certain desires, supplying technical support for a particular kind and scale of human *being:* a scaffold for ambitions that cannot be extracted from its edifice and atmosphere without losing viability. A hard nut to crack.

Another dream: In medieval England, an anchorite was a person (usually a woman) who was bricked into a small cell attached to a church (known as an "anchorhold"), to pass the rest of her life in intense prayer and contemplation.[4] Having received the funeral office from a priest just prior to enclosure, such persons were considered dead to the world.[5] Typically, their cells contained three small apertures: the first allowing for waste export and the receipt of food and water. Another, covered by an opaque veil, would let in air from outside. The last, at eye level, known as a "hagioscope," afforded a view of Mass and the partake of Eucharist when its shutter was opened. Within this living tomb, the inhabitant sought visitation from angels and God. Thus, the anchorhold was an architectural focusing device for divine light and religious illumination. Though locked in, the anchorite's dream was to have her life enlarged through communion with an infinite being, a goal pursued not despite the cell's physical shell but *through* it.

Today, we can discern a secular parallel in the phenomenon of *hikikomori*—a Japanese term that describes the acute social withdrawal, isolation, and confinement of shut-ins, whose only significant connection to the outside world is through the Internet and video games.[6] Like the anchorites, they trade physical mobility for concentration on a seemingly infinite dimension—the virtual scene. In so doing, they exemplify the enticement of the screen as hagioscopic aperture; the promise of rebirth in multiplayer game worlds and social media platforms; the scroll's endless horizon; limitless hyperlinks; felicitous visitation by suggested content; and home delivery. They are avatars for a broader social fantasy that seeks virtual replacement for life beyond the hearth.[7]

Were it not that I have bad dreams… But they arrive. "I am thinking of those nights," wrote Kafka, "at the end of which, having come out of sleep, I awakened with the sensation that I had been shut up inside a walnut shell."[8] Against the promise of unlimited extension and remote

    Poetics of Encryption

control, the inability to extract oneself from certain platforms, surveillance systems, and other infrastructures becomes a waking nightmare. Who can forget the oppressive mediatization of the COVID-19 lockdown, with its discipline of videoconferencing and live newsfeeds? Meditating on Kafka's fragment, the philosopher Gaston Bachelard considers the shell's interior: this kind of dreaming "goes into the walnut's every wrinkle, becoming familiar with the oiliness of its two halves and with all the masochism of the interior prickles on the shell's underside."[9] This vision is instructive. The cell's interior feels comfortable as long as one does not move, or grow. Wriggle too much and it pokes.

The nightmare nutshell is an exoskeleton that we have been sutured into against our resolve or better judgment. A sovereign must be able to choose new garments, to put things on or take them off at will. Detainees, on the other hand, find themselves worn by their suit. Imagine an anchorite undergoing a change of heart: having initially welcomed the wall's final bricks, now beginning to scream in terror, begging for emancipation—only to discover that, though her cries are heard, the matter will not be revisited. Of course they begged for help—begged God for release! Who can imagine that they did not suffer the worst regret inside their living tombs?

A species of horror obtains in the idea that we can no longer exist outside of our shell/cell—that we are locked in for good. Lost, somehow. It obtains, furthermore, in the strange presentiment that whatever *we* are, today, it is a species of invertebrate. The shell does not only imply an externalization of the brain but the rest of the body too. It suggests softening muscles, loss of posture, and general flaccidity. A key figure from the alt-right has attempted to remedy the prevailing mood of impotence with a spurious argument drawn from male hierarchy in lobsters.[10] Men are, apparently, more crustacean than commonly thought, and must embrace this fact. Under the circumstances, saner persons among us feel like Jean-Paul Sartre, who, following an experiment with mescaline, would suffer the recurring hallucination of being chased around by crabs.[11]

Bad dreams and waking life converge in this age of techno-burial, in which one finds subjectivity and political agency smothered by layers of infrastructure that begin proximate to one's body, but which ripple outward towards the stars. For certain artists, cracking open the shell, or crypt, in order to address the kernel within is of the highest priority. Others aspire to map "every wrinkle" of the techno-shell's interior layers. This chapter enters their work.

Orpheus and the World-*Kamára*

Let us tug on a red thread that runs through artworks that are concerned with recovering what is locked inside a techno-shell. The artists considered here do not exhaust this tendency. Rather, the following readings elaborate some symptoms of what we may call a contemporary *poetics of interiority.* Since *poetics* is at issue, we begin by taking up the ancient Greek myth of Orpheus and Eurydice.

This tale concerns a poet who charmed his way into the underworld, in order to recover a great love who was stolen away from him. That love was Eurydice, bitten by a viper, captured by death, and so imprisoned in the house of Hades. In order to effect a rescue, Orpheus, the paradigmatic artist figure, used his special talents to gain entry into this dark and difficult realm. His effort was rewarded. He located Eurydice and won the principle of her release. Yet, she was only discharged on the condition that he not look over his shoulder during their ascent to the world of the living, to check if she be following. Thus, it was demanded that Orpheus trust Hades, god of the underworld, rather than indulge his own curiosity (a difficult promise for an artist to keep). The hero agreed, and so off the lovers set towards an exit from that place, ascending, together, for a time...

Of course, the story does not end here. Poets rarely follow orders. It will be picked up later. For now, it is notable that a particular characteristic of this myth is echoed in art that is concerned with search and recovery—namely, its spatial imaginary. Indeed, an Orphic poetics of interiority abides in works that take on very real (and in no way metaphysical) conditions within the technosphere. Contemporary Orphic quests foreground the functional texture of searching, both on and offline—the labor of finding one's direction *inside* a network of passages. Diving deeper into the shell's interior in order, perhaps, to move beyond it; or to recuperate the possibility of a human image itself, at a time when material facts on the ground (and above it, too) appear to be closing in—swallowing, burying, or in-crypting it ever more deeply.

Authored three years after the release of Google Street View, and standing as the first significant video work with visual content drawn from this resource, Jon Rafman's *You, the World and I* (2010) retooled the ancient myth of Orpheus for a world caught not *on* but *in* camera. Rather than descending into a subterranean domain, its narrator seeks Eurydice inside a platform.[12] Announcing the always already buried quality of life in the Technocene, all protagonists in the

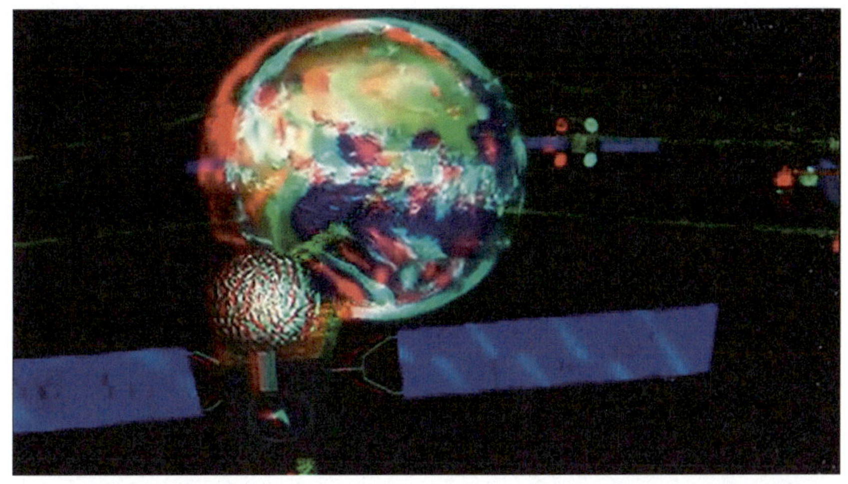

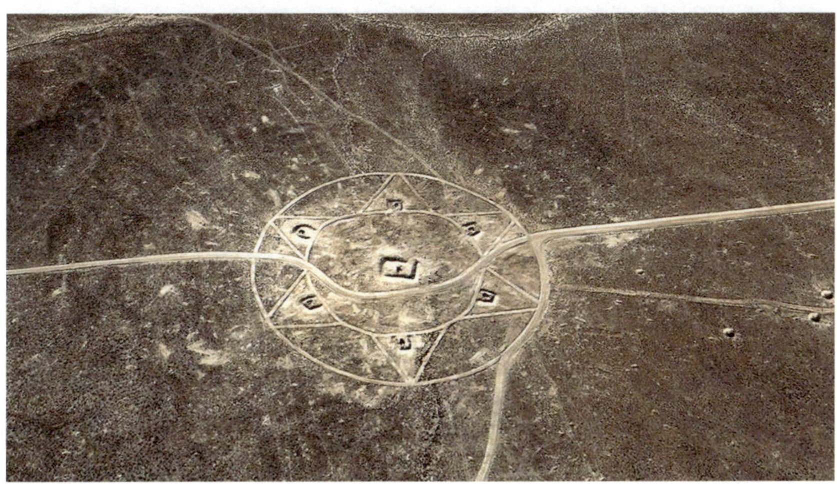

Jon Rafman, *You, the World and I,* 2010
Video, sound, 6:23 min.

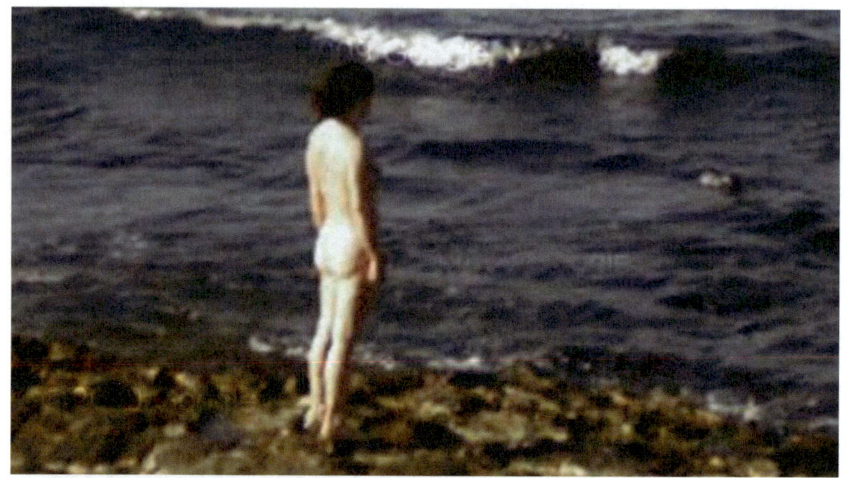

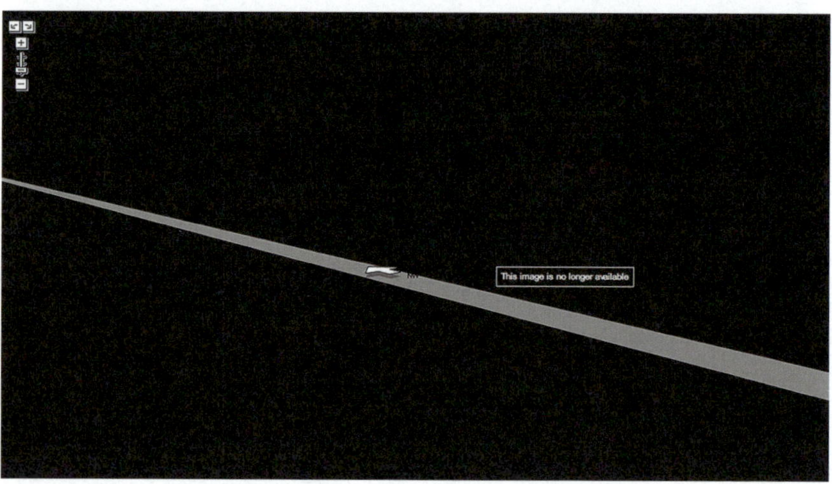

Jon Rafman, *You, the World and I,* 2010
Video, sound, 6:23 min.

                                        Poetics of Encryption

narrative—persons on the street, Rafman's Orpheus, and Eurydice—
are seen to be located beneath or within a planetary surveillance
system. The work's drama turns around the loss and recovery of
identity.

Thematically, *You, the World and I* transposes the early Greek
conception of Orpheus as revealer of mysteries into the figure of a
platform user, parsing the inner space of a gigantic image-machine
in an attempt to recover a picture of their lost love. In this respect, the
work allegorizes the search function, conflating this most ubiquitous
aspect of Internet use with a profound rite—framing the user as a
seeker through their filiation with the mythical protagonist.[13] The
latter's status as both poet and adept (founder of a mystery school)
begs the question concerning user-effected *poiesis,* as opposed to mere
browsing. *Pace* mytho-logic, this is a question of initiation. For the
followers of the ancient Orphic religion, the trial involved successfully
navigating the underworld; shunning its river of forgetfulness, concealment, and oblivion (*lēthē,* per Classical Greek) to drink, instead,
from a lake of memory and truth.[14] *You, the World and I*'s premise
concerns the narrator's struggle to recover a photographic representation of his departed lover. His success hinges upon remembering the
exact time and place where she was captured by a Google Street View
camera, and then retrieving her from the map-archive. Plotting her
whereabouts within the system is a performance that is both art and
craft (*technê*). The operation involves passionately identifying some-
one, not confusing her with another, and not forgetting. At first, the
viewer's own lesson consists in successfully recognizing these conditions, not mistaking them for alternatives, and—one presumes—
being able to apply them skillfully: a lesson for all *users.* But the true
initiate of Rafman's artwork acquires a deeper and more disturbing
instruction. Namely, that their everyday lifeworld is the house of
Hades. Moreover, that they have confused themselves with Orpheus
when they are, in fact, Eurydice—captured and enclosed within
a tomb.

The video begins with a God's-eye perspective above a spinning
globe, before cutting closer in to parse ancient sites like the Pyramids
of Giza (crypts for kings), and geoglyphs including the Westbury
White Horse. The montage is a visual genealogy of megastructures
that goes on to encompass sprawling cityscapes. At the apex of this
trajectory towards increasing complexity and scale, cataloguing
humanity's ever more outsize register, the video features a satellite
constellation surrounding the planet, red beams of light bouncing

between them—passages that, both literally and figuratively, ensnare you, the world, and I. The initiatory wisdom of this representation, and the video, more broadly, is our *being-within* a new form of mega-structure. Rather than a defined architectural figure, rising up from the ground, within the horizon's visible boundaries, this megastructure wraps itself around and captures the whole earth in its net. It is a *world-camera,* with countless eyes and other sensors facing inward, arresting all of terrestrial life, rendering it a *world-picture.*[15]

At this point, one must observe that, in Greek, *kamára* refers to a barrel-vault or ceiling, of the type found in Classical gravesites. It is *built enclosure.* The Latin *camera* still denotes "room"—with the architectural implication that a network-object comprising a satellite constellation and hundreds more cameras at street level must amount to a labyrinth. In this light, the subterranean and grave-like house of Hades, with its countless passages and adjoining chambers (requiring adept *technê* to successfully navigate, at the risk of forgetting oneself), and the world-camera collapse into one: the vision of a new under-world—a *world-kamára* that grows and grows. Soon there will be mega-constellations comprising tens of thousands of satellites, in addition to the hundreds already in orbit, and the billions of extant networked cameras on earth—some installed at fixed locations, many more in mobile use. Much, in the Western political bloc, is compro-mised by the Five Eyes that make up a global surveillance regime, along with the countless tracking systems deployed by the private sector—not least, the *Nine Eyes of Google Street View* (the title of a celebrated photography series by Rafman, 2008–ongoing).[16]

It is here, within, that the poet sings a song of disorientation and entrapment—having both discovered the situation and lost himself. For, inside the world-*kamára,* Orpheus and Eurydice are inverse doubles: two sides of a coin spinning along the symptomatic axis of gender, oscillating between seeker and sought, watcher and watched, living and dead, subject and object. Turning like the globe, this shifting gestalt flickers in the manner of so many transitions between night and day; or a candle burning within a *camera obscura.* It is a melancholy illumination.

Beyond Rafman's piece, more explicitly political rhapsodies of infrastructural interiority abound in recent art. These are songs of counter-mapping, united by critical and embodied trajectories towards the obscure interior of a given system or platform, in order to recover concealed information. This new Orphism is a quest for material insight, rather than emotional or spiritual transcendence.

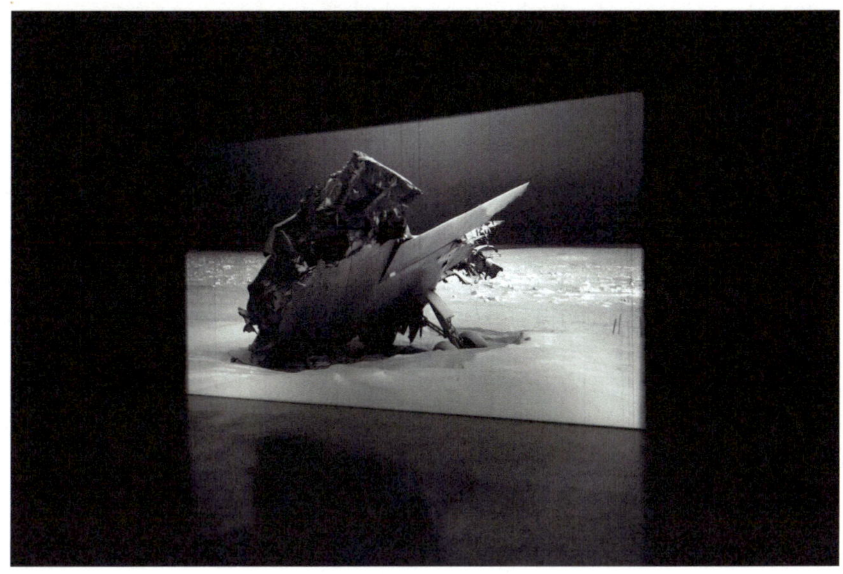

Charles Stankievech, *The Soniferous Aether of The Land Beyond The Land Beyond,* 2013
35 mm film installation with Dolby Sound, 10:18 min.

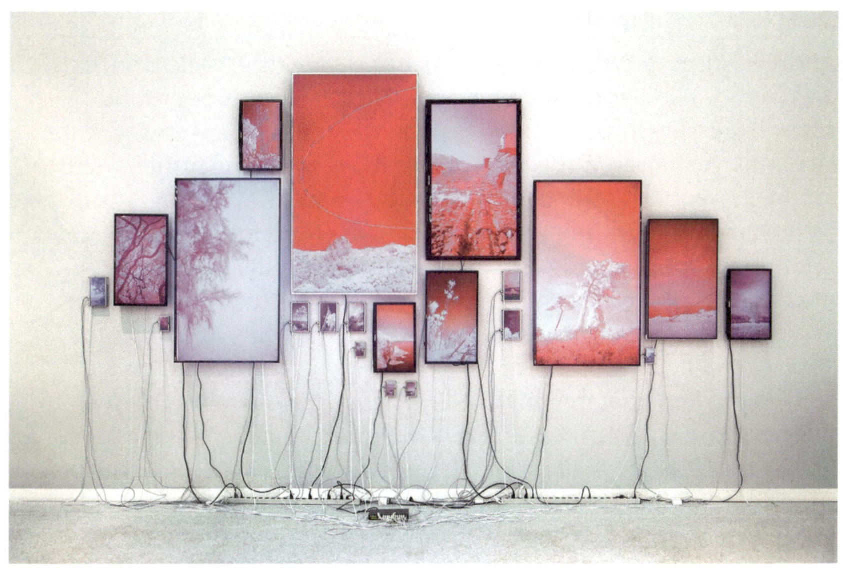

Evan Roth, *Red Lines,* 2016–20
Network performance
Installation view: Carroll/Fletcher at the Armory Show 2017,
New York City, March 2–5, 2017

Black Site

For, despite Internet-enabled apps promising users power over information and the "world at your fingertips," common modes of interface with the technosphere supply only partial perspectives. Newly encrypted geography stands to be deciphered. As the task of decoding grows more urgent, mines, cables, server farms, and security systems begin to feature in exhibitions.[17] Against limited or manipulative depictions, proffered by states and corporations, artists seek to supply alternative spatial and technical metonyms for an inside view. Their images are meant to enable the efficacious plotting of subject positions—(new) possibilities for figuring identification or dis-identification with(in) the system.

Running throughout this type of work, artist-seekers attempt to uncover or de-crypt backend materials, hardware, or processes. *Qua techné,* their investigations foreground the labor of gaining entry and finding one's direction inside the space. Diving deeper, on to recovery. Such approaches include attention to the geology of media, as in the work of Revital Cohen and Tuur Van Balen (discussed on pp. 25–27); the documentation of network architectures such as undersea cables, as seen in Lance Wakeling's video *Tour of the AC-1 Transatlantic Submarine Cable* (2011); and Trevor Paglen's better-known *Landing Sites* (2015).[18] The questing ethos also extends to exposing hidden labor conditions, such as those at various Google facilities, as detailed in Andrew Norman Wilson's film *Workers Leaving the Googleplex* (2011), and his *ScanOps* (2012–ongoing) image series—featuring found scanning errors in Google Books data, wherein glitches, the scanning site, and the hands of the employees who digitize the printed matter are made visible.[19] After digging in another archive, Simon Denny (re)incarnates a chilling Amazon patent diagram for a "system and method for transporting personnel within an active workplace"— now universally referred to as the "worker cage."[20] Denny's project *Secret Power* also showcased leaked NSA documents known as the "Snowden Files."[21]

Lest readers imagine that the link between geography, buried information, and imprisonment is overstated, Lance Wakeling's *Field Visits for Chelsea Manning* (2014) homes in on the issue. The third in a trilogy addressing what the American artist refers to as the physicality of the Internet, the video work is presented as a first-person travelogue, documenting sites where Manning, a former Army intelligence analyst, was detained before being convicted for supplying US diplomatic cables, battlefield videos, and other classified information to WikiLeaks. The locations include Camp Arifjan in Kuwait; the Marine

Corps Base in Quantico, Virginia; Fort Leavenworth, Kansas; and
Fort Meade, Maryland. Like the other videos in the trilogy, *Field Visits*
addresses "the vulnerability and weakness of the human body in
relation to the systems governing the movement of information, partly
through [Wakeling's representative] failure to access high-security
locations."[22] This issue is said to take on "a greater intensity in relation
to the story of a former soldier who was imprisoned and tortured."[23]
But, of course, in the context of our discussion, what is most remark-
able in Wakeling's Orphic journey is that it shadows Bradley Manning's own personal and political passage, undertaken while moving
through a sequence of prison cells, to eventually recover *her*self as
Chelsea. Echoing their previous release of classified files, she was
eventually freed.

All Orphic artworks take the form of dis-closure, thereby re-center-
ing the subject's position in an encrypted and networked landscape.
While the fate of a detainee animates *Field Visits for Chelsea Manning,*
most of Wakeling's footage features prosaic slices of Americana:
Civil War reenactments, a barbershop quartet, retired pilots watching
planes take off and land, and more. Through fixing his gaze on "forms
of recreation and play that cling to frameworks of technological and
governmental power structure,"[24] Wakeling documents the elusive
visibility of the world-*kámara.* A similar strategy of oblique disclosure
obtains in his tour of sites where the transatlantic cable surfaces.[25]
In that video, visual and narrative attention oscillates between the
inhuman scale of global communications hardware and the trivial
details of his experience, as an individual, trying to comprehend or
measure up to it—stalking information pipelines on foot and by train.
In both artworks, what is sought is not so much a central place, but an
efficacious vector for making "sense" of otherwise obscure pathways
within the geography of media, and the mediation of geography—
a specific way to engage with a web of sites; indeed, a *web-site-specific*
aesthetic that is up to the task.

The carceral archipelago of a billion eyes is all-seeing. On the other
hand, it maintains black sites where its activity cannot be observed.
To some degree, images of fiber-optic cables entering the sea symbolize the gates to this underworld; marked paths into the disciplinary
architecture of the world-*kamára.* At the same time, they announce
artistic concern for the threshold between hope and resignation. The
stakes do not only concern people. In fact, imprisonment is a condition applicable to all non-human others. For certain artists the stolen
figure may even be the ground itself (with respect to ecology).

For an artist like Evan Roth, it is not just about depicting cables, but about the question of how such cables (as signal examples of the techno-burial) mediate our perception and relation to landscape. At a beach in South Africa, the southernmost cape of Hong Kong, and elsewhere, Roth sought out locations where the fiber-optic tendrils of global power disappear and/or emerge from obscurity. In contradistinction to Wakeling's focus on the human life around the transatlantic cable, and Paglen's subaquatic photo-documentation of the same fiber-optic line, Roth trains an infrared camera not on the wire but the terrain containing it—his frames rendered in burning crimson. The various clips that make up his project *Red Lines* (2016–20) are not a picturesque valorization of the landscape outside/beyond cyberspace. Indeed, the infrared constitution of these images assures that they remain uncomfortably colored. Any virtual picture of the world that is conditional upon the delivery of data by fiber-optic cable relies upon infrared signaling. The Internet is, Roth states, "an infra-laser light, blinking through glass."[26] This electro-magnetic filter, stacked atop more obviously "real" geography, made up of minerals, molecules, biology, and so on, is increasingly powering the radical rearrangement of the latter. Its overlay is what turns a landscape into, additionally, a netscape—rendering it more intensively exploitable. "Filmed" in the same frequency wave at which the Internet modulates, if Roth's work does not always show a cable, then this is because this is unnecessary. It is, after all, pushing the whole pictorial proposition through one, in a gesture that parallels facts on the ground.

This claim does not only relate to the camera mode employed, nor the resulting visual effect. Despite being displayed in a gallery, the videos are (also) sited elsewhere: Roth calls them "network located" artworks—each scene shown, on screen, runs from a feed that issues from a server located in the country where the video was shot. Fusing gallery installation and a kind of geo-spatial drawing practice, a series of red lines (in laser beam) are traced, from the room where the screens are displayed, across continental divides, under oceans, through the actual network, until distant points are connected. If the videos are ever downloaded before being played back, or if they are taken offline, then any saved files count (for Roth) as documentation rather than actual artwork. The project is thus more *in* the lines than, as the common designation would have it, *on*line.[27]

As the strange red skies and snaking cables of Roth's installation intimate, all is not well. As initiatory representations, in-line landscapes appear wholly taken. In meditating upon them, one is reminded that Anthropocene discourse delivers an uncomfortable insight concerning the world-picture: in modernity the "natural" environment was so resolutely captured by human techniques of visualization, or sensing—enabling environmental abuse—that any future images of the planet will necessarily bear the red marks of trauma. Going forward, the world-*kamàra* and the picture of the world cannot be disentangled.[28]

Cave, Cloud, Hell

The Greek underworld is a cave system. Counterintuitively, so is the contemporary infrastructural complex, despite incorporating air-traffic and orbiting satellites. This is certainly the case when it comes to its linguistic baggage. Etymologically, the Latin *infra* (below) begets *infernalis,* and thereupon the hellish "infernal" and its associated fire through the Christian tradition. Acceding to this chain of identification, recent artistic representations of massive *infra*structures include caves, crypts, stones, mud, and the forge within their iconographies. Their direct affront to the slick design-rhetoric of consumer technologies does not, therefore, prosecute a new Luddism. They are a return of the repressed.

Julian Charrière's *Metamorphism* (2016) is a series of boulder-like objects created by melting together mainboards, hard drives, and CPUs from laptops and mobile phones in a furnace, along with other stones and soil. In this work, the technological is *baked into* the world. Quite apart from irregular, lumpish forms, the sculptures propose (the) earth suffused with man-made technology. Whether the inner fact comprises working components like pipelines and cables, or else anthropogenic pollution so extensive that it amounts to a distinct geological stratum, both sides of the coin represent an un-grounding with implications for a contemporary Orpheus. The title of the series' debut exhibition, *Into the Hollow* (2016), is telling for its cave-like, all-surrounding allusion, and its imperative to delve further.

In a related vein, recent theory conveys a sense of hell within your electronic device—the occluded presence of a social and environmental nightmare, off-screen: media archeology discovers open-pit mines behind the interface, nested within circuit boards, and the degradation of workers and ecosystems too.[29] To borrow the words of media historian and theorist John Durham Peters: Vulcan, not Apollo, is the god of cyberspace.[30] Excavating this seam, Revital Cohen and Tuur

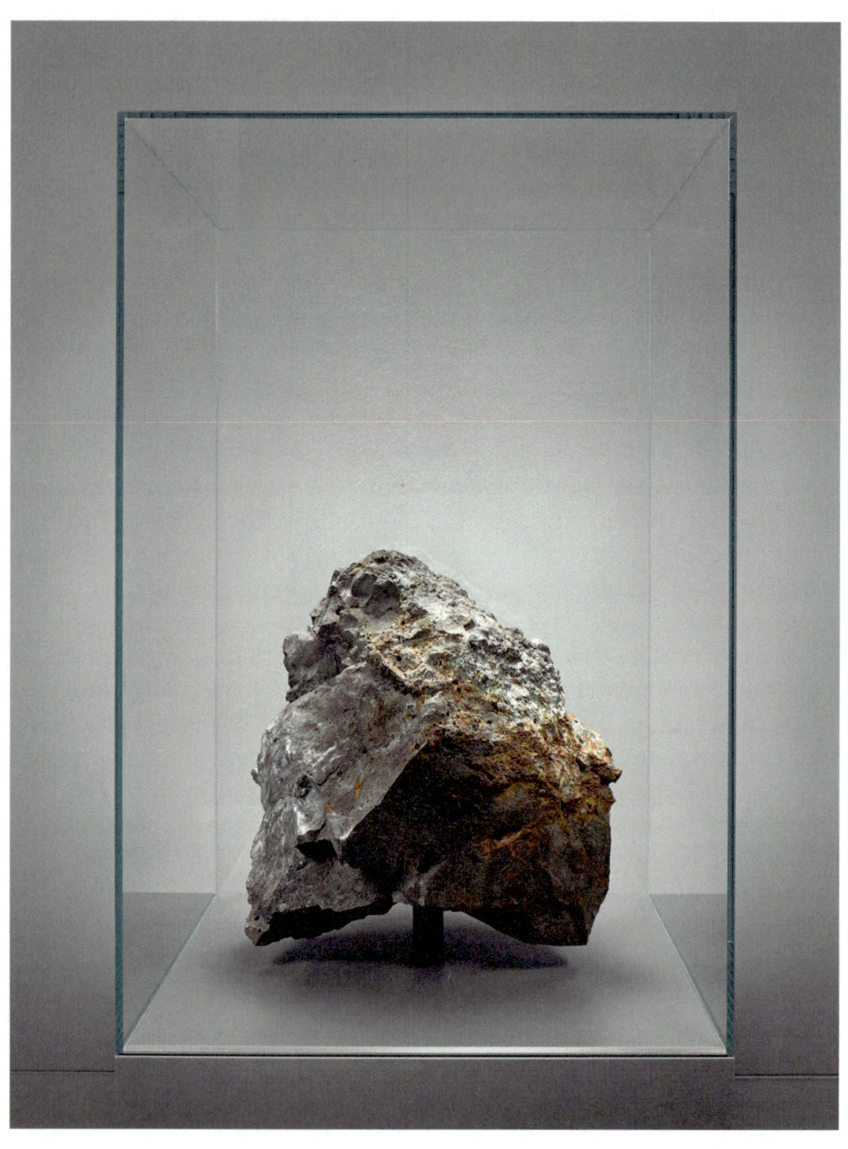

Julian Charrière, *Metamorphism XIII,* 2016
Artificial lava, molten computer waste (Main boards, CPUs, RAMs,
hard drives, cables, etc.), Corian pedestal, steel, white glass,
173×68×68 cm
Installation view: *Into the Hollow,* Dittrich & Schlechtriem,
Berlin, 2016

Poetics of Encryption

Van Balen highlight contested production circuits. As they put it, their artificial mineral-compound/sculpture *H / AlCuTaAu* (2014) was extracted from "40 Kilograms of hard drives [that] were sourced from a data destruction service, a mountain of shiny deformed bricks that were scraped out of the guts of computers."[31] Having employed artisanal techniques that are usually outsourced to underpaid workers in conflict zones, they report on their craft: "Neodymium (Nd) magnets are shredded with a water jet, tantalum (Ta) is filed out of capacitors and the gold (Au) recovered with acids. The aluminum (Al) platters—still holding their ones and zeros—are melted and recast in a sand mould. An artificial ore emerges from the earth, unexpectedly black."[32] Just as with Charrière, anyone who would effectively walk the labyrinth discovers rebirth: earth into machine, and, conversely, machine into dirty, blackened, earth. On the symbolic plane, the exchange of one for the other is close to an alchemical transmutation—the labor of adepts. In a subsequent work, Cohen and Van Balen scatter gold dust, extracted from computer motherboards, onto the soil of a Congolese gold mine (*Retour,* 2015). It is the price of knowledge.[33]

In the same year, we find Mary Mattingly's ongoing photographic series, *Elements,* whose gaze is on the materials that support photographic and computational enterprise. The rare earth elements pictured are harvested and turned into key components of cameras and printers. In her words: "Photography is a construction, fabrication, and truth, and unpacking parts of its complex material ecosystem has become my intimate research subject."[34] The series stands as a conceptual *mise en abyme;* a view *of* and *from* the flow of elements, addressing their impact on our contemporary powers of visualization (through a return to material sources). In much visual culture concerned with ecology (documentary images of profaned landscapes or, alternatively, valorizations of pristine ones in the pages of *National Geographic*), *the status of the medium as a symptom of despoliation goes unacknowledged.* One of Mattingly's key moves is to retool formalism so that it may contribute to a developing materialist (environmental) imaginary.

Such works perform the awareness of a media geologist—one who acknowledges Jussi Parikka's observation that the "deep time resources of the earth are what makes technology happen."[35] The special elements that make up digital electronics are extracted from very specific locations. Moreover, the products that they become are an ecological burden. As McKenzie Wark puts it, channeling Parikka, "Cinema is like a bright brief digital dawn across the surface of

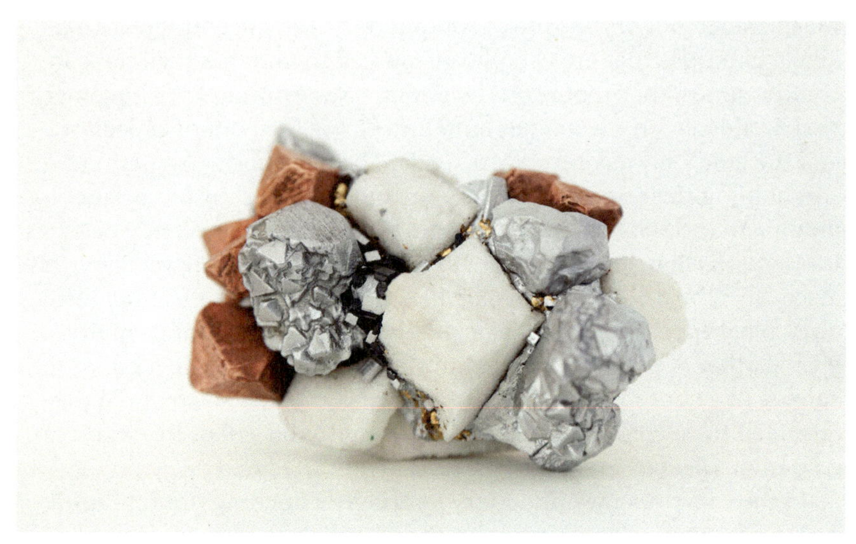

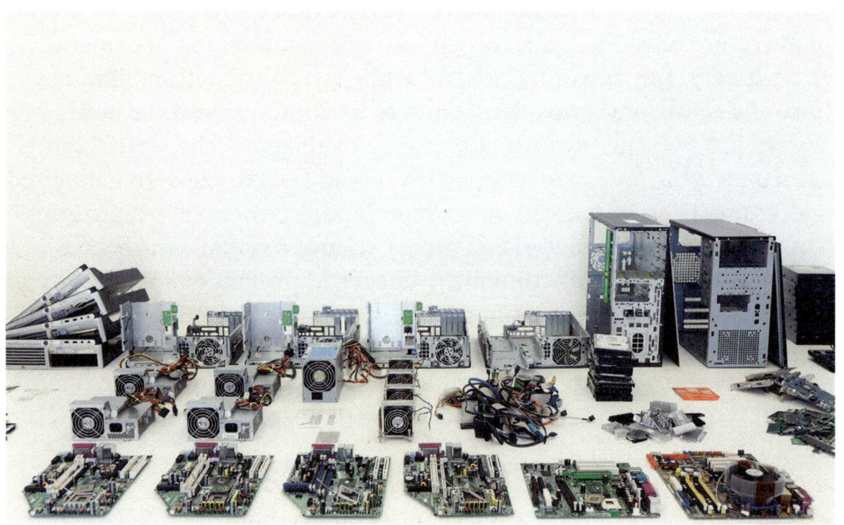

Revital Cohen and Tuur van Balen, *H / AlCuTaAu,* 2014
Aluminum, copper, gold, tantalum, whetstone, 12 × 7 × 6 cm

Assorted tools, computers, and machinery
Installation view: *Arbeid van de Dag* (Labor of the Day),
De Brakke Grond, Amsterdam, 2014

Poetics of Encryption

devices destined to spend the eons again buried in the analog night.... The deep time of the earth is quite literally strip-mined to make the quick-time movies of our era."[36] In this respect, what Charrière and Cohen and Van Balen's works seem to propose is working-*through* facts on the ground: situated awareness within the megastructure or initiatory cave/hell as a path to eco-social transmutation.

To the extent that working through technologically ungrounded earth (navigating its labyrinth, or understanding the world-*kamára*) is a material enterprise, eco-political seekers cannot ignore the question of embodied subjectivity. In view of this, the melancholy narrator of Rafman's *You, the World and I* appears in a different light. Though able to search at will, the object of his affection, Eurydice, is only ever seen from behind—until such time as she is no longer discoverable at all. Perhaps it is not so much that his (individual) love is lost, but that his general mode of loving is not viable. Indeed, in facing her back, the viewer/ narrator's gaze has switched positions to that of Eurydice at the beginning of her doomed ascent from the underworld—facing Orpheus's rear. This inversion is highly suggestive as, in this moment, it repositions the narrator as the one who is lost and/or unrecovered. This turned table would seem to indicate that there can be no curative treatment for you, the world, and the I, while an ideology of untethered observation— floating above the earth, like a cloud or satellite—holds sway.

Today, data is stored in clouds and shares float along with exchange rates. The new revolution is seemingly untethered—wireless and mobile—with bubbles drifting through the worlds of finance and

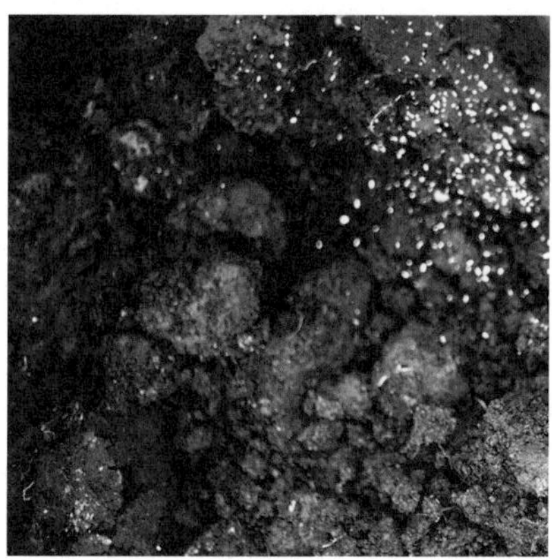

Revital Cohen and Tuur van Balen,
Retour, 2015
Gold from computer motherboards
scattered on the soil of a Congolese
gold mine
C-Type Print, 75×75 cm

philosophy alike.[37] Just some of the buoyant rhetoric attending a "weightless economy" and the rise of "immaterial labor."[38] In addition to this ethereal framing of our digitally informed culture, today's experience of geography—as mediated by IT—imparts a sense of displacement, hovering, and even teleportation. Sitting at our desks, corresponding with persons on the other side of the world, we find ourselves situated in one place *and* another. Every day, millions of people have out-of-body experiences, enabled by avatars on social media, or in multiplayer game worlds. Meanwhile, the ubiquity of Google Earth and air travel make us accustomed to the God's-eye perspective of satellites, in orbit, beyond gravity.

This is surfing—skipping along a vast surface, unencumbered by drag—a synchronic movement without a vertical, lacking depth. Critical engagement with such agendas is an urgent task, as the ideology of dematerialization makes us confuse ourselves with gods—pushing aside the issues of inequality and just distribution of resources that, necessarily, attend all embodied human needs. To judge the moral weight of these visions of the contemporary spirit we need only look for the bodies, and they are everywhere: we shoot videos from hobby drones and real people from military ones, always acting at a perceived distance—Zeus issuing thunderbolts from The Cloud. The Cloud is a Green Zone, a Mac Store, a white cube. Everything else is earth, littered with bodies and discarded junk, scarred by terraforming and a War on Terror—to keep the wells open and the mines producing. Below the Olympian heights of the new

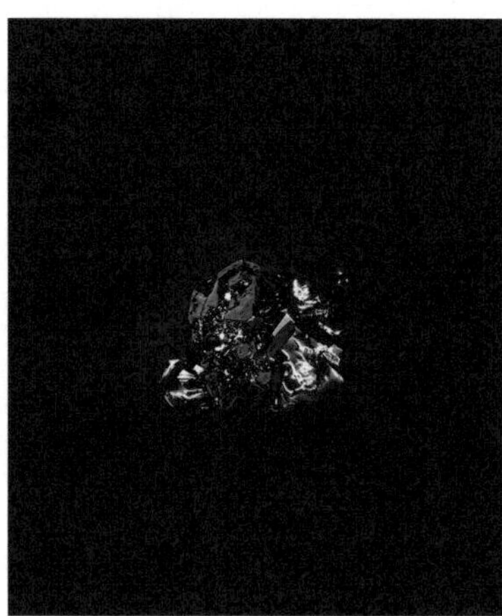

Mary Mattingly,
Elements (Gallium), 2015–
Rare earth elements
in photography

Poetics of Encryption

techno-demiurge there is trauma, applied to the earth as a planetary body as much as to people. Indeed, while an outside perspective may eschew political culpability for environmental and social ruin, it (at best, unwittingly) allies itself with the captor. Otherwise, it is the naïve view of a captive, from *within* a hell they cannot even recognize.

Caduceus

Against the apparent flattening of space and time proposed by communication technologies, recent geopolitical theory has set out to map the technical integration of the globe not only along the horizontal axis, but also along the vertical.[39] Such analyses constitute the figure of *spaceship infrastructure.* Sovereignty, the king of infinite space, apparently sits at the controls. In this (putatively good) dream, enclosure is a cockpit.[40]

According to Diedrich Diederichsen and Anselm Franke, curators of the exhibition *The Whole Earth: California and the Disappearance of the Outside* (2013) at Haus der Kulturen der Welt in Berlin, 1960s space exploration ushered in novel cultural values that were not generated by looking out, but by looking back at our own planet. It was as a result of this endeavor that an image of our terrestrial globe was captured by astronaut William Anders, *Earthrise* (1968). Later that year, the photograph was featured on the inaugural cover of an American countercultural magazine, *The Whole Earth Catalogue.* It would also appear on Buckminster Fuller's *Operating Manual for Spaceship Earth* (1968). Both publications were signal moments popularizing holistic "systems" thinking, associated with cybernetics, globalization, and environmentalism. While imagining the earth as a total mechanism, with mankind at the helm, such publications exemplified an ascendant discourse of planetary stewardship.[41]

A ship is a totally designed environment. Would-be pilots must understand its layout. But with planetary stewardship in mind, what kind of vessel are we in, today?[42] According to Parag Khanna, a prominent voice in neoliberal strategic studies, society is undergoing "a fundamental transformation by which functional infrastructure tells us more about how the world works than physical borders." On the other end of the ideological spectrum, Benjamin Bratton holds that technical architecture is also an institutional form. Making layered infrastructure (more) visible is the first step towards operating what we may call *spaceship infrastructure.*

Both figures seek a higher-resolution analysis of the world's interior situation; one whose architectural figure is not rendered in plan (viewed from above), but section. Herewith, Khanna's explication of living within: "There is no undesignated space…. [Even] the skies are cluttered with airplanes, satellites, and increasingly drones, layered with CO_2 emissions and pollution, and permeated by radar and telecommunications."[45] Bratton similarly speaks of the interior. His model "does not put technology 'inside' a 'society,' but sees a technological totality as the armature of the social itself."[46] We "dwell within" an "accidental megastructure … a new architecture" that "divide[s] up the world into sovereign spaces."[47] This megastructure incorporates "infrastructure at the continental level, pervasive computing at the urban scale, and ambient interfaces at the perceptual scale,"[48] amongst other things. For Bratton (and reflected in Khanna's comments on the sky), maps of horizontal space (planar geography) "can't account for all the overlapping layers that create a thickened vertical jurisdictional complexity."[49] The Stack, he writes, "is that new *nomos* rendered now as vertically thickened political geography."[50]

The presence of mines, cables, and so on in recent art has already been noted.[51] Such projects dig *down* into matter, in order to master otherwise hidden reality principles. But one should also understand that the critical spatial axis upon which they operate is bi-directional; it projects upwards, too, into the sky. Like recent theory, art also probes the atmosphere as a feature of our enclosure. Against misty incomprehension, the aerial hardens—reread not as ethereal or open, but as closed and full: subdivided by legal writ, saturated by sensor waves, brimming with aircraft and particle pollution, externally contained by a net of satellites. In a photographic work by Amy Balkin it has clear outlines. The artist describes her *The Atmosphere: A Guide* (2013/2016) as a "poster-essay depicting various human influences on the sky and their accumulated traces, whether chemical, narrative, spatial, or political."[52] Visually referencing the 1972 Cloud Code Chart, issued by the US Department of Commerce, National Oceanic and Atmospheric Administration, it is "an interpretive aid for looking up"[53]—a guide that visualizes the occupation of "present, past, and future atmospheres, from sea level to the exosphere,"[54] as well as consequent "downward influences."[55] A selection of these occupations, laid out in grid format for easy identification, range from the ocean's surface, through LIDAR (Light Detection and Ranging), to climate modeling, space junk, and more. While presented on a two-dimensional page, Balkin's critical line(s) of flight move through layered situations.

Poetics of Encryption

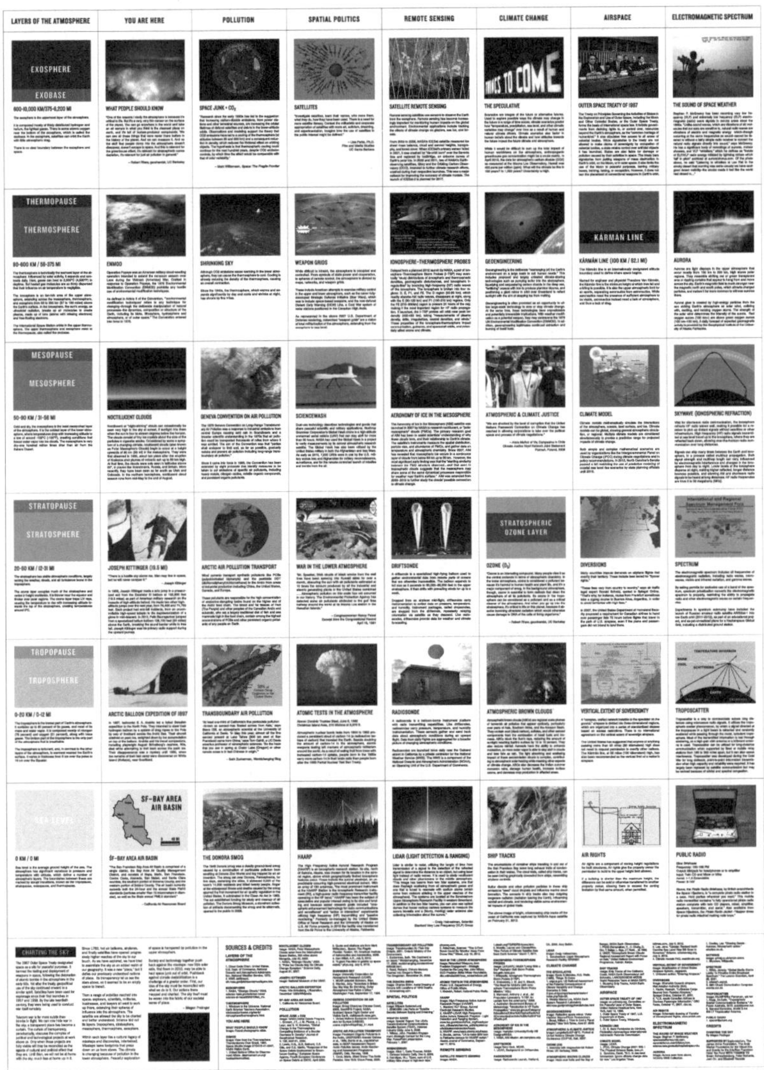

Amy Balkin, *The Atmosphere: A Guide,* 2013/16
PDF file and poster-essay, 121.9 × 81.3 cm

Elsewhere, in a work that I commissioned for the 2015 exhibition
Rare Earth, at Thyssen-Bornemisza Art Contemporary in Vienna,
the British artist Suzanne Treister offered a wall drawing that similarly
proposes a species of full-spectrum imaging of space, material,
technology, and power. In her *Rare Earth* (2014), the history and
affordances of rare earth elements are visualized.[56] Taking the form
of a mandala or cosmological figure, her picture visually encompasses
concentric layers of being and influence, rippling outwards from the
material itself, through extractive, scientific, industrial, medical, and
military applications—and on to cultural and philosophical impacts.
An epic mapping of how such elements underpin contemporary life,
as well as certain worldviews, Treister's diagram is both pedagogical
and visionary.

Taking an even broader perspective, Serbian artist and media
theorist Vladan Joler has proffered his own line-diagram of "today's
full stack"—a global condition that he officially titles the *New
Extractivism.*[57] Joler's document pretends to the status of delivering
(or recovering) an operating manual for this planetary edifice. Its look
brings this implication home—a crisp schematic charting the use and
control of space. In line with the realism of current infographics, the
work is art for the age of data visualization and graphic user interface;
wherein "the facts" and "choices" are put at user disposal through
putatively transparent visual mediation. The piece initially took the
form of a PDF containing a densely annotated "map," released on the
dark web as part of the 2020–21 Yerevan Biennial, before it was
reworked as a video guide.[58] Qualifying its massive scope of address,
which ranges from Earth's crust to the exosphere, Joler's introduction
points out that his diagram's consistent visual style belies a more
hybrid assemblage "of different concepts."[59] It is, he proposes, a
"semi-coherent picture"[60] that relies on allegories: "All [the] allegories
and concepts gathered here add up to a blueprint—for a machine-like
superstructure; a super allegory that encompasses the whole
world."[61]

Among numerous dystopian elements, the diagram details "capture agents": platforms (such as Google, Facebook, and Amazon)
figured as black holes, whose event horizons obtain "where the cost
of opting out is too high."[62] Following capture, users enter the "Platopticon"—a system of enclosure wherein millions of prisoners each
have their own cave/cell, upon whose screen-walls contemporary
shadows pass, in the form of an interface running personalized
content, modulated by live data tracking the prisoner's attention

and interactions.[63] In Joler's account, this cave-interface "is the office cubicle of [unpaid] immaterial labor."[64] Within, prisoners (*hikikomori; anchorites*) attend the "projected algorithmic spectacle of images,"[65] by scrolling, liking, sharing, commenting, or creating content. At the same time, their every movement or emotional reaction is being recorded, and this data becomes a resource for multifarious exploitation. It is a "closed circle"; a "bubble" whose exterior—composed of proprietary data and code—is invisible to the detainee.[66]

If we are to take *New Extractivism* as a manual for exiting the Platopticon, then one's escape vector must consist in a first moment that punctures the spectacular interface. A second must pass through hardware. A third, code, and so on, through many more layers of the stack in the direction of self-control—a status that is in stark contrast to alternative terms employed throughout Joler's document: *user, product, prisoner/worker, dividual.* In the model, such terms denote a human being whose body and mind are being exploited and managed as an "extraction stratum." But there is more. The whole planet is penetrated and bled by the superstructure—every data probe furthering exploitation of natural resources. Thrice, the PDF features illustrations of a long screw whose downward drilling transports previously hidden being(s) to the surface, for exploitation. Such is the power of the vertical axis for the New Extractivist sovereign.

For some artists, however, the critical vertical axis is not extractivist in the malignant sense. As such, it is best figured not as a screw with a spiral thread but as the Caduceus. Carried by the mythical Hermes, who, like Orpheus, was a messenger between worlds, this magical staff comes wrapped in two snakes whose bodies spiral together. According to Hermes's well-known vocation, this figure symbolizes virtues aligned with negotiation, eloquence, trade, and interpretation (*hermeneutes*), relating to the traffic between celestial and terrestrial domains. Additionally, its alchemical (Hermetic) implication is the union of opposites—wherein the bottom delivers the top, the inside delivers the outside, the smallest gives the largest, the most closed renders the most profound, and so on.[67] Recent art concerned with infrastructure shares this aesthetic logic of inversion: indeed, works that probe the deepest and most hidden places propose to extract and reveal wisdom; to bring truth to the surface; and, ultimately, to elevate the critical perspective.

In terms of figuration, sorties into house of Hades discover that the individual persona has been swapped for a digital doppelganger composed of "n-dimensional statistical projections."[68] The collective Critical Art Ensemble describes this found "data body" as "the fascist

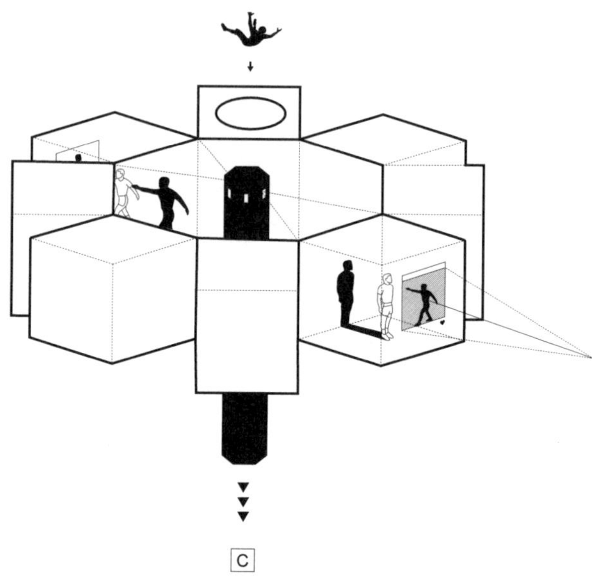

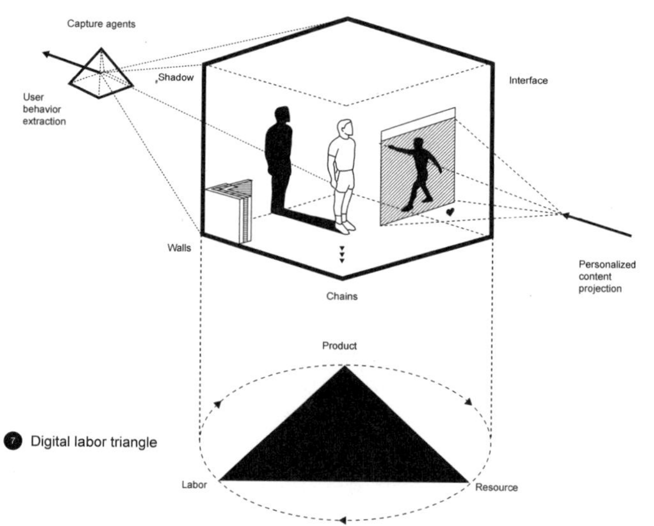

Vladan Joler, *New Extractivism* (detail), 2020
Website, PDF file, and video, 17:33 min.

Poetics of Encryption

sibling of the virtual body," which exists "in complete service to the corporate and police state."[69] *Vice versa,* excavating dividuation mechanisms employed by New Extractivism implies the recovery of a free human: in the downward spiral of infrastructure art, a new Eurydice is plotted or accurately sensed within a cave-cubicle. Simultaneously, in the upward spiral, she is released/extracted from her static and grounded position, delivered to a higher plane of operative facility (not least, politically). The Caduceus is thus a dialectic of decryption–encryption. The revealed subject (whether prisoner or capture agent) is supplied through a decrypting action that takes place on a certain epistemological level. However, on another, the subject remains encrypted. Indeed, somewhat counterintuitively, the rationale for de-crypting (rescuing or enlightening) a person is the assumption that they have a profound aspect that transcends statistical projection; a form of being that is being wronged. On the other side of the coin, mapping the extractive ensemble consists in pointing out black boxes without necessarily breaking them open—a contemporary equivalent to *here there be monsters.* These black boxes remain functionally secure, neither cracked nor slain. They have been handled through sublimation.

Joler admits aporia with respect to his map: "What we have here is an almost fractal allegorical structure—an allegory within an allegory within an allegory."[70] Bratton declares something similar: "This model is of a Stack that both does and does not exist as such: it is a machine that serves as a schema, as much as it is a schema of machines."[71] He goes on, "Perhaps the image of a totality that this conception provides would … make the composition of new governmentalities and new sovereignties both more legible and more effective."[72] What one takes from these statements is something akin to the philosopher Ian Hacking's position on representation. On some level, any representation misses the full mark. However, it may be considered correct if it allows one to intervene in the matter at hand, somehow. If you can operate on the thing by virtue of your representation of it then you have a measure of the latter's success. In our view, both Bratton's and Joler's maps function as spiral staircases within the stack. What the latter's work indicates, along with Rafman's Orphic tale and other artworks in this chapter, is that allegories stand to be "discovered," so to speak, by artists in the microcosm, the macrocosm, and all medial stack dimensions. Bearing our own endeavor in mind, we also admit that art criticism smuggles its own allegories into the field of representation, continuing the fractal.

Generally speaking, the affordance of the allegory with respect to the domain it strives to *capture* or *encapsulate* is the operative issue. Does Bratton's "image of totality," or a particular artistic critique of infrastructure, move the dial? If it is hard to assess its impact on "governmentalities," one must allow its efficacy within the more capacious field of "new sovereignties": emerging *kings of infinite space*. In a parallel allegory, Joler speaks of "Our imaginary hero … swimming against [the] platform's gravitational force."[73] Uniting both references is the figure of an unrestrained human vector through vertical layers of jurisdiction, engaging each of their respective designations (or scores) in turn. What Bratton terms the "design horizons" of each layer may be probed for exploits. Layers may be redesigned in their own code. And they may also be translated into others—i.e. allegory.[74] Elsewhere, I have explored this concept as a method for "errant curating."[75] Here, let us recognize that maps of the stack powerfully explicate the world-*kamára* by allowing artists to plot the seeker/Eurydice within a nest of vaults—concentric layers of infrastructure, whose points of interconnection may as well be tributaries of Lethe to non-initiates.[76] As a corrective, blueprints are prescribed by artists/thinkers for their initiatory power. These are what license an ascendant persona or individual, capable of enlightened vertical navigation through the stack's layers; against the flat stasis of dividuation, capture, and dead-end.

In fact, sequential decryption/translation of the stack's layers stands in curious parallel with the Hermetic account of the soul's

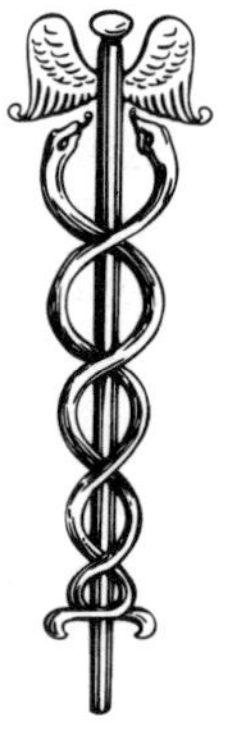

The Caduceus of Hermes

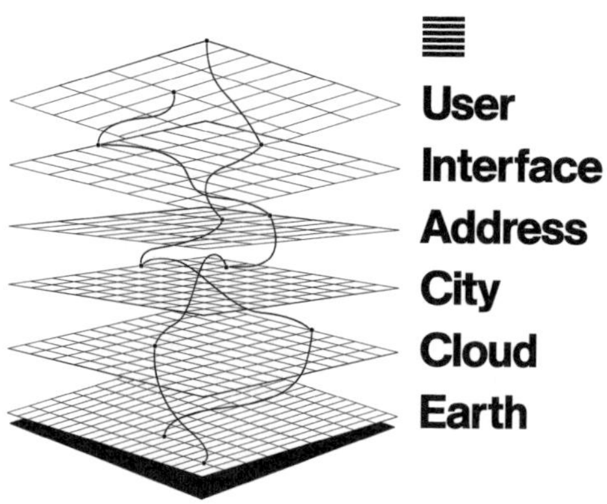

Metahaven, *Diagram of the Six Layers of The Stack*, 2016

Poetics of Encryption

ascent through the planets after death, to the supra-cosmic place of absolute power.[77] The classic description of this journey is given in the *Corpus Hermeticum,* a key text of Renaissance Neoplatonism, which makes use of pre-Copernican cosmology. The Ptolemaic astronomer imagined that the transparent spheres of the seven planets lay between him and the pole star. In the words of musicologist Joscelyn Godwin, Hermes Trismegistus "taught that these have to be crossed one by one on the upward, and at each sphere one had to lay aside the negative tendencies ruled by the planet in question." He continues, "Perhaps this is why the path of the soul is not an unimpeded straight line but a serpentine path."[78] Let us briefly note that the *Corpus Hermeticum*'s early-modern translator, the epochal finder and interpreter of ancient texts, Marsilio Ficino, led an Orphic cult within the Medici Court.[79] In the twentieth century, Carl Jung's psychology offered a restatement of this vision, as "integration of the personality or way of individuation,"[80] with the planetary portals standing as challenges presented to us by life and the archetypical contents of the unconscious.

Just as I do not attribute a Ptolemaic cosmology to Jung, so Bratton's own work cannot be considered anything other than post-Copernican. He does not discuss any correspondence between a "soul" and an extraterrestrial body. Nor does he address inner psychological structures. Yet, while *The Stack* is not a return to Hermetic theology, it does carry over the diagrammatic imaginary of nested spheres (*qua* Ptolemy) and an associated mytho-graphic agential

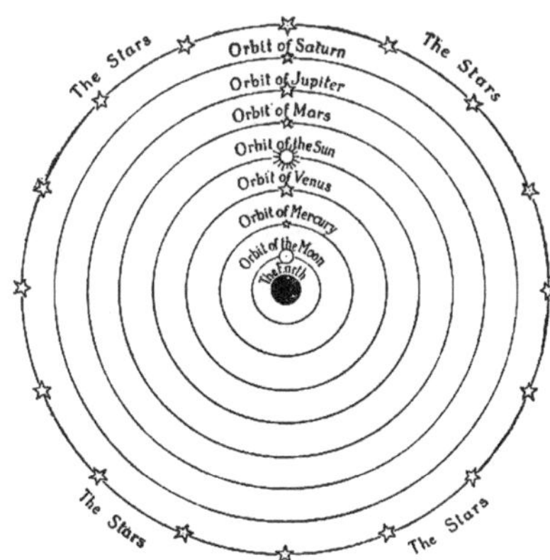

The Ptolemaic Idea of the Universe

structure. For, the emblematic drawing of the infrastructural situation that is supplied in the book, by Metahaven, is only a partial perspective: each of the multiple layers of infrastructure that make up "the stack" in fact envelops the planet. They are *planetary* layers, or spheres wrapped around spheres. With Bratton, the stakes may be termed *intra-terrestrial.* As far as this spatial imaginary relates to political agency, I understand that a successful political navigation is a vector through the layers, skillfully dealing with each in turn. This vector may even be an ascent. Indeed, it is interesting to note that the user occupies the top layer of Bratton's stack, the last sphere, just as the Hermetic goal-self was ascribed to the outermost planetary layer—the pole star. Both Bratton and Hermes Trismegistus employ the same core architectural figure, then: in section, this comprises concentric rings. With the introduction of a horizontal axis they are hemispheric vaults—*kamára.* Both planetary imaginaries thus concern power and individuation—specifically, addressing how an important aspect of the person is articulated through relations with the *kamára.*

Balkin, Joler, and Bratton's works do not advance an explicit humanism, let alone a natural order. However, they do allegorize ascendant physical and intellectual human agency. In this they manifest hope that Eurydice may be recovered from her hellish office cubicle, viewing live video of a night sky packed with pollution, cameras, weapons grids, and space junk. It is an admirable dream.

Cave, Grave, Cockpit

Earlier, it was mentioned that there was more to the Orphic myth. Let us continue: Although he swore not to look back over his shoulder during ascent (to see if Eurydice were following), Orpheus could not help but turn and gaze. Just like that, Hades snatched her back into the deepest recesses of the underworld, forever. In my view, the specific nature of his error was a turn-back towards materiality (the pit) while otherwise leaving that place for a higher realm. For, a key thing about initiatory descent that must not be forgotten is that *it is supposed to effect an upward movement or elevation of the person* (if we are using the Classical language—*the soul*). Orpheus's looking back is a re-assertion of descent (a fall) that cancels out any elevation (especially for Eurydice, his double). His mistake is tantamount to killing her. And it gets worse. After this, Orpheus goes on to become a proto "incel": "Ashamed and appalled by his failure, he spends the rest of

Poetics of Encryption

his days in melancholy misogyny, eschewing all women in speech and song."[81] Though the point is that no living woman can compete with twice-dead Eurydice, it is, of course, "disingenuous to dismiss women in general because his pride failed one of them."[82] That, at least, would seem to be the judgment of the living women who feature in the myth—avenging maenads or bacchants (elemental earth goddesses that hark back to pre-patriarchal societies) who choose to sacrificially dismember him as punishment for his slander. Orpheus entered the cave, the underworld, and it seems he never truly left.

In contrast with the critical dynamism of both (web-)site-specific practices and media archeology, elsewhere, Rafman presents us with another reverie of interiority: it is a body in a tight, dark space whose only light source is a screen. The work borrows its architectural vernacular from so-called "troll caves"—*ad hoc* constructions created by users endeavoring to offer total attention to their chosen virtual reality. These are frequently build-outs of beds, sometimes chairs and desks, which incorporate technical equipment—consoles, keyboards, etc.—within easy reach. For *Cockpit* (2014), Rafman places a computer inside an office cabinet and invites viewers to climb in and watch *Mainsqueeze* (2014)—a montage of fetish clips from the darkest corners of the web. A work of sculptural ethnography, the artist's cave re-hearses an apt "found" paradigm for a vapid (if not kinky) embrace of *being-within*. It is a proposition that concerns the will to self-obscuration through cocooning, in the vein of *hikikomori*. Perhaps, also, the apocryphal "blue pill" of *The Matrix*—which may also be described as cynical identification with one's position inside a "filter bubble."[83] The sculptural aspect of this work does not so much address digging deeper, *on to* discovery, as burrowing and settling into a grotto—and possible grotesque.[84] It is in this respect that one recalls the substance of Plato's celebrated allegory, wherein Socrates likens non-initiates to prisoners, shackled in a cave. Lacking familiarity with the sun/truth, these unfortunates erroneously take "the shadows of the artifacts as *the unhidden*."[85]

The cave is baked into the troll. Characteristically ugly, they turn into stone when exposed to sunlight.[86] Not so much constrained by the underworld as suffused by it, they are a recognized social and media typology.[87] As mythic trolls would steal human maidens, so their meat-space analogues, self-described "involuntary celibates," demand unlimited license over women.[88] Here, we must revisit our comment on the potential non-viability of the (general) mode of loving pursued by Rafman's Orpheus, extending this to the fetish element in *Cockpit/*

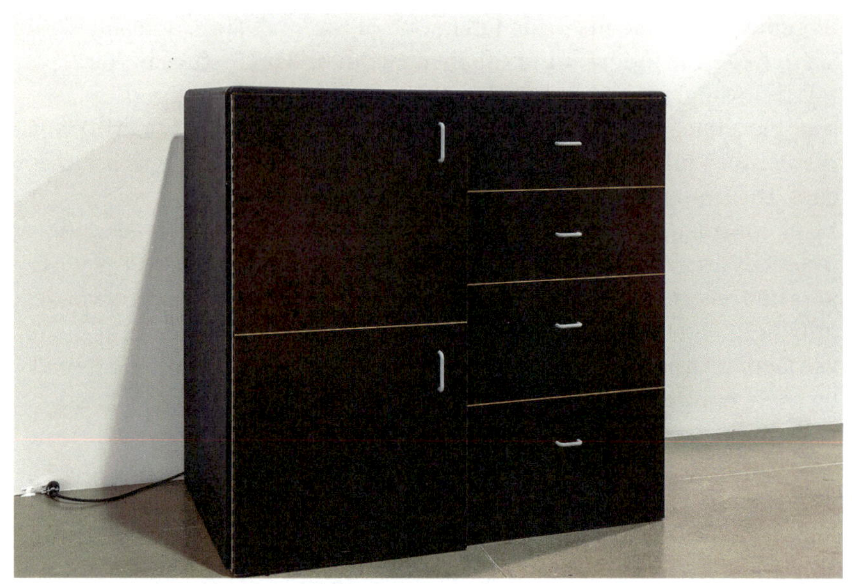

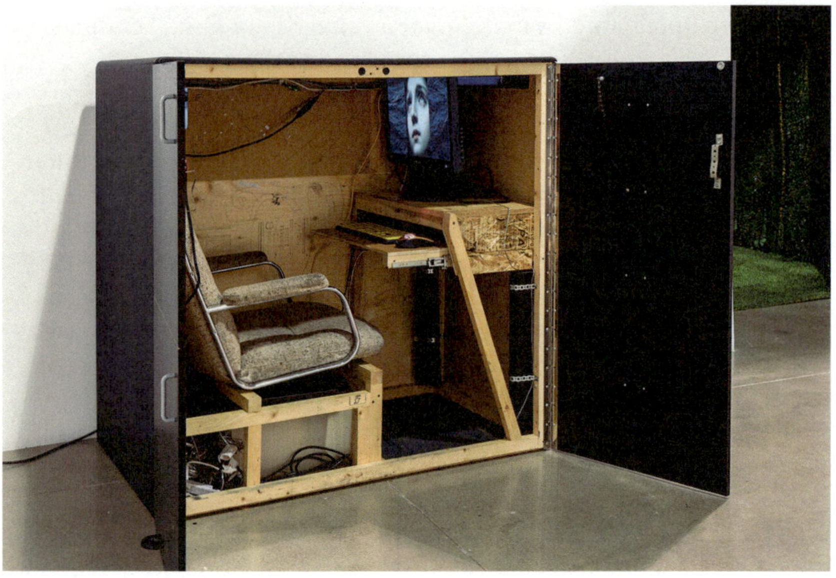

Jon Rafman, *Cockpit,* 2014
Wood, chair, screen, 124.5 × 124.5 × 76.2 cm

Poetics of Encryption

Mainsqueeze. Orpheus *does* want to leave the underworld. The troll, on the other hand, burrows in to the point of effacing distinctions between *enfer*-structure and their own person. It is self-inhumation; the closing-up of a funerary pit. The troll is, as the poem goes, "not waving but drowning"—though they may not know it.[89] What is telling about Rafman's *Cockpit,* as opposed to slick commercial versions (such as the Bauhütte *Gaming Bed*), is the abject quality of the would-be convenience—from its poor materials to its tight enclosure.[90] There is a masochistic aspect to these prosthetic caves. In them, the otherwise dynamic and expansive human body is put under pressure, *squeezed,* as the system closes in.

Beyond Rafman's work, the Brazilian-American artist Juliana Cerqueira Leite takes on the relationship between technology and corporeal enclosure, in a sculpture entitled *Anthropometry* (2019). Hers is a systematic and institutional approach to the cock/pit form, first exhibited in 2019 at the National Archaeological Museum in Naples— home to bodies and artifacts recovered from Pompeii (a buried society).[91] In 1986, NASA published their Manned-System Integration Standards (MSIS) handbook, for the design of outer space worksta- tions and habitats.[92] The research for this publication involved analyz- ing affordances of the human body, including a "grasp-reach study" in which a person strapped to a model cockpit chair would reach as far as they could in all directions—their scope of mobility measured in detail. The results went on to inform the future placement of controls in the Space Shuttle. For *Anthropometry,* Leite, sitting on a replica Space Shuttle chair, reenacted the movements within a large clay-lined mold—running her fingers along and through the wet material, its surface recording the measure of her reach. The final sculpture comprises a positive (dry) plaster cast from the mold, attached to a chair—a roughly spherical form whose surface registers a messy index of digits (fingers) as the maximal spatial extension or limit of her human embodiment within the furniture system/discipline. With respect to cockpit design, this recorded limit traces her final threshold before *digital* continuance, onward/outward to and from a machine interface.

While both Rafman and Leite's cockpits stage prosthesis or exten- sion of the human will, they also work dialectically, highlighting bodily compression into a minimal housing or enclosure. Whatever expanded (cyber or outer) spatial domain of action is opened up by these techno-caves, so an inverse trajectory also obtains, characterized by marginal corporeal exercise and an amputatory suggestion.

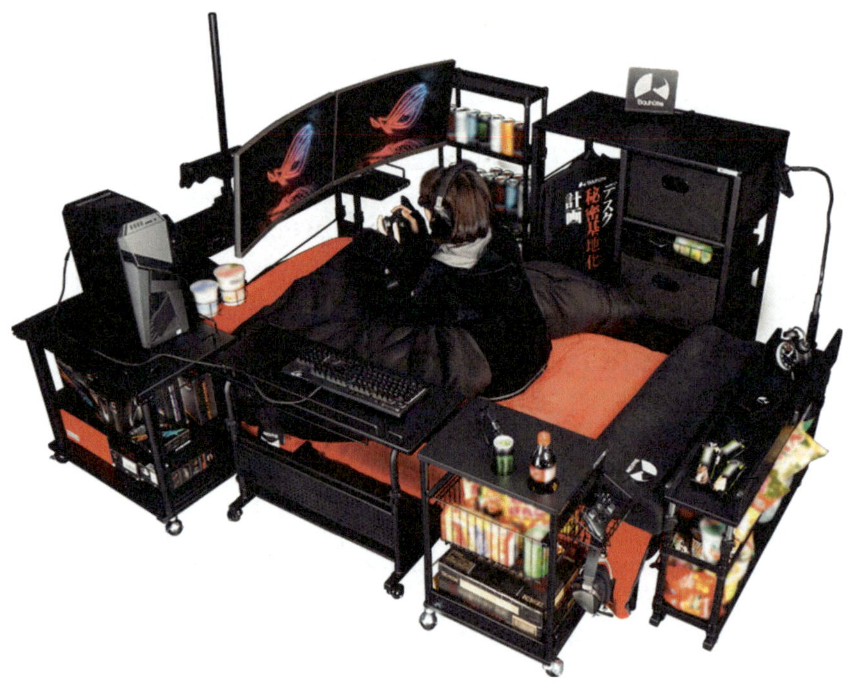

Bauhütte Gaming Bed
Bed Desk BHD-1200BD,
Adjustable Headboard BHB-950,
Gaming Suit "Ninja Onesie"
HFD-4G, Gaming Bean Bag BHB
180, Headphone Hanger BHP-S100,
Energy Wagon BHS-430EW, Slim
Bottle Rack BHS-150, Long Side
Table BHT-800S, Clothing Rack
Table BHT-830

Poetics of Encryption

Philosopher Vilém Flusser once proposed the "manual atrophy" of the button pusher as a liberation from the burden of hands—those tools for *handling* and *working on.* A new life, defined by the finger, concerned with ease and play, was apparently coming into being. But the ambivalence of *Homo digitalis,* his "handless, fingering human being,"[93] is what emerges in such artworks, complicating any recourse to the ludic. Indeed, in *Anthropometry,* Leite's digits would appear to scratch at the walls of a prison.[94]

In fact, both pieces represent the biological person patched into a solid-state circuit; a liminal condition of (human) *being-within-a-machine,* a status philosopher Byung Chul-Han deems "undead."[95] At the end of this atrophy, the *becoming stone* of the mythic troll is recast. In Rafman's work, desire for prosthesis—further reach—effects a metamorphosis from fleshy finger to sepulcher, via microprocessor and keyboard. It is a process of desiccation, hardening, and shell-growth. Likewise, a new view on the *calchi,* recovered from earth composed of compressed volcanic ash—the inspiration for Leite's *Anthropometry* and the rest of her Neapolitan suite of works in plaster. In the latter case, we understand that the Classical citizenry or *people* of Pompeii were utterly buried, only to burn away and become negative spaces within the ground: human caves. These are the molds from which the plaster *calchi* were cast back into positive: a process re-incorporated through Leite's meditation on human representation within a condition of techno-burial, and mineralization by cockpit—*becoming encaved.*

Now heating up, our critical excavation of the cockpit uncovers philosopher Michel Serres's comments on the Space Shuttle *Challenger* disaster of January 28, 1986—in which all seven crew members were incinerated. He describes witnessing the event on television, drawing a parallel to ancient worship of the god Baal. Specifically, he talks about the Carthaginian practice of putting people inside a sculpture and burning it as a sacrifice to this deity. He writes that, in both cases, living bodies were interred within a casket and destroyed in front of a mass audience, and that the difference between the conceptual designation *idol/sculpture* and *vehicle* is what separates the *Challenger* event from a sacrificial rite. The latter concept renders the explosion, and so many more common incidents, like car crashes, "accidents," rather than indicators of structural depravity. Serres reminds us that the difference is *cult*ure-making, but that (at root) both the "idol and the rocket are tombs."[96] The thrust of his comments probes whether scientific societies are still founded on human sacrifice.[97] The question is not so easily answered. If they are not sacrificed *per se,* Rafman and

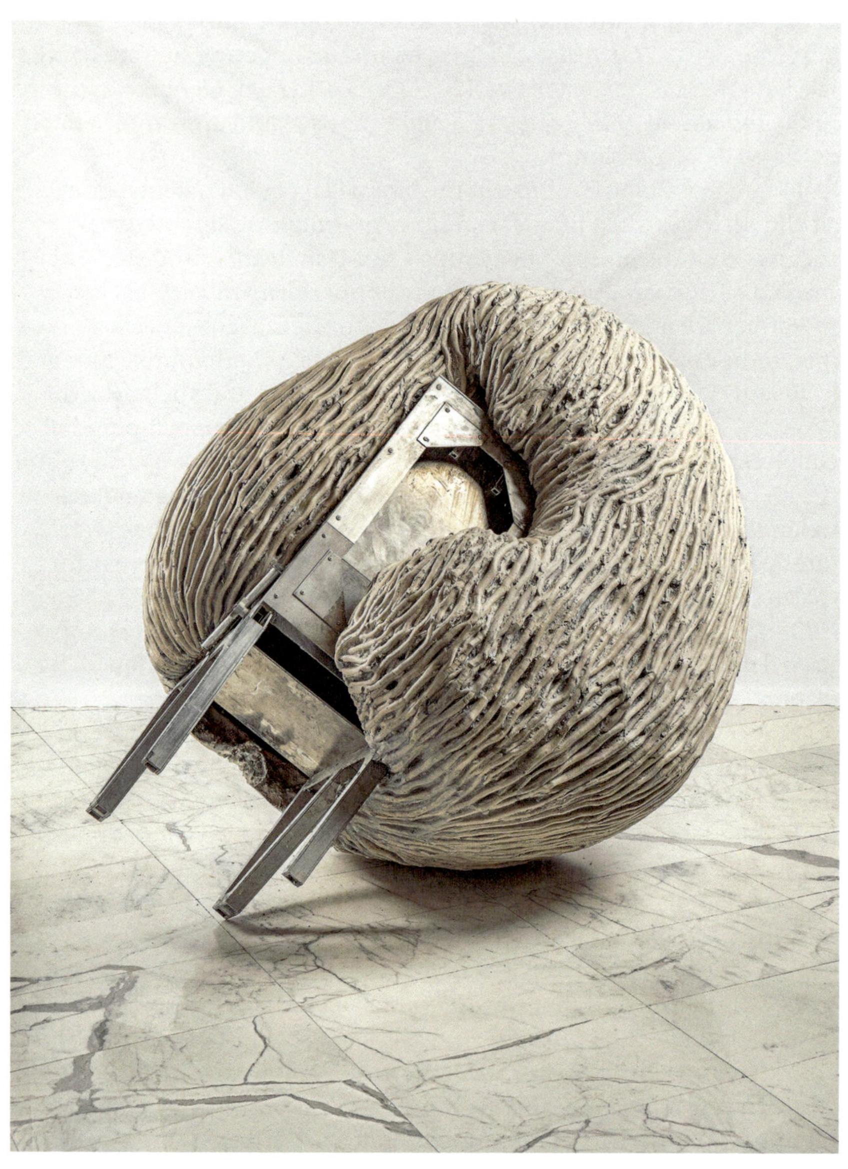

Juliana Cerqueira Leite, *Anthropometry,* 2019
Aquaresin, aluminum, glass fiber, steel, pigment, clay, 170 × 140 × 130 cm
Installation view: *Orogenesis,* Museo Archeologico Nazionale
di Napoli (MANN), Naples, 2019

Poetics of Encryption

Leite's bodies appear demoted—with respect to kinesis.[98] Moreover, when it comes to trolls, incels, or cocks in a pit, the abyss stares back: In 2017, a young neo-Nazi drove a Dodge Challenger into a crowd of anti-fascist protesters in Charlottesville, Virginia, killing one and injuring twenty-eight people.[99] The incident was captured on live television. That same perpetrator had, on previous occasions, assaulted his own mother and threatened her with a knife after she told him to stop playing video games.[100]

At this point, the outline of a new funerary art appears on our radar, along with attendant sacrificial concerns. Moving on from Rafman, Leite, and outright horror, its spectacular plane becomes visible. It is signaled by British artist Roger Hiorns's burial of a military passenger aircraft in 2016—an installation ventured as the first in a series to play out on each continent. With visitors able to enter the subterranean body of the vehicle, through a passage beginning above ground, the artist suggests that "the human occupant of the newly buried plane will become influenced and more attuned to the powerful systems [that] we pass through."[101] This work is, I assert, the creation of a contemporary pilgrimage site under the Orphic sign. It announces, off-screen, in the earth, at the scale of monumental sculpture, an art concerned with modalities of encryption.

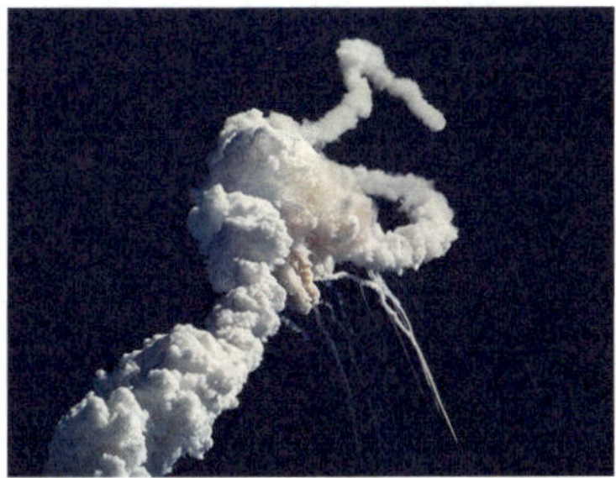

Space Shuttle *Challenger* explodes shortly after take-off, January 28, 1986

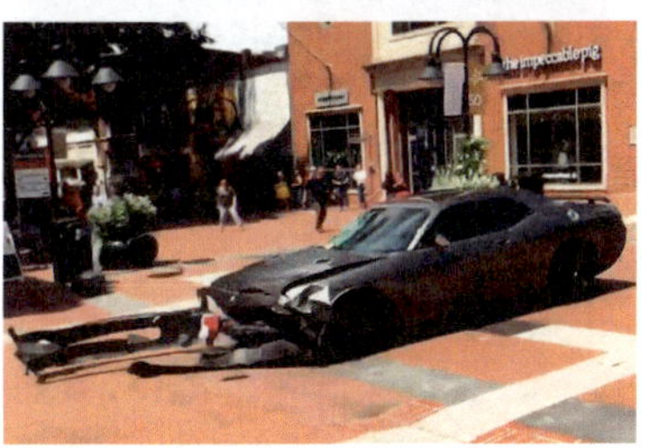

Dodge Challenger involved in a vehicle-ramming attack in Charlottesville, Virginia, August 12, 2017

Coffin

As should be clear, the nature of the crypt is a live issue in contemporary art, but one should not move on without attending to comments offered by another artist from the United Kingdom, the author Tom McCarthy, concerning the "Google era"—so defined by "every moment of our urban transit ... recorded and archived by close-circuit cameras, our location logged by the miniature recording caskets that we carry in our pockets [phones],"[102] and every keystroke and click-through "notated, copied, cross-indexed and correlated with the others."[103] This amounts to the advent of "a communal *black box*—expanding to contain whole populaces."[104] The figure that he invokes is present in all commercial airplanes: famously, it is the flight and cockpit-voice recorder, engineered to withstand even the most violent event—so that its content may be retrieved from a crash site and aid forensic investigation. McCarthy installed such a device (lent by Boeing) at Stockholm's Moderna Museet in 2008.[105] Four years prior, at London's Institute of Contemporary Arts, he set up a large *Transmission Room,* in which feeds from various media sources (from Ovid to stock market prices) were transcribed and then recombined in various metric formats, before being read aloud and broadcast throughout the city over radio. His inspiration was Jean Cocteau's 1949 film *Orphée* (Orpheus), in which the updated Thracian poet transcribes and publishes verses by another rhapsode who, confined to the underworld, is broadcasting on a frequency that can be picked up on a car radio. Of intermittent quality, the protagonist must collage together the snippets that he hears. Here, as before, the techno-Orpheus navigates undeath, both for others and himself, capturing the voice of the buried poet (Eurydice? Him?) through the constitutive act of recording—in this case, a *technê* that involves searching for an adequate or meaningful composition.

One might expect that McCarthy, a novelist, should develop a somewhat logophilic iconography of encryption-as-recording (radio, microphone, etc.). This approach is also apparent in his comments on Bram Stoker's *Dracula* in a recent article. There, McCarthy asserts that boxes and records form the "main props" around which the novel is built.[106] Both come together, he claims, in a single device: the phonograph used by Dr. John Seward to record his psychiatric assessment of the mystery figure (the vampire). McCarthy offers the following rhetorical question: "Don't all the novel's other boxes of undeadness serve as fantastic doubles, phantasmatic satellites

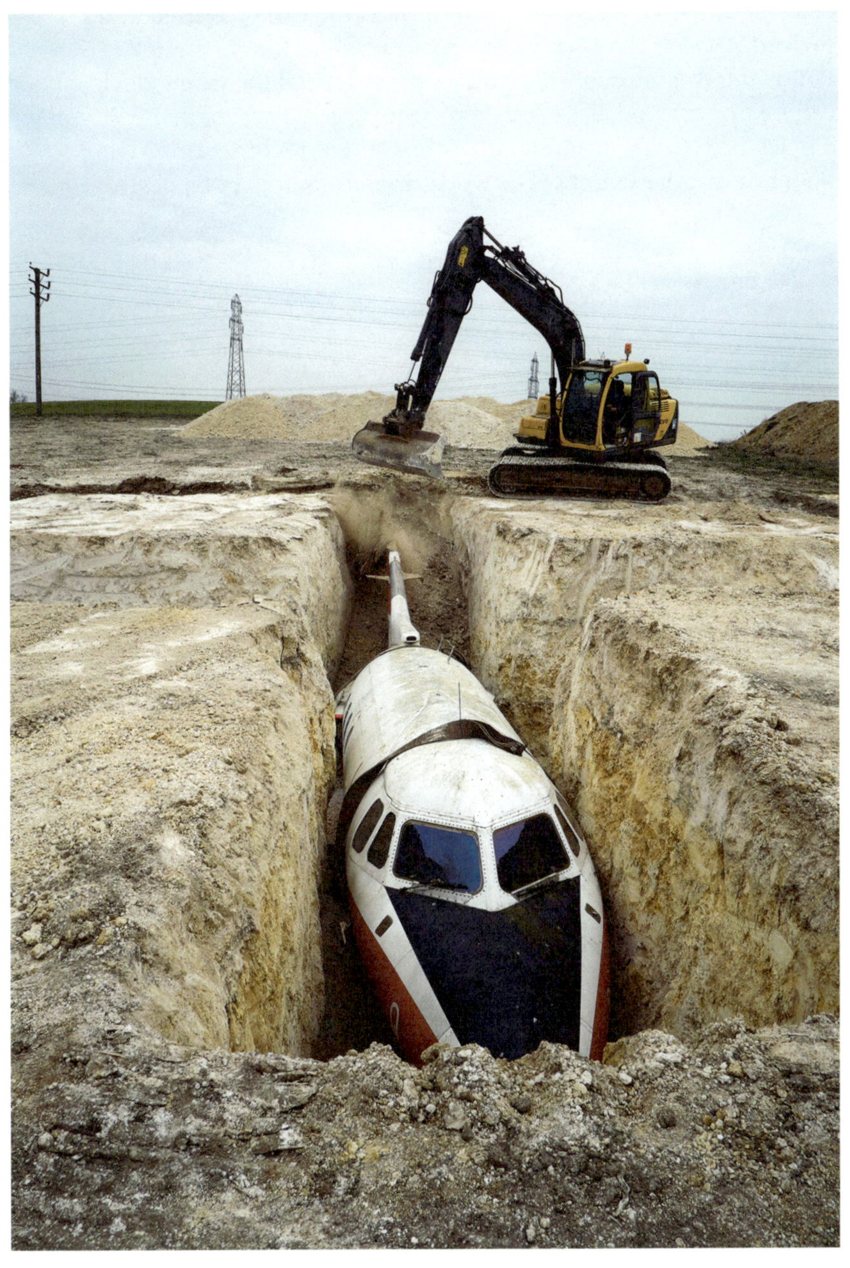

Roger Hiorns, *The retrospective view of the pathway, (pathways),* 1990–2016
Jet airliner, burial, dimensions variable

orbiting the real box, within whose walls life can be buried and revived? Wasn't the Dictaphone a vampire's coffin all along?"[107] Following this train of thought, cameras (visual recording devices) can be understood as caskets too—the *camera obscura* being, literally, a black box. *Qua* communal black box (flight recorder), one cannot help but wonder whether the world-*kamára* may ever be destroyed.

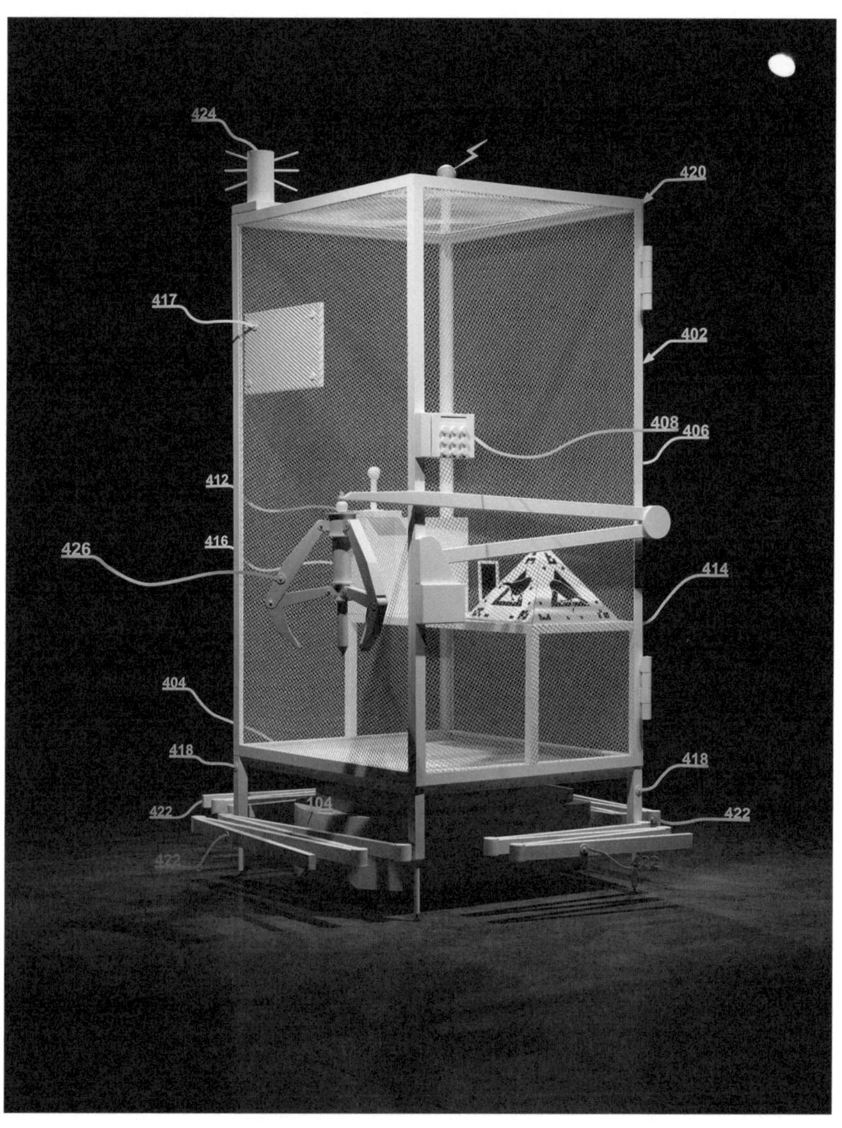

Simon Denny, *Amazon worker cage patent drawing as virtual King Island Brown Thornbill cage (US 9,280,157 B2: "System and method for transporting personnel within an active workspace," 2016)*, 2019
Powder-coated metal, MDF, plastic, digital print on cardboard, iOS augmented reality interface, 286×215×215 cm

Black Box

Cave, Crypt, Hell, Camera, Cubicle, Cockpit, Coffin

These tokens of entrapment encompass one another. However, within their nested matrix there lies another species of container—the *black box* of cybernetics. Beyond capturing the user, this object serves as a key prop in the personal-political drama of being excluded from a hidden order of reality, unable to access or read its code. In fact, this figure is the inverse aspect of the world-*kamára*'s all-encompassing interior. *Hikikomori* and trolls may not dream of puncturing the interface, so complete is their subjection, yet it is more common for users to be aware—and troubled by the sense—that there is *something* behind the spectacle that cannot be known directly. Addressing the deep social import of black boxes, this chapter reverses course from the previous focus on being *locked in* to consider the condition of being *locked out*.

In medicine, the adjective "occult" is applied to a disease or process that is not accompanied by readily discernible symptoms. The Oxford English Dictionary cites the example of blood "abnormally present, e.g. in feces, but detectable only chemically or microscopically."[1] The blood in question is too small to see without a microscope. Playing no part in routine experience, it is occult by virtue of evading the resolution of our embodied perceptual apparatus.[2] This characterization does not only apply to the example given, but to countless technical presences in everyday life that are suspected but only verifiable by looking deeper into the matter. Indeed, within the landscape of surveillance capitalism, a "new economic order [which] claims human experience as free raw material for *hidden* commercial practices of extraction, prediction, and sales," many occlusions obtain.[3]

Nonetheless, investigation does not guarantee enlightenment. Certain mechanisms may be detected yet remain functionally unreadable. For black boxes are a class of occult objects that stand like the dark cuboid at the beginning of Stanley Kubrick's film *2001: A Space Odyssey*—in front of a community of apes, scratching their chins, beating their chests, or prostrating themselves in clueless devotion. They are available here and now, but only to a limited degree. They present as *more than meets the eye*—sometimes maddeningly so. Their hidden remainder, tauntingly disguised, may not be a mystical problem but does catalyze affects in tune with such, including wonder and paranoia.[4] In fact, contemporary life is organized as much around manifest exclusions from a technological interior as around legibility and access. Today, subjectivity plays out amid a landscape of nested black boxes, in relation to which we are always both *within and without.*[5]

The ground upon which contemporary culture rests is deeply encrypted. Set against narratives of transparency, a countercurrent of darkness and opacity casts its shade over the Technocene. Already, a hidden order is enshrined in the *de facto* constitution of enlightened thought: the atomic world of modern science, whose reality exists out of sight. Chemistry and physics, for instance, require systems of description that contradict the logic of basic experience in the manner of Schrödinger's undead cat. In this way, it is an epistemic common-place to consider the lived realm pregnant with secrets. Most people readily acknowledge at least one concealed (under)world, and embrace a certain distrust of the senses in principle. Thus, even as it serves empirical science and healthy skepticism, positivism's hegemony is a font of mysterious—negative—affect in secular life, bubbling away behind the scenes.

Consolidating the occult character of the "enlightened" *dispositif,* on the macrophenomenal level, the all-surrounding technosphere manifests profound obscurity. Though man-made, its scale is too extensive to be experienced in full by any individual. Even particular components outstrip human sensibility through their massive size.[7] This applies not only to hardware, such as pipeline systems and communications infrastructure, but also to the parameters and volume of data employed by powerful AI models—for instance, the 10.5 terabytes of MassiveText used to train DeepMind, which comprises some 2.35 billion documents drawn from web pages, books, news articles, and code.[8] Thus, one observes that large scales can and do function, effectively, as a mode of encryption. This issue is only exacerbated by the fact that the megastructure's physical components—such as undersea cables and discreetly located server farms—are literally buried. Furthermore, much data is locked behind technical and legal firewalls. So it is that, with the intimation of an encrypted world, a quasi-gnostic mood lies coiled within "knowledge societies" whose secular ethos otherwise privileges "universal access to information and knowledge."[9]

Sociologically speaking, there is certainly a gulf between what most people observe in daily experience and the extensive unseen corners of that same "reality," generally understood to be lying beyond the horizon of what is (personally) accessible. Yet it is apparent that both the invisible quality of the microscopic world and the hyperobjectivity of certain infrastructures are amenable to psychological repression.

One can just keep moving and avoid the issue. What is harder to ignore is the fact that the domain of the seen and heard is shot through with another (more proximate) layer of encryption; visible locked boxes that are harder to metabolize within the frame of a critical intellect. These are man-made encryptions that are on display—sometimes literally—as they work *on* and *through* us. Consider computing technologies, such as smartphones and apps, whose inner mechanisms are opaque—whether by virtue of their complexity, their proprietary schema, or, as per usual, both. It is not that these systems cannot be known in principle, but that their kernels are practically obscure. And yet, they occupy the heart of our affairs: our houses, our pockets, our ears, our eyes, and minds. Soon they will be in our brains. They mediate the economy, social relations, sex, dreams, and, above all, attention. They are constitutive pillars for a whole way of life. All told, they organize our fate.

To manage this push and pull with a relentless parade of black boxes, in the most intimate moments of one's individuation, users seek intellectual accommodation. They fudge the terms of relation, imagine that black boxes function in certain ways and not others, hope that they are not up to something, and so on.[10] Otherwise, they let go of the question altogether and embrace jaded capitulation. In such moments, the interface forms the locus of faith's stealth (re)entry into contemporary technoculture. Here, this archaic specter pursues negotiation with reason, coming into conflict with critical enterprise or absorbing its excess through a devil's bargain—one that accepts the limits of individual command over the *logic* at the core of the techno-*logical.* This chapter is concerned with the psychodramatic field of bargaining our way through this bad dream.[11] The fact that black boxes stridently resist intellectual and political recuperation makes for an especially fraught situation, not least since dialogue with the black box is required in order to establish the conditions for (self-)portraiture in this encrypted world. What is at stake in this endeavor is nothing less than the possible image of a "masterful user" in the Technocene—the possibility of free agency.[12]

The philosopher Brian Massumi has written that "affect is a real condition, an intrinsic variable of the late capitalist system, as infrastructural as a factory."[13] Among the panoply of possible responses to inscrutable tech, "wonder" is capitalism's key prescription. And yet, marketeers do not have a monopoly on the imagination. For now, at least, there remains a field of organic response, wherein art may play an important role. If we hope to speak of a contemporary mood, then we must attend our relationships with the surfaces of artifacts that possess inaccessible depths. Our encounter with these occult elements (or companions) is a key locus of desire and disappointment in contemporary technoculture. It is for this reason that artistic critique explores the tension between the visible interface and its opaque backend. The works considered hereafter crystallize different facets of this problematic modus, which should feel eerily familiar to most readers. From these works we glean diagnostic images, and, perhaps, curative proposals.

The Black Box

In cybernetics, a black box denotes a unit of software or hardware that interacts (with the system that it is embedded within) entirely through its interface. The details of its implementation are obscure.[14] More generally, a black box is a device that can be viewed in terms of input and output, observing only their pattern, without any knowledge of a conversion mechanism. What happens inside it is opaque, veiled in shadow: black. In terms of user relation, a black box instantiates an imperfect or partial understanding of a thing that, nevertheless, does not affect one's ability to make some use of it, and to observe its effects in the real world. "The Black Box cannot be opened.... Knowledge gained from examining a Black Box is based on a profound ignorance."[15]

A dark monolith dominates the gallery space, towering over visitors, a droning noise emanating from within that intensifies according to their proximity. Carsten Nicolai's *anti* (2004) is a distorted black object, truncated to obtain rhombic and triangular facets—its shape inspired by the geometric solid in Albrecht Dürer's *Melencolia I* (1514). Wailing, sometimes shrill, *anti*'s acoustic dimension is powered by a theremin—a musical instrument that reacts to the invisible magnetic field of human bodies, thus "enabling an interaction ... while its mechanism remains hidden."[16] According to Nicolai, *anti* "refuses instant recognition" even as it confronts the viewer, "trying to mask its form and disguise its function," but all the while "absorbing information."[17]

Further touching upon *anti*'s symbolic resonance, Nicolai claims that "regular geometric forms represent systematic thinking and the interrelationship between mathematics, optics, art, and philosophy."[18] Certainly, with respect to Dürer's masterpiece, this relationship is set

Poetics of Encryption

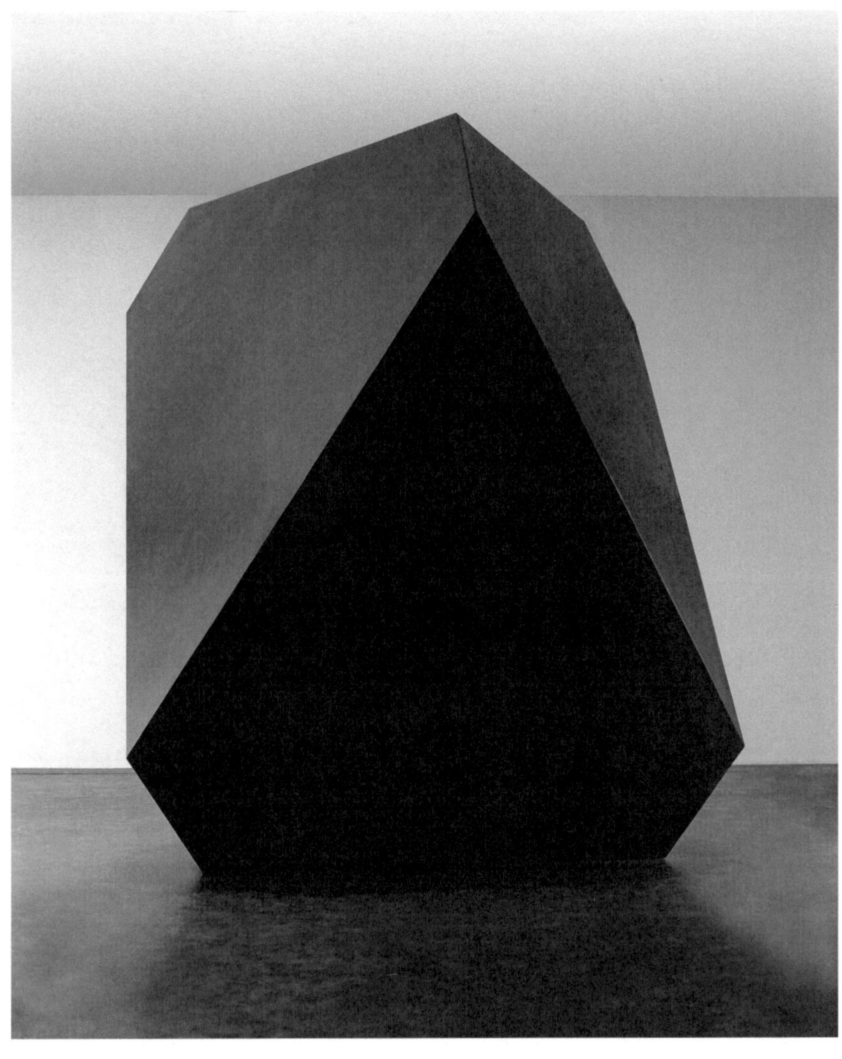

Carsten Nicolai, *anti,* 2004
PP lightweight structure, sound module, theremin module,
transducer, amplifier, light-absorbent black paint, 255×255×300 cm

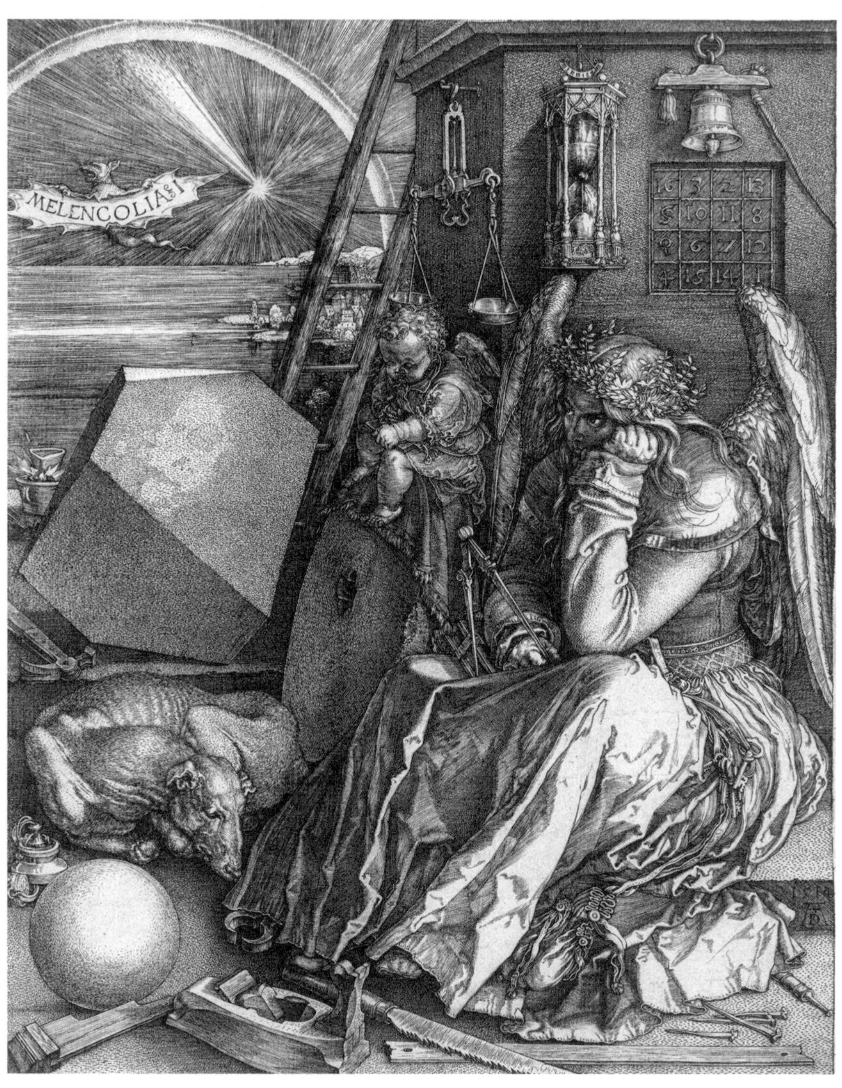

Albrecht Dürer, *Melencolia I,* 1514
Engraving, 24 × 18.5 cm

Poetics of Encryption

within an allegorical frame provided by the title, which leads us
directly to *melancholy*. A sensitive viewer cannot fail to substitute the
figure in Dürer's engraving with Nicolai's gallery visitor—the former
personifying the gloomy humor associated with certain intellectual
labors (whose etched accoutrements include a compass, magic square,
hourglass, and weighing scales). Head in hand, staring into the middle distance, Dürer's brooding muse is sometimes described as figuring the limits of knowledge. Indeed, according to Erwin Panofsky
et al.,

> she is an imaginative Melancholy, whose thoughts and actions all
> take place within the realms of space and visibility, from pure
> reflexion upon geometry to activity in the lesser crafts.... Here if
> anywhere we receive the impression of a being to whom her
> allotted realm seems intolerably restricted—of a being whose
> thoughts "have reached the limit."[20]

"She"—being sketched within the metaphysical coordinates of
Ficino's Neoplatonism, ascribed to Dürer—is "restricted" to the realm
of the senses. Though meditating on geometry, Melancholy does not
access the invisible heart of the matter. This is evidenced, perhaps, by
the rhomboid's reflective surface, upon which the blurry outline of a
face (her face?) can be made out. Frau Melancholy is working hard but
lacks the bandwidth to access a bigger picture—something a true
initiate possesses, according to the Renaissance schema. Thus, she
is thrown back onto her inadequate self-image; into a reality that is
so full of things—ladders, bats, bells, spheres, dogs, and faces—but
wherein, literally and figuratively (with respect to another object in
the scene), *the book is closed.*

When we consider Nicolai's uptake of this allegorical complex, one
understands his comments on the object's "hidden mechanism" and
"disguised function" as reflections on the potential transposition
of Dürer's theme into our present day. Rather than metaphysical,
Nicolai's rhetoric is concrete: *mechanism, function, information.* As
such, *anti* is a drama of exclusion from the interior of a device or system logic. The inaccessible realm is resolutely concrete (not meta) but
nevertheless "masked" and elsewhere. The dark monolith's operation
concerns the visitor's own person, sensing their body, among other
things. Moreover, it works remotely, by way of a procedure that is
obscure (at the very least, visually). The stakes of the relation are not

just physical. Indeed, the mood engendered by this type of situation is at issue in Nicolai's work: *anti* stages a common form of contemporary intellectual labor—*attending a black box as it works on you*—in order to ask *how* this species of relation colors one's own temperament.

The number one in Dürer's title, *Melencolia I,* has been taken to indicate that melancholy is but one of the four humors, conceived as fundamental subject types within the Greek imaginary alongside choleric, phlegmatic, and sanguine. These were general dispositions towards the world at large, effectively written into the person from birth. Rather than proposing adherence to this doctrine, this observation is ventured to suggest the uptake of an anatomical project on the part of artists today, *vis-à-vis* various moods conditioned by black boxes, and, indeed, the black box as contemporary affect.[21] The result is a new visual culture of occlusion, with artists taking on the sprawling landscape of black boxes within which they find themselves—in the Heideggerian sense—*thrown.*

The artist Félix Luque Sánchez also offers an ominous space-making (scenographic) black box in his CGI video work titled *Chapter I: The Discovery* (2009). Marshaling congruent theatrics, his object is a smooth, black dodecahedron, pulsing with light and sound—demonstrating reactive qualities that portend something to be revealed. The box's shiny surface beckons curious persons, responding to their approach with a buzzing, broken, and babbling noise. Sometimes its sonic range and rhythms appear to approximate human speech. Is it a monologue? Or is it kin—communicating, however partially, with them? In the dramatic construction, we see the outputs but do not know what is driving them. Is that rising pitch (and flashing light) a threat of some kind?

The work plays out in a series of vignettes. First, a gallery, occupied by the dark object; later, other scenarios involving the mysterious solid, out there, in the world. So many portentous opening scenes from science-fiction cinema: some sort of alien probe, perhaps, crash-landed in a snowy field; a super-advanced piece of found technology being monitored in a secret lab, a series of contact microphones and sensor cables affixed to its surface. Are these, one wonders, moments from the object's past—a kind of backstory, presaging a gallery encounter? Or, within the video's dramatic universe, do these scenes suggest that there are multiple versions of the device out there in the world? If so, how many might there be? Acknowledging the video's CGI appearance raises a further question: What if these animations belong to the physical object as supplementary materials,

Poetics of Encryption

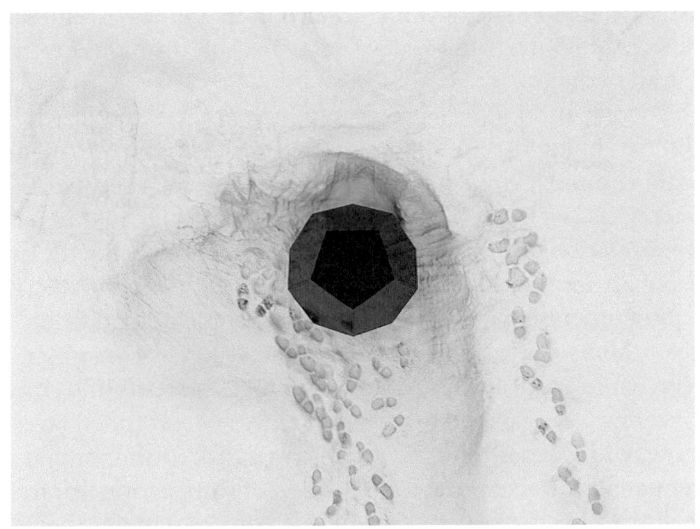

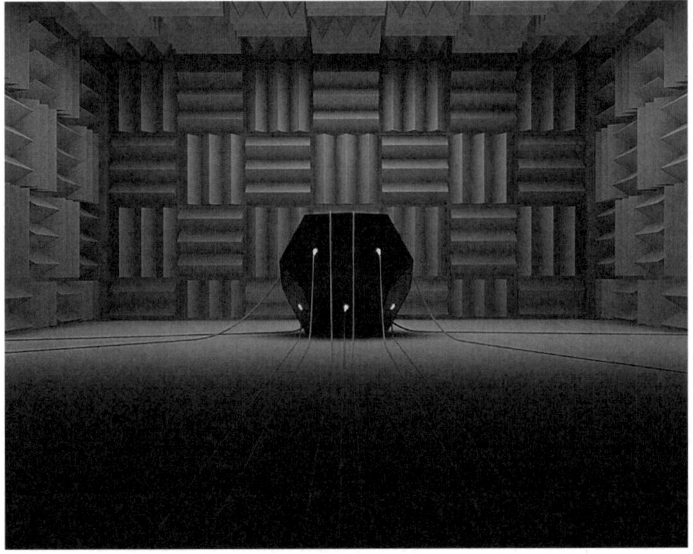

Félix Luque Sánchez, *Chapter I: The Discovery,* 2009
1.6 m³ plywood and Plexiglas sculpture: computer, sound card,
788-LD+ dimmers, ballasts, TL-D 15w, ultra sound sensors, homemade
electronics, MaxMsp programming; Videos: 3d Max, After Effects

like instruction manuals outlining appropriate modes of contact? Questions proliferate. The mystery deepens. Yet, throughout, the object is all surface.

Both Nicolai and Luque's projects leverage the aesthetic import of a certain psychological oscillation, between attraction and alienation, which late-capitalist subjects feel in the presence of a compelling container. This is a locus of affect attending *packaging* that is set into an uneasy relationship with *content* (that which is contained). In the absence of an accessible center, the outside becomes a fetish. The online phenomenon of "unboxing," where people upload video footage of themselves opening parcels (to reveal new consumer products) while carefully describing the process, exemplifies interest in the interface as a layered experience. Having unwrapped layers of packaging, while describing the process in a procedural tone, the unboxer usually offers a forced expression of satisfaction upon the release of the (invariably mass-produced) item. Serving as the dead-eyed simulacrum of a fulfilled quest, requiring no travel or intellectual penetration, unboxing represses the issue of a technical, economic, or political backend, fixing upon the commodity as (false) kernel. As an affective performance, unboxing represents the diminished progeny of wonder—a more ancient relation to the inaccessible. Against it, the probing imperative of critical reason bristles.

Ultimately, it is not that black boxes are necessarily bad, or up to no good. It is just that they often require an act of faith that they are not. Children of the *Aufklärung* are supposed to demand more light, not less, and man-made black boxes are all the more suspect for being the fruit of (scientific) rationalism while proposing that users disengage from its performance, to some degree, when interacting with them. There is, after all, a possible universe where anyone (on principle, in terms of human intellect) is capable of understanding whatever another human has designed. When a user does not meet this theoretical selfhood in practice, their critical agency is disturbed, and the hum of the device has the potential to sound more like a growl. Indeed, the confidence that a device *is* knowable can be an apologia for ignoring its workings: it is to accept alienation. However, all too often this is a lived science fiction, premised on the idea of a one-to-one relation between theory and practice that is too ahistorical a concept to be applicable today, given the sheer abundance and sedimentation of extant technical systems. It is the science fiction of our *scientism,* spuriously guaranteeing the legibility of the world we live in—a world saturated with specialized constructs, though

we are long past being able to read the book. It is a *faith* structure,
a mania. As information technologies proliferate within surveillance
capitalism, reordering life at an ever-increasing pace, the faithfulness
of users grates against the scientistic ideology of the free subject.

Mysticism meets the fetish for the commodity and its secret here,
a secret embedded in the dark logic of exchange and exploitation—of
workers, environments, attention spans, worlds.[22] The fetish object is
everything one wants from a new smartphone, car, or high-end oven.
It is a black mirror, offering images even as it circumscribes clear vision.
In fact, corporate tech behemoths aim to establish black boxes where,
previously, an open system might have offered more affordances. Black
absorbs light. Keeping things proprietary means stopping the sun
from rising over the internal horizon of the device, restricting users to
prescribed inputs (e.g. "pay as you go"), and receiving prescribed
outputs. When it comes to computing power, so many commodities
could do more than what they are marketed for. But why pay once when
you can pay thrice? This brings us to the title of Luque's artwork,
Chapter I: The Discovery. If this named discovery is a case of finding a
fully formed inscrutable object in the world, then will there be a *Chapter
II*? That is, a second moment in which one may find out more about
this mysterious thing? Given the lack of a sequel, it appears that the
work only concerns the initial encounter—establishing, aesthetically,
the principle of perennial limbo. Rather than any further character or
plot development, in some future, the proposition is suspended. It is
a pregnant metaphor for so much experience in the age of black boxes.

The black box is a smoke screen, behind which the true forge
of contemporary life smolders—under the sign of Vulcan, or
Tezcatlipoca.[23] The latter was a central deity of the Aztecs, associated
with prophesy. His name is often translated as "Smoking Mirror"—for
the black reflectors made of obsidian (volcanic glass) used for divination under his sign. The blackness of such mirrors was that smoke,
clouding and altering a reflection of the world, and in so doing,
providing a picture not of what (already) is, but of *what might be.*
As twenty-first-century smoking mirrors, Luque and Nicolai's icons
reflect the iPhone's obsidian character—crystalline and jet-black,
though forged not in the natural furnace of a Tequila volcano but
a neo-alchemical crucible. It is in such research and development
laboratories that, we are told, visionaries operate, willing the future
into being. Staring into the black mirrors with which they have
equipped consumers, smoke (and the fire of the neo-colonial forge)
begins to speak riddles, to cast spells; to babble, whisper, shout, and

cajole. Beyond echoes of pre-Columbian magic, European divination through crystal gazing (running from the Druids through to carnival sideshows) flickers in the collective unconscious of those who are interested less in what they are *looking with* than *what they see.* With respect to Plato's cave, the bright icons of the graphical user interface (GUI) stand akin to shadows, standing in substitution for the unhidden/sun; a folly re-presented in Saint Paul's diagnostic concerning obscure sight: vision *quasi speculum in oenigmate*—"as in a mirror darkly."[24]

Black denotes the screen or veil separating a viewer from what is inside. It invokes an epistemic relation. This is not only an optic metaphor but, in some products, a literal condition. However, with respect to certain objects, and the works thus far considered, another occlusion may be observed: the smooth geometric surface design of recent consumer electronics (presaged by Dürer's rhomboid, and echoed by Luque's dodecahedron) suggests plenitude—fullness, self-sufficiency, and frictionless value proposition. Such devices set their own terms of use. A digital politics registered, once again, in the human digitus, its image apparent in an early series of photographs by the artist Britta Thie. *Sweat on Retina* (2012) comprises various scans of turned-off (black) iPhone screens, each bearing the greasy marks of fingertips in patterns ranging from the seemingly random to the loosely calligraphic. In contrast to the buried-but-alive fingerings of Juliana Leite's *Anthropometry* (attempting to claw a way out of the techno-cave; a work, it should be noted, that employs tropes of volcanic burial), Thie's photographs capture the non-stick exterior of a box whose interior is fundamentally inaccessible to the embodied user. While on first view, the images engage the history of painterly abstraction, suggesting a logical next step whereby the screen takes the place of the canvas, the messiness—and diminutive scale—of the artist's bodily interaction hints at something more. Indeed, their sweaty pawing at *it* suggests a field of effort that straddles both work and (stunted) eroticism. This spatial rhetoric stages a reverse situation to the *untimely entombed,* yet it similarly reduces the user's person(a) to the index of a poor interaction with some interface.

What is the difference between opening the black box—cracking the system—and unboxing? The latter would appear to be the epitome of the commodity fetish, and the former closer to its refusal. Yet, Luque's *Chapter I* suggests that things are less clear. The video components of the exhibition, all of them apparently disclosing historical facts about the ambiguous object in question, might at first appear

Poetics of Encryption

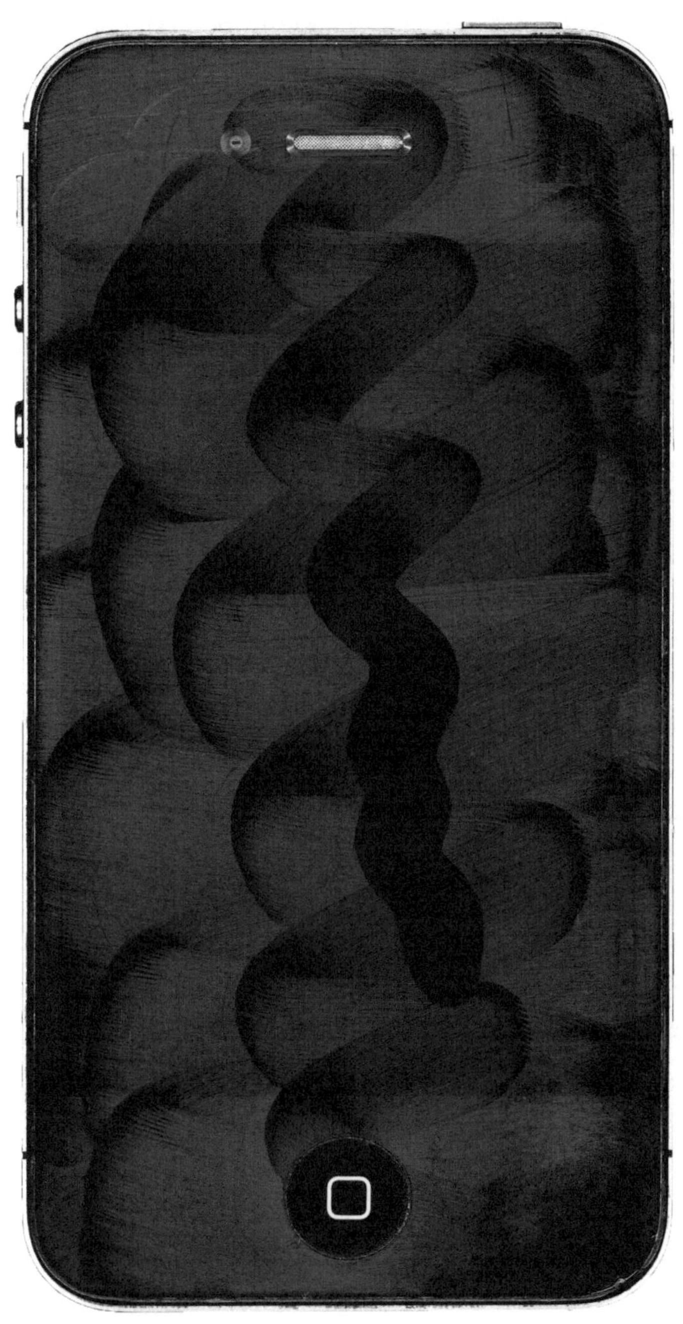

Britta Thie, *Sweat on Retina,* 2012
Digital scan of iPhone 4 touchscreen, dimensions variable

to be a kind of penetration of its mystery. And, yet, one must eventually realize that each is a spectacle, nothing more, sliding across the surface of another black box: the screen. The exhibition's visitors are also unboxing: pulling back one veil only to find another. In a related fashion, Thie's finger movements are not subject to friction, but neither do they penetrate.

While the works discussed here do not open up the mechanical underworld of the device (crypto-physical reality), through a *theatrics of the enclosed* they nevertheless prepare the ground for ideology critique: late-capitalist dream analysis. Illustrating this tendency, a work by another German artist has pictured the manufactured *sleep of reason* at the point of interface. Taken in the brightly lit and slick style of commercial photography, Susanna Hertrich's *Robot* (2010) features a woman lying on her side, cozily dozing in crisp white sheets with her left arm draped tenderly across her bed partner: a slick black polyhedron. It is the literal intimate embrace of the alien device—the *robot*. It is, according to Hertrich, a portrait of "man–machine synthesis."[25] In her vision, the object has no obvious independent function but to "serve as projection area for its respective user."[26] Robot (from the Russian, *robota*) means *to work*. There is no denying the potential pleasure of distance from inner workings. But images like this seem to provoke the question: Where is the pain? For, as always in the psychoanalysis of dreams, it must be somewhere.

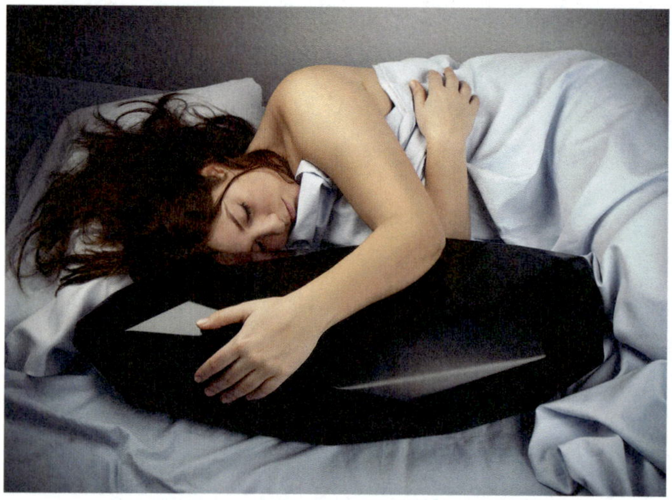

Susanna Hertrich, *Robot,* 2010
C-print on alubond with acrylic coating, 80 × 120 cm

Poetics of Encryption

Blackboxing

"When a machine runs efficiently, when a matter of fact is settled, one need focus only on its inputs and outputs and not on its internal complexity. Thus, paradoxically, the more science and technology succeed, the more opaque and obscure they become."[27] So wrote the late Bruno Latour, describing the social process of "blackboxing." However, blackboxing is not only a social effect but also a design agenda. To a certain degree, it is an imperative. Indeed, as Garnet Hertz puts it, blackboxing facilitates the creation of those "building blocks from which new technologies and infrastructures are built."[28] Additionally, in consumer tech, it clears the ground for ease of use, not least as a computer system "is almost incomprehensible if thought of in terms of its millions of transistors, circuits, mathematical calculations, and technical components."[29] What is required, therefore, is a mediating figure that hides such mechanics. Yet, as Latour indicates, this substitution muddies the waters between transparency and opacity. As a consequence, in a landscape that is ever-more filled with blackboxed systems, artistic icons for the technologically enclosed or obscure inevitably abound. Beyond recourse to an art that figures literal black boxes, such as Nicolai's opaque rhomboid, a counterintuitive aesthetic emerges, wherein translucent tokens also stand for what is hidden, or the process of making secret.

"The more the small item (smartphone) I hold in my hand is personalized, easy to use, 'transparent' in its functioning," writes Slavoj Žižek, "the more the entire setup has to rely on the work being done elsewhere, in a vast circuit of machines that co-ordinate the user's experience."[30] Widening the frame, he continues: "The more our experience [appears] non-alienated, spontaneous, transparent, the more it is regulated by the invisible network controlled by state agencies and large private companies that follow their secret agendas."[31] In this hidden field we also find "ghost work," repeatedly mentioned in Joler's New Extractivism diagram—the stress put upon real bodies, often in the developing world, out of sight, out of mind; a tendency exposed in a 2019 book by Mary L. Gray and Siddharth Suri.[32]

Let us be *clear:* For those who would critique technology's impact, perhaps the most disturbing species of icon for the black box figures it as *transparent.* This image is where the real ideological serpent bites—a viper to the user's Eurydice, or (running the allegory through its biblical metamorphosis) the snake offering questionable fruit to some Eve. How else to decode documentation from 2006 of the Apple

Store construction site on New York's Fifth Avenue? Before completion, this cube-shaped building was clad in jet-black wooden hoarding. A black box erected only to be *performatively cast aside* upon the work's completion—unboxed—to reveal a transparent glass cube. At the time, the event's visual politics were contested. Some radical groups in the Middle East interpreted the black cube as the architectural analogue of the Kaaba (a building at the center of Islam's most important mosque, whose Arabic name translates as "cube"), unjustly profaned through conversion into a consumer icon. Some Western press observers did, in fact, refer to the building as "Apple Mecca."[33] With this issue playing out in the midst of the spurious War on Terror, it is easy to see how the new edifice afforded religious/identitarian projections—notwithstanding the fact that the offended audience accessed information about the structure through the Internet. Today, in the aftermath of the controversy caused by WikiLeaks and Edward Snowden, we cannot help but understand the transparent cube as a veil of another kind.[34]

Indeed, in the immediate wake of Snowden's 2013 disclosure of the Five Eyes Alliance global surveillance system, spanning state and consumer infrastructure, we find certain artists attempting to complicate the notion of transparency. Specifically, we find them attempting to illustrate how transparency effects blackboxing. Paralleling the conceptual hardening of the sky mentioned in the previous chapter, their agendas assert the latent politics—or prejudice—within the translucent, filling in some of it, or attempting to calibrate intellectual

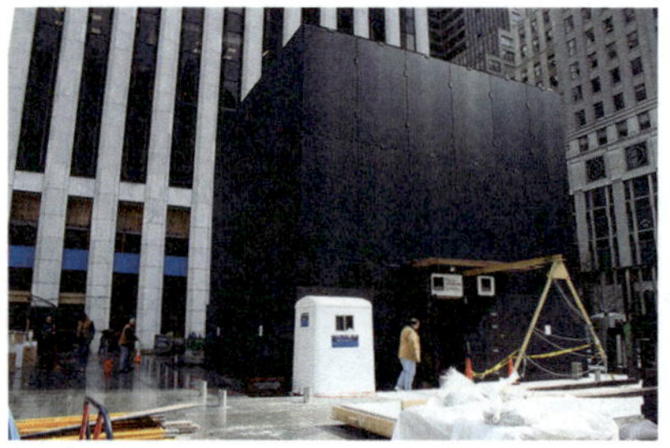

Apple Fifth Avenue under construction, 2006

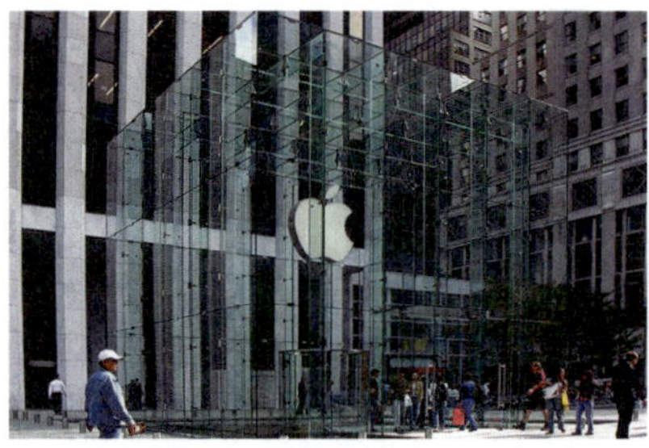

Apple Fifth Avenue, 2006

Poetics of Encryption

perceptions to see through its charade. For, one might initially associate transparency with a certain absolute: a one-to-one assurance of accurate vision. Yet there is a second etymological sense of the term. After the Latin *trans* (across, beyond; through) follows *parere* (come into sight, appear; submit, obey), its latter aspect involving the act of surrender: to submit to inspection, to obediently perform. Within the concept: a disciplinary kernel.

In his 2013 exhibition at my project space, Import Projects, Berlin, titled *Invisible Measure,* the artist Beny Wagner undertook a transmedia meditation on "narratives hidden in plain view"—probing the aesthetics and rhetoric of transparency as a "vehicle for ideological social reform."[35] Reflecting upon how, over the last century, the concept of transparency evolved alongside a gradual shift from material to immaterial labor processes, the exhibition comprised the eponymous video essay, a series of Plexiglas sculptures, a sound piece, and a digital-print reproduction of a found painting. The first of these was a filmic reverie structured around the uptake of glass in modern architecture, with a voiceover composed of extracts from the influential book *Glass Architecture,* written by the critic and poet Paul Scheerbart in 1914. Throughout the video, Wagner's camera captures the shimmering appearance and disappearance of urban surfaces, their physicality briefly brought to light in moments wherein visual opacity is effected by solar or artificial illumination. Through so much glimmer, combined with the voiceover's enthusiastic pronouncements concerning the holistic merits of the material, our contemporary built environment at first appears to live up to Scheerbart's now century-old vision of a glass world so virtuous that it "would rather break than bend." And yet, as indicated through the further inclusion of Plexiglas manufacture in the movie, the ethos of the crystal palace has since warped, becoming subject to a newer material reality where transparent structures can be, in Wagner's own words, "as malleable as each of our individual desires."[36]

Accompanied by three totem-like Plexiglas sculptures, *Contract, Light Politics,* and *Without Seams* (all 2013), as well as another wall-mounted work shaped like a fig leaf, Wagner's exhibition dug into the newer substance. As the first manufactured material to effect transparency without the compromise of fragility, Plexiglas allowed for more visual permeability in material culture. And yet, as the exhibition text explained, its story is murky: following its invention in Germany—in 1933, the year Hitler came to power as Chancellor—it was immediately put to military use. According to the artist, "today's inheritors of the

Plexiglas patent, while proud of their product's optimization of our ability to see, are keen to obscure this genesis."[37] We can understand how Wagner's cognizance of this occluded history found an interesting foil in the enthusiasm of Scheerbart—a turn of the century German— not least given the forty-fourth of *Glass Architecture*'s numbered theses, titled "Vanquishing vermin": "That in a glass house, if properly built, vermin must be unknown, needs no further comment."[38] A functional reflection of the dialectic of enlightenment if ever there was one. Thus, *Invisible Measure*'s video and sculptures asserted the intersection of the aesthetic and the question of political imperatives.

Performatively, Wagner's *Invisible Measure* did not attempt to synthesize a single perspective, but rather envisioned the image and concept of transparency through something approaching the logic of refraction. Through the exhibition's looking glass, the discourse of transparency was seen to express—among other things—a trajectory of the German hygiene concept. The sound piece and "painting" appeared to further indicate its passage into the present day. In these works, Wagner took Transparency International (TI), the global anti-corruption organization, to task, casting a critical eye on its latent claim to purity. Founded in 1993 by Peter Eigen, former manager of programs in Africa and Latin America for the World Bank, the organi- zation maintains two ranking systems for countries: the annual Corruption Perceptions Index (CPI), and the Global Corruption Barometer (GCB).[39] By their reckoning, transparency is quantifiable— through survey and in-depth statistical analysis. Wagner's sound installation *Through It Appearance* (2013) was based on an interview with Eigen, whose booming disembodied voice was broadcast through the galleries, suggesting a position of hidden omnipotence—authority and judgment residing out of sight. More cutting, however, was the inclusion of a digital reproduction of a painting that Wagner had photographed on the wall of Eigen's office—a gift, according to the latter, from former trainees in Africa—depicting him with white hair, wearing a white shirt and sitting at the center of a table in a manner art-historically evocative of the Christ figure, his person and speech attended closely by a group of all-Black listeners—the painted hues of their bodies in visual keeping with the rest of the landscape.

Clarity about what transparency means in political terms, and to whom, was at issue in Wagner's project. As the only work of appropria- tion in the exhibition, the reproduced painting gestured towards structural racism in the World Bank/TI system, as much as to the prospect of an individual white savior complex. Bearing this in mind, it is notable that if corruption is endemic to political black boxes—indeed, if it "happens in the shadows," to borrow a phrase from TI's website—then the imperative to transparency is also, in cybernetic terminology, a demand for more "white" boxes. In less metaphorical language, TI pursues this demand through metric analyses that impute crimes to persons, even "without reliable information" to go on—according to one independent report that also concluded that the CPI was "of uncertain value to poor countries."[40] Transparency, it seems, retains an obscure aspect even when institutionalized.

> In Dresden, where I studied, there is the Deutsches Hygiene-Museum where an anatomical model of the human body from the 1930s is displayed. A life-size figure made of glass. Under the transparent shell of the "glass woman" one can see each and every human organ. It's time for me to remake the GlassHuman.[41]

This statement comes from another German artist, Tillman Hornig, when asked about his future agenda. The retrospective import of this comment is significant when considering his previous works: sculptures made of transparent glass, cut to match the scale and format of laptops and smartphones (*GlassBook,* 2013–present; *GlassPhone,* 2014–present), and often pictured as if in use, in the style of stock photography. In both series, an oscillation between the surrender of human life to computation (making it trans-apparent), and the invisibility of the latter is on view.

Hornig's mention of the transparent woman relates to the 1936 object created by Franz and Fritz Tschakert as a follow up to their immensely popular *Transparent Man* (1927).[42] Depicting "the human body as a machine: understandable, immaculate and, if well cared for, durable," the figure is also described by the museum as "the reification of modernism's image of the human being [conveying] faith in the link between science, transparency, and rationality."[43] As characterized by the historian Jeffrey Schnapp, both figures were "consecrated symbols of the Health Museum movement, worldwide messengers of Scheerbart's 'new glass environment [that] will completely transform humankind,' the model citizens of the glass utopias of the day," and, during the period of Nazi rule, icons of eugenics.[44] In light of his previous body of work, Hornig's comment raises the specter of an updated *Gläserne(r) Mensch/Frau*—signified by the transparent affect of consumer tech.

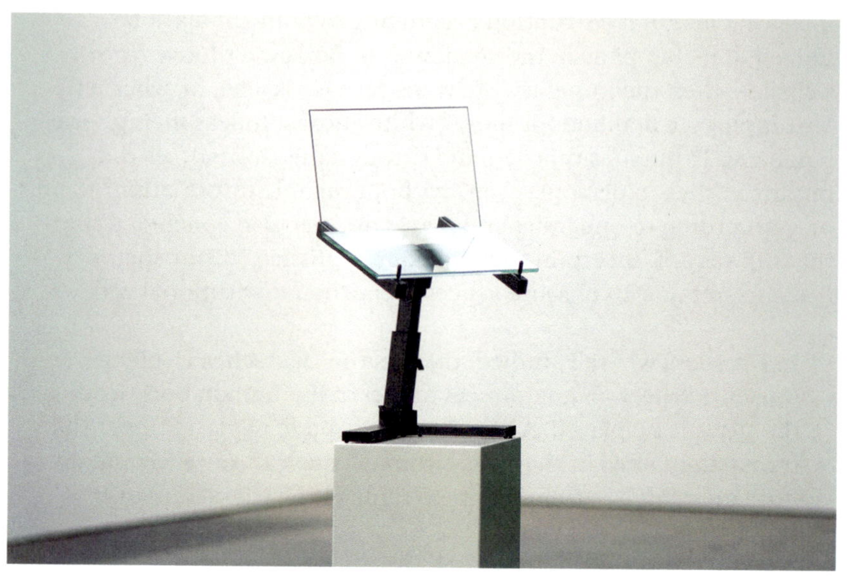

Tilman Hornig, *GlassBook,* 2013–
15 in. *GlassBook* on stand. Installation view: Art Berlin Contemporary, 2015

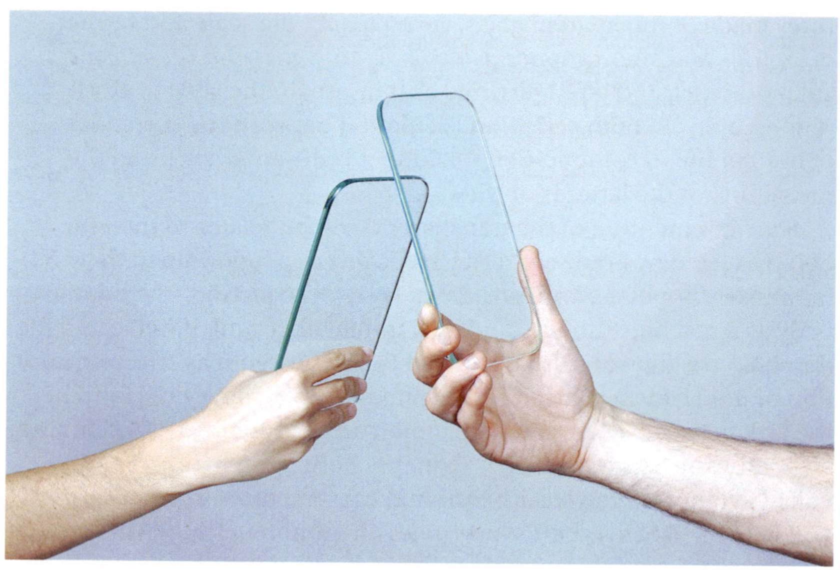

Tilman Hornig, *GlassPhone* (*Stille Nacht* no. 13), 2020
Photograph printed on glass, 40 × 60 cm

Poetics of Encryption

In both series, the glass stand-in is less visible than the device invoked. However, within Hornig's photographs, this disappearing act establishes the dramatic principle of the depicted scene: the "coming into sight" of the pictured users. Offering a visible parallel to unseen surveillance techniques, Hornig's transparent sculptures serve them up for inspection. It is a move that parallels the computational staging and/or extraction of the data body—that "fascist sibling of the real body" whose real home, as we have already observed, is not a crystal palace but a cave/coffin.[45]

What Hornig's glass works convey is that, counterintuitively, the computer cannot be seen. While ubiquitous and proximate it is, effectively, blackboxed—receding from view even as it occupies the central space of attention. But how does this happen? On the one hand, powered by the phenomenon of Moore's Law, tech is ever shrinking. "In no other sector are the tendencies of technology and design towards their own vanishing so clear,"[46] writes philosopher Johannes Thumfart in an exhibition text about Hornig's work: "A true obsession to minimize everything reigns, which has already compressed the capacity of the room-sized machines of the fifties into the size of a pants pocket."[47] To this we must note the further movement from pocketsize to subcutaneous, with "significant research efforts on a global scale" pursuing the end goal of an effective brain–computer interface.[48]

Crucially, this scopic vanishing is a useful register of its phenomenological disappearance—something that is much harder to attend, and which the artist's work fixes upon. As intensely *ready-to-hand,* tech is seamlessly incorporated into the choreography of desire and action throughout society. In its everyday mode, it may even be unreadable. By Thumfart's account it comes across as being without qualities, pushing the user's intellect towards anything but itself: "It is easier to believe we are looking at different things, when in fact we are just staring, over and over, at the same screen."[49] We have already stated that this hides (its) power. Thumfart paints the picture more starkly: "Instead of a new golden age, we are witnesses to the dawning of cyber-totalitarianism, invulnerable as it remains without a face, without a form, without a space, without a body."[50] It is a stark claim, and one that stands to be modified in light of Hornig's images. As seen in certain photos where the user's distorted face is reflected in the surface of the transparent object, we understand that part of the phenomenological invisibility of cyber-totalitarianism is that it leads users to confuse it for themselves. Transparency is a hall of mirrors.

Qua mirror, the screen may propose a human image—representative of a familiar world. But a *sous-face* obtains beneath it, which departs from phizical value.[51] Code and logic do not have any color, or sweat. Through the looking glass, their coded agency *counts,* but may not always *account* for a life that one might hope to live.[52] Contemporary society is profoundly disciplined by this digital *Übermenschlichkeit* (overhumanity), yet most of us are adrift on the screen. Its constantly changing skein, the façade, dazzles as it occludes a travesty of unified subjectivity. Users may delight in the way it refracts; the way it seems capable of producing a panorama of selfhood. Its glittering mutability hints at proliferation and rebirth—a billion selfies. But within this image matrix (using the term in its traditional sense, as *womb*) many fail to discern their twin: a real yet foreign body. Their digital doppelganger, *sous-face,* or shadow, is not a photograph or a status update, much less a manifestation of playfulness or open possibility. It is a cluster of instrumental functions that would collapse the person into its own image: one's "real" body at risk of becoming the avatar of this virtual twin. In this sense, we are living the emergence of machines in the areas we once thought of as our ghosthood—(sub)consciousness, memory, desire, and more.

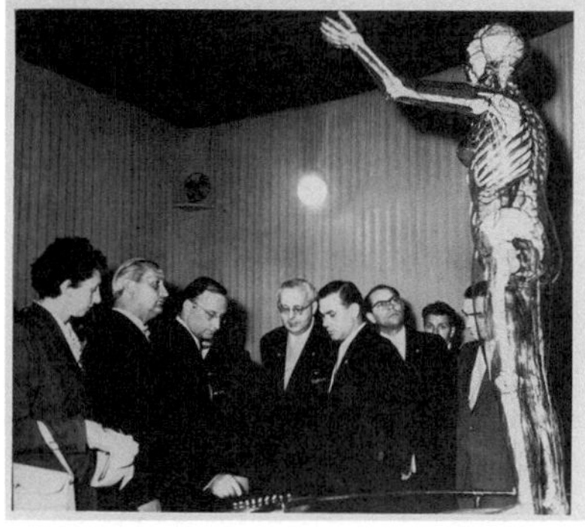

Opening of the National Hygiene Exhibition—
Guests of Honor in Front of
the *Gläserne Frau* (1935–36), 1961
Baryta photo paper, 10.5×14.8 cm

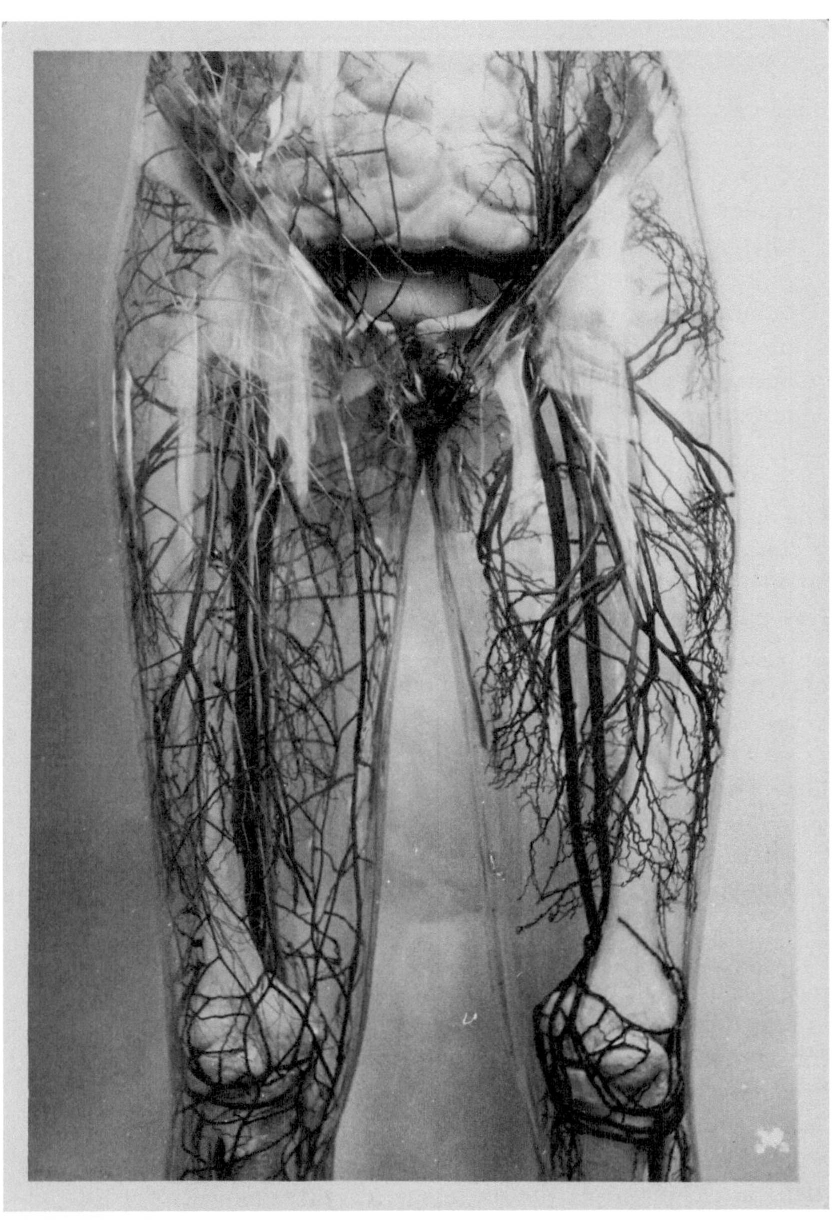

"New image of the vascular system of the *Gläserne Frau*"—Genital area and thighs, 1950–69
Baryta photo paper, 14.9×10.4 cm

Black box image culture meditates on this situation: on remote (yet proximate) control; on the flatness of the "self"-portrait offered by the black mirror—the data body first outlined, discursively, by Critical Art Ensemble in 1995, decades before the complex of massive data capture and deep learning arrived on the scene. In an incredibly prescient diagnosis, their account proposes that

> the most frightening thing about the data body is that it is the center of an individual's social being. It tells the members of officialdom what our cultural identities and roles are. We are powerless to contradict the data body. Its word is the law. One's organic being is no longer a determining factor, from the point of view of corporate and government bureaucracies. Data have become the center of social culture, and our organic flesh is nothing more than a counterfeit representation of original data.[53]

The data body is thus a person opened up to technical inspection; a performing body whose auditorium is not so much a playhouse as it is an operating theatre, or worse.[54] It is, as the example of the *Gläserne Frau* indicates, a tool that exposes the subject while at the same time muddying the waters with respect to the boundaries between person-hood and a technical phenomenon to be managed.

Black Lives

The data body has assumed prominence in the last decade as a kind of contemporary portrait subject, whose strange double figure appears in various artworks. Clad in heterogeneous visual markers, while manifesting a disciplinary flattening of the (human) life to which it refers, the artistic data body portrait re-presents the subjection of human depth to the surface effects of algorithmic operations—as a consequence of automating the interpretation of images. As artist and research scientist Adam Harvey observes, "There is no *true* 'face' in facial detection, only probabilities and thresholds."[55] In a data body portrait such thresholds are a central visual concern. By fixing upon them, artists propose a double image: as well as representing the distorted "human" sitter, the strange figure also stands for the like-ness of the machine-artist at work; specifically, the system's character as typically *receding from view:* works of data body portraiture employ

Poetics of Encryption

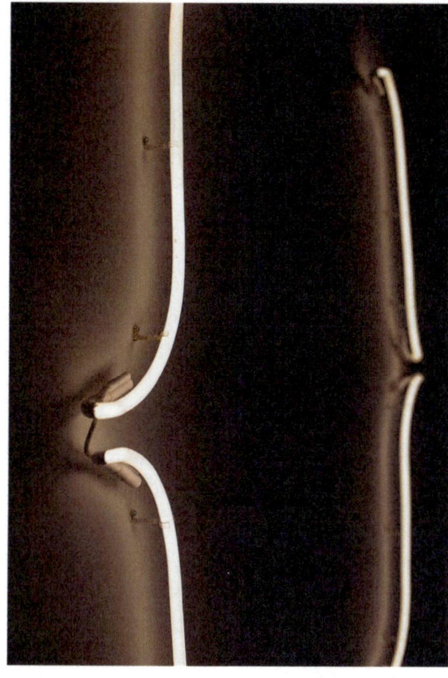

Mimi Ọnụọha, *Classification.01,* 2017
Custom hardware (camera, sensor),
neon, 201.4 × 180.3 cm

a negative strategy in order to approach the evasive bot, making it
visible through the deracinated, reduced images of people that it
supplies or "sees" while—simultaneously—obscuring itself. In a key
sense, this double portraiture attempts a (higher resolution) image
of the *inter-face,* the liminal site wherein the subject and object of
machine vision converge. All the better to free the human from the
anti-culture of machine vision.

Mimi Ọnụọha's *Classification.01* (2017) is a sculpture that outwardly
consists of two white neon curly bracket symbols mounted on a wall.
When more than one viewer approaches, the work employs a nearby
camera-computer system to determine whether to class them as
"similar" according to a variety of algorithmic conditions. The brackets only light up if the terms of classification are met, without, however, sharing the decision's guiding code or rationale—leaving viewers
to speculate as to what conditions have been satisfied or unmet.
Classification.01 represents an open question about the *how* of taxonomy. Crucially, the depicted brackets not only represent a box to put
people in, but also the bracketed process that underpins the delivered
sign. Ọnụọha's visual icon symbolizes more than a formal operation;
it also speaks about how computation encodes the social. The

Nigerian-American artist puts it thus: "We are grouped and sorted by models, computers, and algorithms. These algorithmic classifications are more likely to be perceived as true than human sortings, regardless of how arbitrary they are. And things that have been perceived as true have real and true consequences."[56]

Indeed, AI classifications of people are rarely made visible to the people being classified. As black box AI assumes a larger role in society, its side effects also gain prominence. While artificial intelligence is able to churn through massive pools of data in order to solve challenges that humans struggle with, "understanding how it makes its decisions is often very difficult to do, if not impossible."[57] If there is no way to determine how an algorithm came to a result, real epistemological and ethical challenges will obtain in fields from medicine through to government.[58] Indeed, "When an AI model works it is not as easy as it should be to make further refinements, and when it exhibits *odd* behaviour it can be hard to fix."[59] An odd descriptor for some of the more egregious AI operations encountered in the field.

"I, the man of color, want only this: That the tool never possess the man"—so wrote Franz Fanon in his classic work on the psychic construction of Blackness, *Black Skin, White Masks,* published in 1952.[60] But it does. While examining constructions of the data body, a host of artists have diagnosed the computation of Blackness as an acute symptom of White supremacy; a toxic hygiene carried into the algorithmic dimension. As a graduate student in 2015, the coder and artist Joy Buolamwini found that a facial analysis system being used to ascertain gender was better able to detect her when she wore a White mask. "In my case, a white mask was a closer fit to what the system had learned was a face than my actual human face."[61] Buolamwini would go on to be among the first to research and analyze the pronounced bias towards White males exhibited in commercial AI, and consider its ripple effects in domains including safety and employment—coining the term the "coded gaze" to describe algorithmic operations that serve the latent (hidden) "preferences, priorities, and at times prejudices of those who have the power to shape [AI] technology."[62]

In this regard, the *material culture of the black box* and the *matter of Black lives* (namely, that they matter) come together—as the most acute symptom of a more general trauma attending algorithmic governance. Consider the fact that certain software used by a United States court to calculate risk assessment was found to be biased against Black prisoners—prone to label them nearly twice as likely to

reoffend as White people (45 percent versus 24 percent).[63] "If you're
not careful, you risk automating the exact same biases these programs are supposed to eliminate," stated the lead statistician of the
non-profit Human Rights Data Analysis Group (HRDAG), whose work
on a different report proved that an AI called "HunchLab," employed
by the St. Louis Police Department to predict future crime hotspots,
could get stuck in a feedback loop of over-policing majority Black and
Brown neighborhoods.[64] The prospect of living under the technical
reification of normative categories may only be acceptable if those
categories are agreed upon to begin with, but even when this is the
case, actually implementing them in the tech is a different matter.
Without piercing the black box system's rhetorically transparent
screen, one cannot trust that the delivered portrait does not smuggle
in confusion or systemic prejudice. For, as a cybernetic rule of thumb,
"inside every white box there are two black boxes trying to get out."[65]

As black box AI's social penetration continues apace, the inscrutable systems that would screen the human scene for undesirables
come into sharper artistic focus. One person pursuing this task goes
by the legal name of "American Artist"—an ambivalent denotation
that both insists, in their account, on the "visibility of blackness as
descriptive of an american artist," as well as its erasure by algorithm:
their chosen moniker is unable to be "validated by a computer as a
person's name," and is also (mis)recognized by search engines that
offer famous white figures, instead, in response to the prompt.[66] Their
video installation *2015* (2019) is a twenty-one-minute, single-channel
video that interpolates the visitor as a police officer—driving through
the freeways and side streets of Brooklyn. The video is offered as a
view through the windscreen of their squad car; a transparent lens
overlaid with an Augmented Reality (AR) textual interface whose
content appears to be predictive policing updates in real time.
Superimposed on buildings and tarmac, words including "BUR-
GLARY," "RAPE," and "MURDER" scroll, along with statistics concerning their frequency, flashing maps, and more. Occasionally, a notice
announces: "CRIME DETERRED." "But where's the potentially
criminal activity? Through the windshield, we only see an intersection, a few parked cars, some nondescript buildings. It's clear now.
Aided by algorithms developed by tech firms like PredPol, the police
car transforms the world out the window into a criminal landscape
by targeting locations and imagining infractions."[67] In this manner,
the work pictures the fact that police are, according to the artist,
"armed with much more than guns, that armature takes the form of

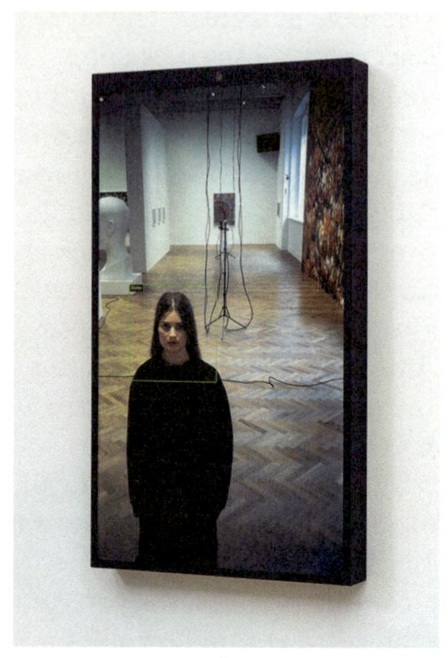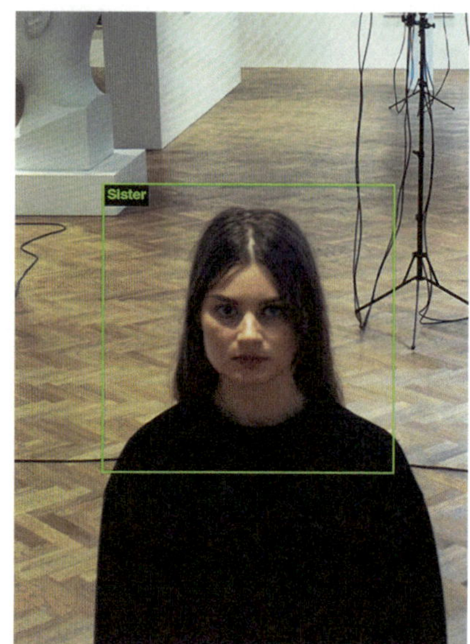

Trevor Paglen and Kate Crawford,
ImageNet Roulette, 2019
Screen, camera, computer elements,
aluminum frame, 149.86 × 89.85 × 29.85 cm

so-called neutral technology, that crime forecasting is the same-old anti-black policing, albeit with shiny new information systems and sophisticated artificial intelligence."[68]

Moving beyond dramatic representation, Kate Crawford and Trevor Paglen's *ImageNet Roulette* was a website-artwork that went viral upon its release in September 2019.[69] Users were invited to uploaded photographs of themselves, which were then tagged/labeled by an AI trained on the "person" categories extant in a key dataset known as "Image-Net."[70] While White users were regularly assigned inaccurate descriptions (Paglen's publicity headshot, for example, was tagged as belonging to a "microeconomic expert"), people of color were more likely to be labeled with racial and other slurs. Pejorative categorizations were not only confined to race, however, but also registered in misogynistic, cruel, and absurd language. While the visual component of the project comprised photographs of people, it was more a (self-)portrait of the ImageNet AIs—a project that, in Paglen's telling, let the training set "speak for itself."[71] Claiming to demonstrate "why classifying people in this way is unscientific at best, and deeply harmful at worst,"[72] Crawford and Paglen's *Training Humans* exhibition took place at Fondazione Prada's Osservatorio venue in Milan in 2020, and featured

  Poetics of Encryption

a physical display summarizing the outcomes of *ImageNet Roulette.*[73]
In language alluding to eugenics, Paglen characterized the exhibition
as showing how AI training set images are part of a "long tradition of
capturing people's images without their consent, in order to classify,
segment, and often stereotype them in ways that evoke colonial
projects of the past."[74]

Yet there is a further turn of the screw to consider: ImageNet was
created in 2009 by researchers at Princeton University and Stanford
University, who assembled its collection of over one million photo
portraits by scraping them from the Internet. They then hired Amazon
Mechanical Turk workers to categorize the images.[75] In Paglen's words,
"the prejudices and biases of these low-paid, crowd-sourced laborers
are inevitably reflected in the AI system that they helped create."[76]
One suspects, however, that in addition to bigotry, the objectionable
labeling may also indicate individual rebellion against the form of
alienated toil undertaken by the laborers; a kind of crude industrial
sabotage whose indiscriminate, racist fallout recapitulates the anti-
social nature of "ghost work."[77] Perhaps the only way for the invisible
personnel to be seen was through toxic semaphore.[78] As a result of
media attention given to the project, ImageNet would remove 600,000
images of people stored in its system.[79] Could it be that this scrubbing
more perfectly repressed the unhygienic trace of the human backend?
And what are we to make of the fact that "toxicity" is a given across
all of AI and not only facial recognition?[80]

An obvious mode of pushback against all of this obtains in artistic
attempts to renovate AI-informed data bodies—to bring them more
in line with "real" humanity and/or some concept of a democratic
subject. Such attempts simultaneously perform rectified (human) labor
conditions when training AI—the artist's passionate effort replacing
the ghost worker's alienated slog. Joy Buolamwini and Timnit Gebru's
Gender Shades (2018) is a good example in this regard. Preceding
Crawford and Paglen's *ImageNet Roulette,* it also took on bias in AI facial
recognition. They did this first through an academic paper outlining
how popular applications display obvious discrimination on the basis of
gender or skin color. They argued that such results issue from erroneous
or incomplete training data sets, while pointing out consequent risks for
the effectiveness of certain medical applications.[81] Following this
diagnostic, the pair then offered an image prescription, something that
we may understand as a better engine for machine portraiture: a novel
"benchmark data set," facilitating new criteria for facial comparison.
Buolamwini and Gebru's set contains the data of 1,270 parliamentarians

from three African and three European countries. Thus, they claim to have created "the first training data set containing all skin color types, while at the same time being able to test facial recognition of gender."[82]

Performing Encryption—Masking and Cryptonomy

"Whereas photographers initially saw the world warped through their own camera's viewfinder system, or flattened into a silver-gelatin print," writes Adam Harvey, "the computer vision operator sees a world twisted by algorithms which in turn reflect a world constructed from warped and biased training datasets."[83] Clearly, this is a situation in need of redress. But reforming offending tech does not always appeal. Citing the "Law of Mutual Reciprocity," cybernetician Ranulph Glanville reminds us that "since the Box is Black to the observer, the observer may be Black to the Box."[84] For artists who choose not to renovate training data sets in their critical response to AI, the latter is a technical and poetic strategy. This tendency may be termed *performing encryption.* Borrowing the formulation from the Swedish dance phenomenologist Suzan Kozel, its dramatic modus involves, among other things, "manipulating degrees of luminosity, playing with focus, legibility, brightness and obscurity."[85] When it comes to performance: "Encryption is not a wall, it is a re-patterning or a distortion, of a flow."[86] Throughout, it is a dance of masks.

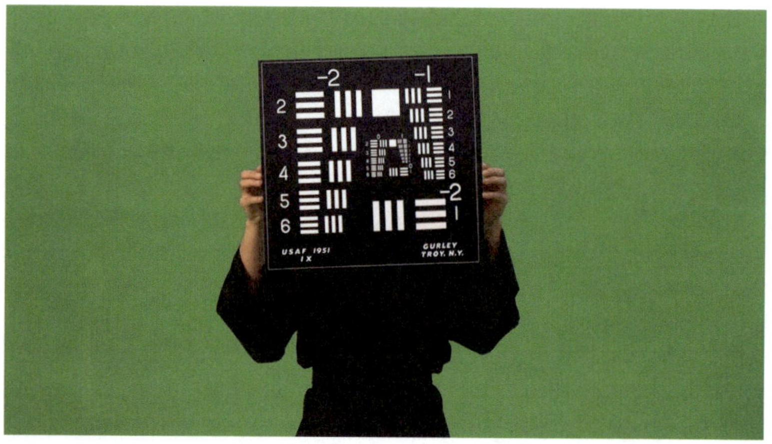

Hito Steyerl, *How Not to Be Seen: A Fucking Didactic Educational .MOV File,* 2013
Single-channel high-definition digital video and sound in architectural environment, 15:52 min.

Poetics of Encryption

As Hito Steyerl's *How Not to Be Seen: A Fucking Didactic Educational .MOV File* (2013) asserts, being visible within the "world as picture" to powers that control computer vision may facilitate one's ultimate disappearance. In a droning monotone, the video's voiceover charts a catchment area that spans being "female and over fifty," or "being spam caught in a filter," to being "an enemy of the state." The result: being "eliminated, liquidated, and then dissimulated,... eradicated, deleted, dispensed with, filtered, processed, selected, separated, wiped out." By way of contrast, the narrator observes that "today, most important things want to remain invisible. Love is invisible. War is invisible. Capitalism is invisible."[87] For heroes and villains alike, *how not to be seen* is of paramount concern, and a set of technical strategies.

Such concern was taken up in Trevor Paglen's 2014 collaboration with Jacob Appelbaum, wherein the pair deployed a transparent visual marker for cloaking or disappearance. Following the former's investigative work on military "black sites"—normally unseen nodes in the prosecution of the so-called War on Terror, such as the National Security Agency (NSA) headquarters, and numerous secret prisons where torture was conducted—*Autonomy Cube* would become a signal work in an artistic tendency to *seize the means of obstruction*. Commissioned for the 9th Berlin Biennale in 2016, it took the form of a clear Perspex cube that was meant, in Paglen's own words, to be both "seen" and "used."[88] Offering museum visitors a way to disappear from digital surveillance, Internet-connected computers housed within the

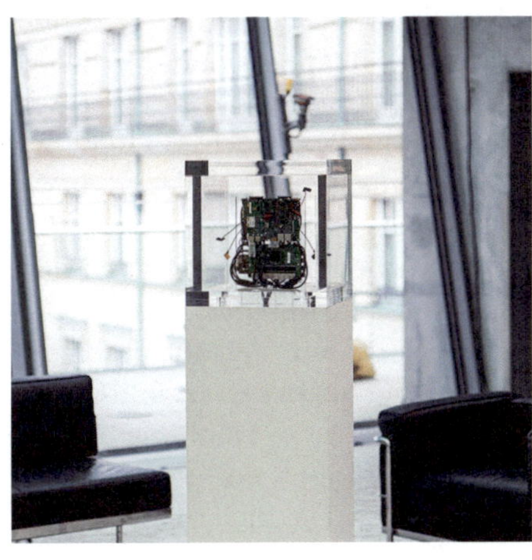

Trevor Paglen and Jason Appelbaum,
Autonomy Cube, 2015
Plexiglas cube, computer components,
49.85 × 49.85 × 49.85 cm

sculpture created an open Wi-Fi hotspot wherever it was installed. Rather than a normal Internet connection, the sculpture routed all Wi-Fi traffic through the secure encrypted protocol of the Tor network— a global network of volunteer-run relays designed to help anonymize data. In addition, *Autonomy Cube* became a part of the Tor network, relaying Tor traffic.[89] This was a case of performative IP *masking.*[90]

Black Box culture circles around the themes of cloaking, veiling, screening off. However, as the above indicates, it is not just about attending a masked player, as audience. It is also about the art of donning disguises that are fit for the Technocene stage. Pursuing propaganda of the deed in line with antecedent Tactical Media, Adam Harvey's work has gone deep into the issue of facial anonymization. His *CV Dazzle* (2013–) trialed a low-tech camouflage strategy against machine sight. Utilizing bold patterning to break apart the expected features targeted by computer vision, proving "that faces, or other objects, can exist in a dual perceptual state: visible to humans yet invisible to machines," his project prototyped certain makeup, hair style, and fashion accessories that would "target" or "evade" the common Viola–Jones Haar cascade face detection algorithm included in the popular OpenCV framework.[92] These were, by design, cheap or free, and thus accessible to a broad audience. Following his thesis, various "looks" were produced for *DIS* magazine, and later as a series for the *New York Times* (*Look 5,* 2013). Approaching viral success, dazzle would go on to be adopted, periodically, by groups active during street protest. But just as a human face changes over time, so detection software continues to increase in power. Like beauty, dazzle fades. Because computer vision is a probabilistic determination, the "right look" is, therefore, about discovering how to appear one step below the threshold of detection. *CV Dazzle* is not a reified image but a generative "strategy"; a protocol that must be continually reviewed in light of developments in surveillance tech.[93] Façades must keep changing at pace with ever-developing code. Whatever "art" is created while addressing the issue stands to be superseded by further switch-outs (in a manner that parallels the march of software updates). In this way, a succession of dazzling masks must be worn, one after the other, to blind the changing machine viewer(s). The history of art follows.

Harvey's further work also attempts to stake out a hiding place for the human body within the machine's blind spot. For example, *Hyper-Face* (2016) prototyped a camouflage pattern designed to undermine computer vision algorithms by providing abundant "false faces" (reducing detection and recognition confidence scores). *HyperFace*

Adam Harvey, *CV Dazzle Look 1,* 2010
Original look for CV Dazzle thesis at NYU
Model: Jen Jaffe / Hair: Pia Vivas

Adam Harvey, *CV Dazzle Look 2,* 2010
For *DIS* magazine
Model: Irina / Hair: Pia Vivas / Creative
Direction: Lauren Boyle and Marco Roso

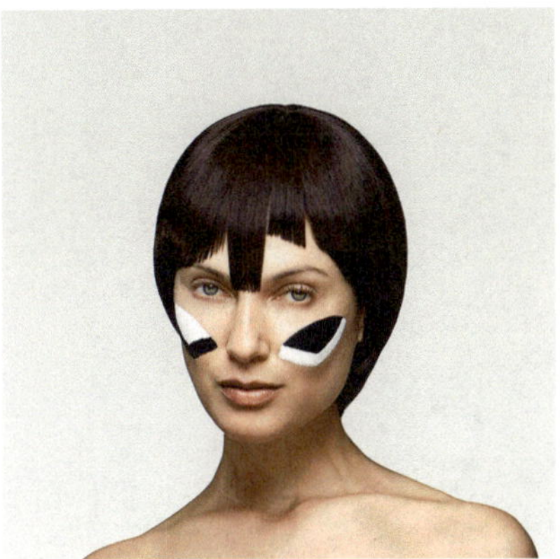

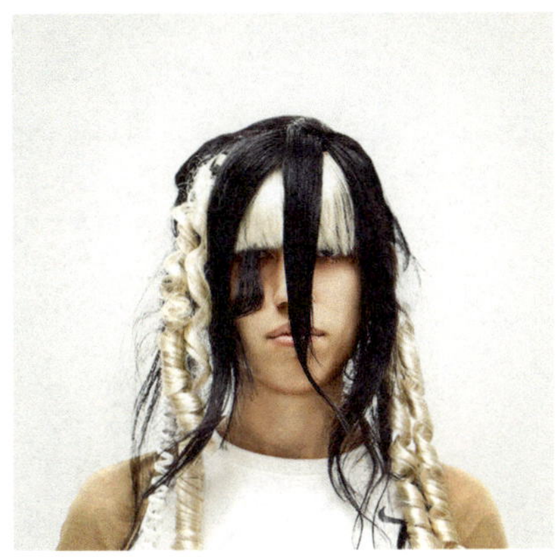

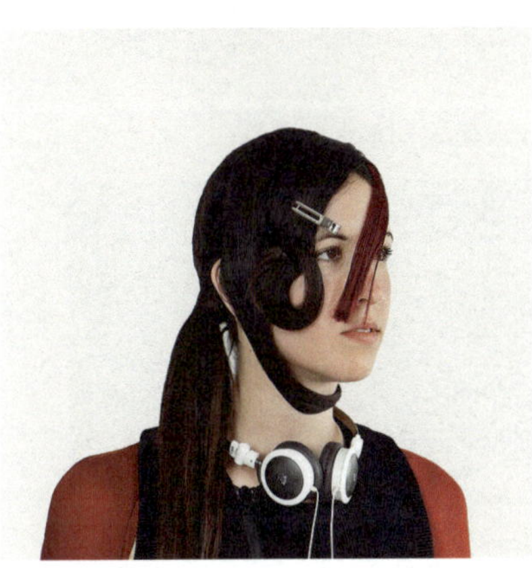

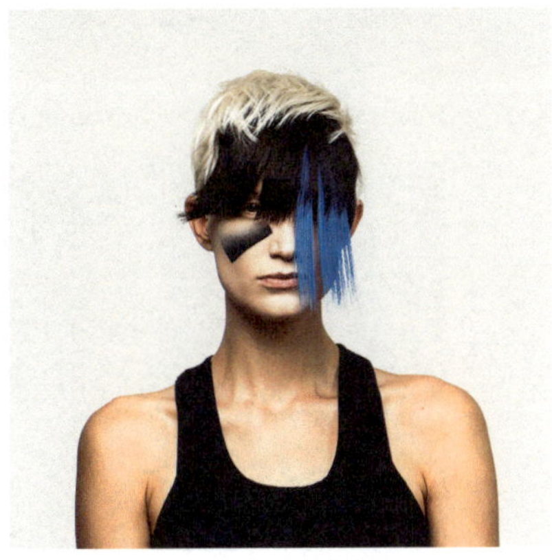

Adam Harvey, *CV Dazzle Look 4,* 2010
For *DIS* magazine
Model: Maria / Hair: Pia Vivas / Creative
Direction: Lauren Boyle and Marco Roso

Adam Harvey, *CV Dazzle Look 5,* 2013
Commissioned for the *New York Times*
Model: Bre Lembitz / Hair: Pia Vivas /
Makeup: Giana DeYoung / Produced by
John Niedermeyer and James Thomas

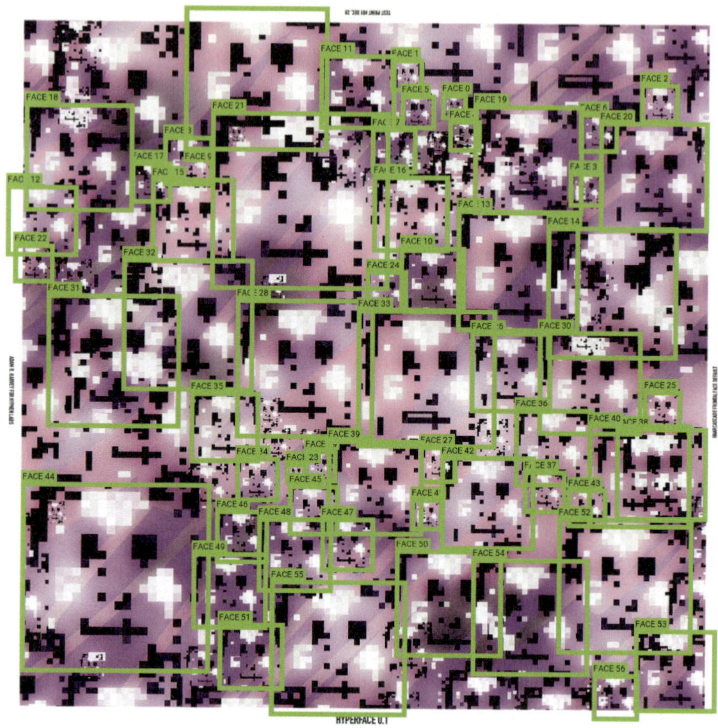

Adam Harvey, *HyperFace* render, 2017
Haar cascade face-detection output on *HyperFace* pattern

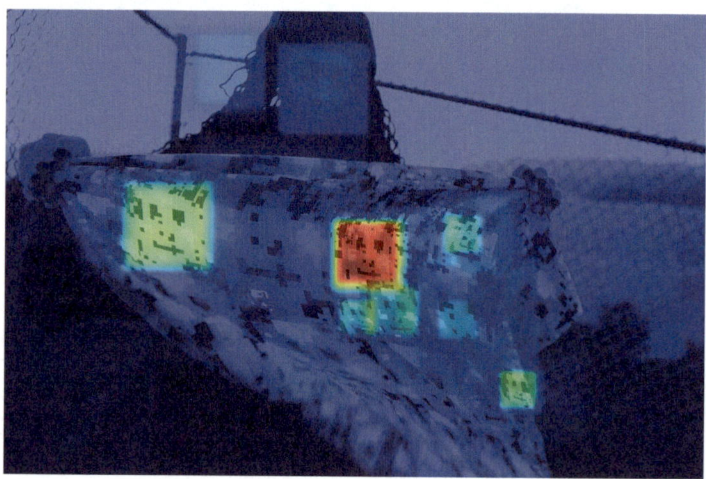

Adam Harvey, *Hyperface* test image / saliency visualization, 2017
Model: Ashley Baccus-Clark

extended the *CV Dazzle* strategy through an inverse operation. While *CV Dazzle* targeted the facial area (the figure), *HyperFace* aimed to alter the surrounding area (the ground)—providing a backdrop teeming with triggers for detection, exploiting the default frontalface profile used by OpenCV. As with *CV Dazzle,* this strategy implies constant updates, with Harvey advocating for the creation of additional patterns targeted at "convolutional neural networks or HoG/SVM-based edge detectors."[94] *HyperFace* was launched as a textile print at the 2017 Sundance Film Festival. Here, it was presented as part of Hyphen-Labs' NeuroSpeculative AfroFeminism (NSAF), a Black world-building project manifest through product design, virtual reality, and neuro-science narratives, focusing on the topics of privacy, transparency, identity, and perception.[95]

In focusing on making faces undetectable (as faces), we may characterize Harvey's projects as repelling machine vision. Conversely, the results are visually fascinating to humans. This double-sight, or split viewership, is an aesthetic motor in the contemporary dance of masks. We also see it in Zach Blas's *Facial Weaponization Suite* (2012–14), four "collective masks" that were the result of a series of public workshops. Each was modeled from the aggregated biometric data of participants and comprised visually amorphous forms putatively undetectable as "human" by facial recognition tech.[96] One of these masks explored a complex described by the artist as the "tripartite conception of blackness" (a useful formula for the topics raised in the preceding section), incorporating "the racist inability of biometric technologies to detect dark skin, the favoring of black in militant aesthetics, and black as that which informatically obfuscates." Another, titled *Fag Face Mask,* was generated using biometric capture of "many" queer men's faces as a response to certain pseudo-scientific studies claiming the ability to determine sexual orientation through facial data.[97] A third engaged feminism's relations to "concealment and imperceptibility, taking veil legislation in France as a troubling site that oppressively forces visibility."[98] The last apparently considered the deployment of biometrics as a security technology at the Mexico–United States border, and its relation to nationalist violence. All the masks intersected with the use of masking in social movements, in Blas's view, "as an opaque tool of collective transformation that refuses dominant forms of political representation."[99]

In both Harvey and Blas's works, performing encryption is seen to involve spectacular or dazzling visual effects as a response to the technical lay of the land, rather than as a result of some creative caprice. One is tempted to suggest that the visual strangeness of their masks registers the outsize effort/labor involved in evading the machine-capture agent; or that, in a kind of visual transposition, they are masks depicting the strangeness of the surveillance AI's gaze in relief.[100] The dance of masks is a play of double vision, as we are reminded by William Blake:

> What to others a trifle appears
> Fills me full of smiles or tears;
> For double the vision my eyes do see
> And a double vision is always with me.
> With my inward eye, 'tis an old Man grey;
> With my outward, a thistle across my way.[101]

If the journey *into the crypt* (explored in the previous chapter) may be characterized as Orphic seeking, then performing encryption may be likened to performative identification with Hades, god of death—the underworld. Hades *the unseen* is the one who captures and keeps; the one who sets the terms of use. The one who cannot be compelled. This is a suitable dramatic frame for work that *does not enter* another's crypt but which itself *in-crypts.* If this aesthetic strategy may be approached through psychoanalytic language, we may also call it a process of "cryptonymy." It is a nested artwork—one that contains a whole *other layer* of reality; an encrypted layer, installed within the digital infrastructure (code). Cryptonymic work is a response to the contemporary landscape of black boxes, but one that eschews melancholic affect and/or attempts at cracking. Instead, it takes up the *work of occlusion* as its own task. Such work unfolds the novel artistic program of *performing the hidden* (making the act of hiding public) in ways that move beyond the visual rhetoric of the (facial) mask: a cryptonymic aesthetic.

The term "cryptonymy" issues from Jacques Derrida's introduction to Nicholas Abraham and Maria Torok's re-reading of Freud's Wolf Man—a book focused on psychoanalysis; specifically, the articulation of something "encrypted" in a psyche that is registered through cryptic speech.[102] In setting the stage for the authors' excursus, Derrida makes the point that what is encrypted is *both* living and dead. Commenting on Derrida's claim, the theorist Max Haiven explains that "encryption names a process where a constitutive and essential part of a system (language, philosophy, society) must be sealed in a

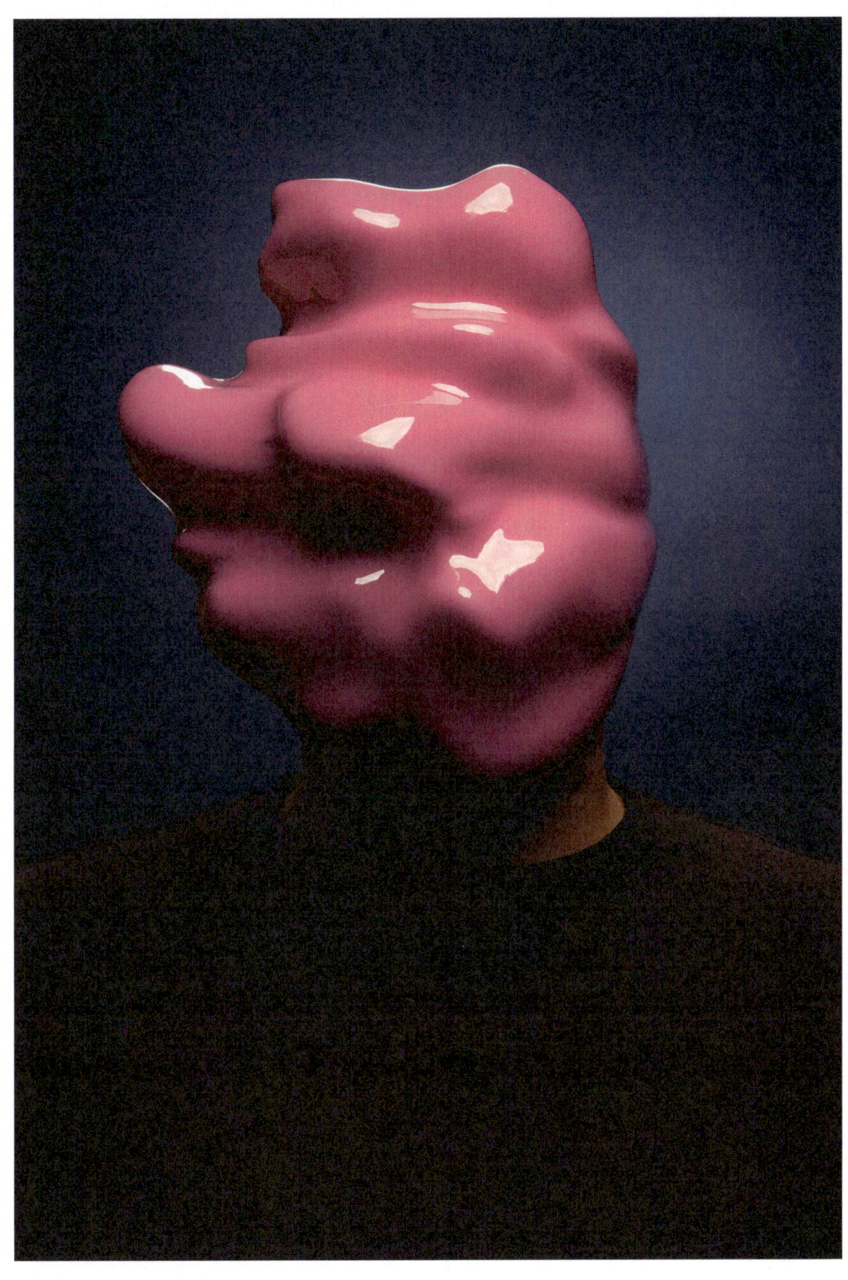

Zach Blas, *Facial Weaponization Suite: Fag Face Mask,* 2012
Vacuum-formed plastic mask and protestor

structure, a crypt, where its status as living or dead is unknown."[103] Bolstering the previous observations on the funerary function of the barrel-vault/*kamára* (latent within the world-camera), Derrida's argument highlights the architectural component of the crypt concept: an arch. What this indicates, in his view, is that encryption provides structure—being *constitutive* of an edifice. Indeed, Haiven notes, Derrida "uses the metaphor of the archway (a term that shares an etymology with crypt in French) to illustrate how a crypt is, in fact, part of a system of mutual supports."[104] Haiven further explains that

> encryption is the process by which a lost object of projection and attachment is secretly maintained in a state that is both life and death. This act of inner encryption exhibits outwardly as encrypted speech or utterance that evades or actively avoids decryption *in order to preserve the system or structure between life and death.*[105]

With respect to our current concerns, a "cryptonymic" system need not be speech *per se.* It may be an artwork whose compositional structure straddles life and death (visible and hidden) in favor of never resolving this tension. A *cryptonymic aesthetic* holds part of the artwork (or exhibition) away from view as a key aspect of its mode of exhibiting. While performing encryption, cryptonymic art goes beyond masking a person or body in the service of privacy, opening onto broader textures of the inaccessible. Perhaps in order to exhibit anything but the ostensible contents of a crypt. By way of example, my own curated project, *Treasure of Lima: A Buried Exhibition* (2014), was a collection of forty works buried in a locked box at a secret location, on an island in the Pacific Ocean that it is illegal to visit; the exact GPS coordinates encrypted, and the resulting eight-hundred-character cipher 3D-printed as a steel scroll, then sold at auction without decryption key—in order to facilitate the visibility of a narrative, legal, economic, biological, and ecological framework, rather than art objects.[106] Among other concerns, a key question (contained within the project title) was whether the exhibition might be considered open or active only if it remains buried.[107] And conversely, whether it may be deemed closed if the contents of the box are recovered and viewed.

A year later, another signal project, *Don't Follow the Wind* (2015), took place in the Fukushima nuclear disaster exclusion zone—initiated by Tokyo-based artist collective Chim↑Pom and curated by Kenji

Poetics of Encryption

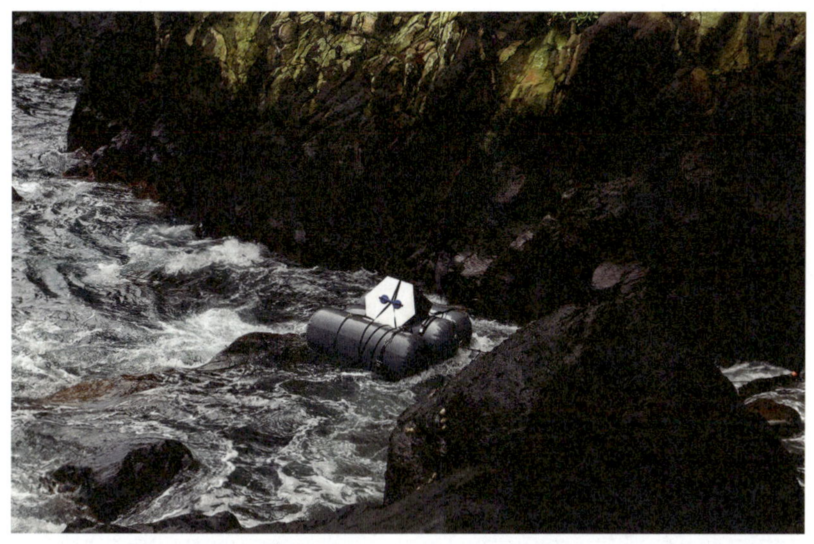

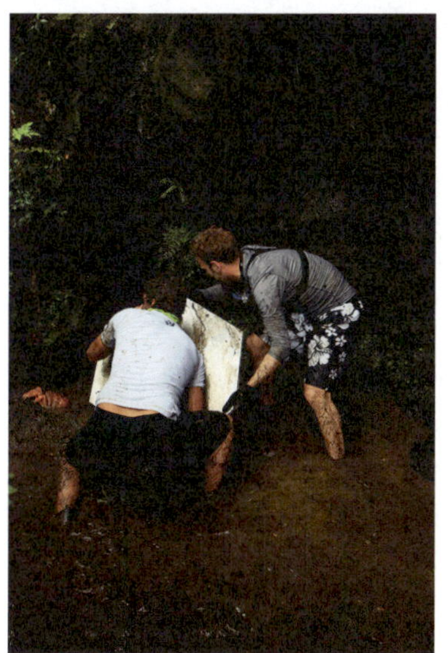

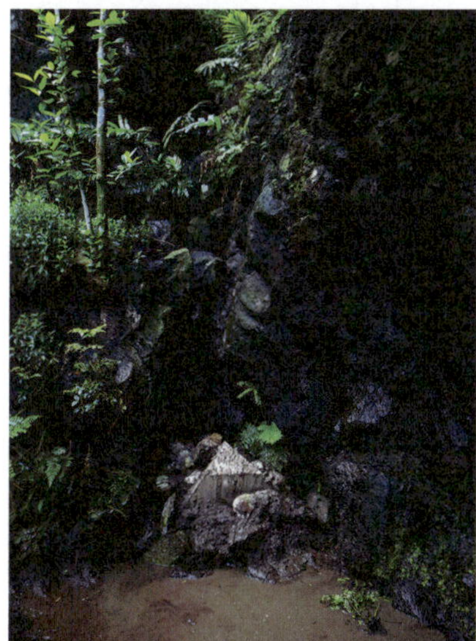

Treasure of Lima: A Buried Exhibition, 2014
Project of the TBA21–ACADEMY, Isla del Coco, Costa Rica, 2014

Kubota, Eva and Franco Mattes, and Jason Waite. Despite the exhibition being officially "open" from March 2015, the artworks on site remain functionally inaccessible to the general public until the radiation dissipates enough for the area to be safely entered. As with *Treasure of Lima: A Buried Exhibition,* the question of the show's status as open or closed obtains. Following on from this enterprise, Eva and Franco Mattes would proffer further performed encryptions—first, through a series of video interviews with hundreds of Internet content moderators (*Dark Content,* 2015) released only on the dark web (the encrypted layer of the internet).[108] Another of their dark web exhibitions (only accessible to those using the Tor browser) was the online group exhibition *Time is Out of Joint,* commissioned by the 2020–21 Yerevan Biennial, notable for the release of Vladan Joler's *New Extractivism* PDF, discussed in the preceding chapter.

Recently, the pair have also begun to develop a sculptural cryptonymy. Their *Circuits* (2022) is a pink cable tray that hosts two microcomputers and a coil of Ethernet wires—the electrical components transferring image files back and forth, constantly, throughout the assemblage. With its color recalling interior flesh, this infrastructure sculpture is located in the corner of the gallery on two walls—like an empty picture frame that has been pressed into position by some giant thumb. Circulating within its cables is a day's worth of photos shot by the artists, taken from their personal archive. But, of course, these photographs are invisible to gallery visitors. *Circuits* thus dramatizes the issue of translation, or—in musical terms—transposition. It shows how something can be present in one mode and absent in another. This has a bearing on our wider relation to cultural and informatic goods. The vast majority of images do not exist in the form of printed photographs, hung on a wall or featured in books. Instead, they obtain as files that are constantly copied and transferred between devices and data centers. In this sense, *Circuits* is a display of contemporary images in their most common form. It points to the perceptual difference between image(s) and reality, providing the former with body. In a similar vein, the pair's *Untitled (P2P Server)* (2022) consists of a server connected to the open Internet, sharing a video via torrent on a peer-to-peer network. This server has no output/monitor, and so the register of the data artwork is limited to blinking lights and the noise of the server's cooling fan. And yet, this artwork is being distributed across many nodes in the network. On the conceptual level, the piece is differentiated from *Circuits* by making visibility or decrypting (and hence accessing) the hidden file contingent upon joining the

Poetics of Encryption

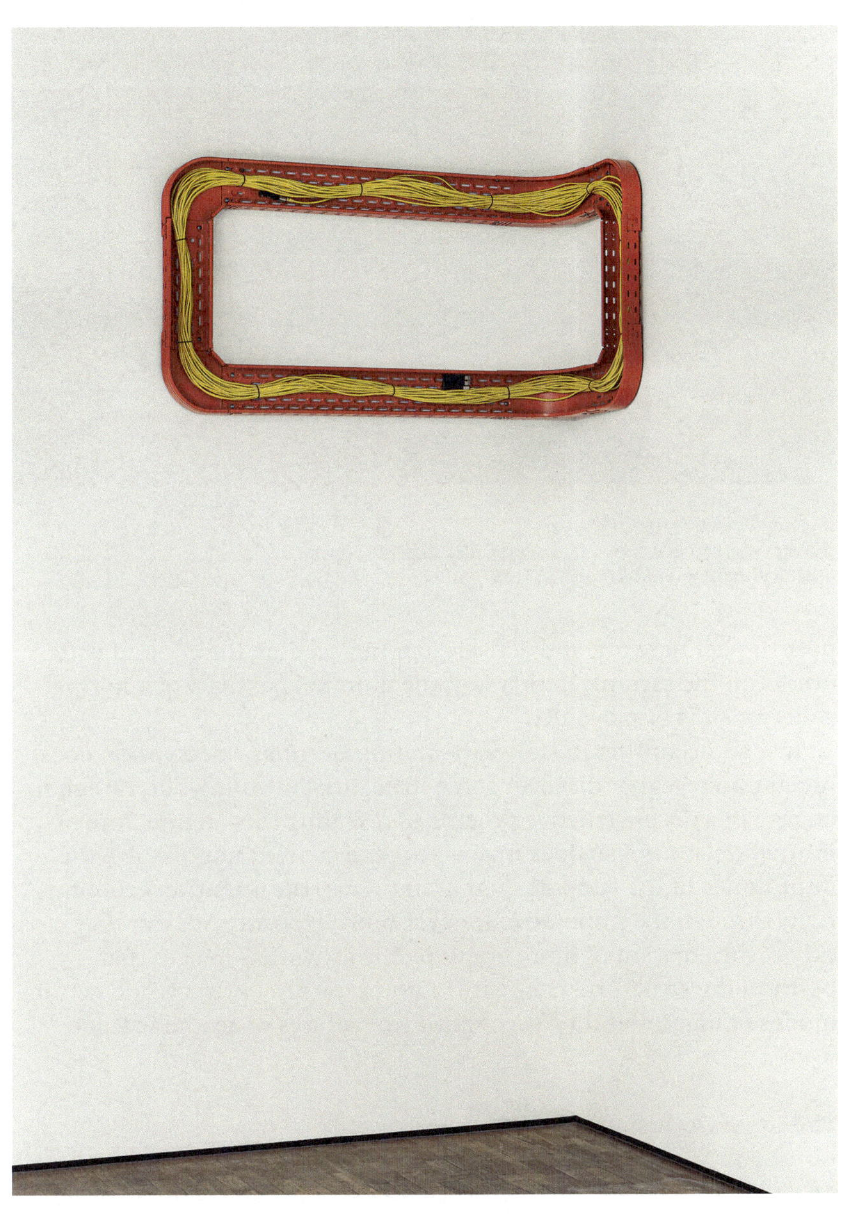

Eva and Franco Mattes, *Personal Photographs May 5 2011,* 2022
Powder-coated customized cable tray, Ethernet cables, 33 digital images, single-board computers,
metal cases, micro SD cards, USB flash drives, Ethernet adapters, custom software,
142 × 80 × 54 cm. Installation view: FMAV, Modena, 2022 / Collection of Comune di Modena

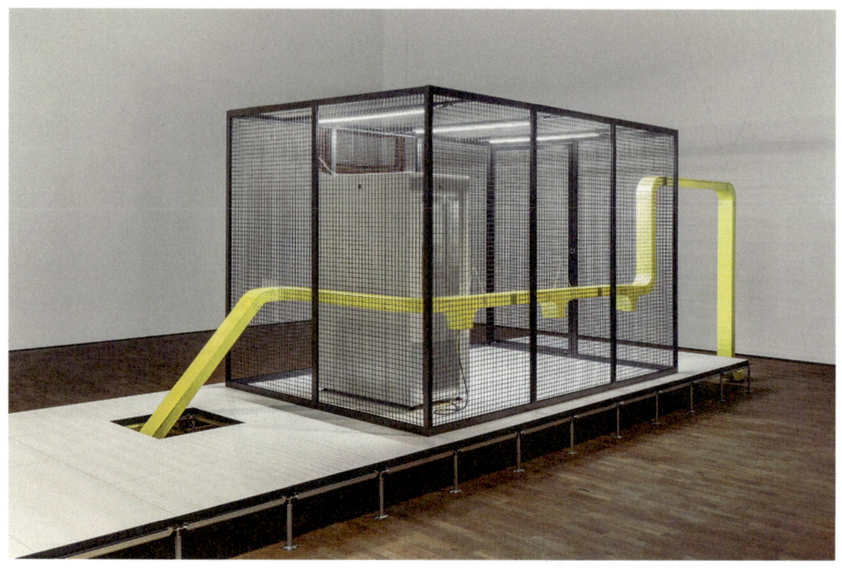

Eva and Franco Mattes, *P2P,* 2022
Server cage, server cabinet, rack server, file, Torrent software,
Installation view: FMAV, Modena, 2022

peer-to-peer network and actively sharing/seeding the content with others on the torrent. In this way, the nominal passivity of a normal gallery visit is also avoided.

Just as, according to Haiven (restating Derrida), "decryption does not aim to reveal or discover some 'true' final meaning but, rather, to engage in a deconstructive process of revealing this architecture of mutual reliances," so does uncovering the content not dissolve the importance of the support.[109] At a time when the attention economy rams through the imperative for ever-more exposure, we can only expect the creation of more cryptonymic artworks—pieces that perform the structural necessity of non-exposure, privacy, and certain modes of inaccessibility as constitutive features of aesthetic value.[110]

The Great Occlusion

As previously touched upon, the seeming transparency of the device or system masks its power and entanglements with the material (world).

     Poetics of Encryption

However, in addition to its hidden engagement with open-pit mines, servers who-knows-where, slave labor, and more, another key occlusion issuing from the functional transparency of a device is the computer's role in constituting the reality principle itself. Indeed, computers are fundamental to the construction and ongoing maintenance of both social and scientific facts. In the words of Thumfart,

> Only the computers of banks and stock markets materialize property. Only the digital archiving and normalization of social relations on microchips produce stable, continuous contacts. Only the recording and comparing of our data by medical computers make it possible to speak of health. In some countries, computers are already calculating the results of elections by themselves.[111]

He continues: "Because of their indispensability to modern physics, computers also define what we consider to be real.... De facto real is what can be calculated by computers."[112] And this can end, too: "Where computers fail, the horizon of our binding reality also ends."[113] As Thumfart's comments indicate, the desire to totally avoid, crack, or escape black boxes runs up against their role in the constitution of the world as we know it. Indeed, the black box constitutes both baby *and* bathwater in contemporary knowledge production.

So what does it mean to let go of trying to crack the black box? Already, the depunctualization or breaking apart of consumer technologies into their components is highly difficult, due to the specialized engineering and manufacturing processes employed in their creation.[114] But the problem goes way beyond devices. As developments in AI gather apace, and as the specters of Artificial General Intelligence (AGI) and Artificial Super Intelligence (ASI) take shape on the horizon, depunctualization is totally out of the question. This opens onto a very strange vista indeed—namely, to scenes wherein, through the exercise of hitherto unimaginable computing power, technology's hidden interior turns both the past and the present inside-out, scrambling the longstanding contrast between memory and oblivion, and what was left of the fidelity between muse and artist. Let us now turn our attention to this.

Black Hole

As an optic metaphor for intellectual limit, the blackness of the box emanates from a solar myth latent in Plato's allegory of the cave, and further imaginaries of enlightenment. While the philosopher imagined that prisoners might eventually turn their attention to the sun, gaining direct access to true "forms" of reality and, thus, freedom from conceptual bondage, in the Technocene things are different. With respect to the profusion of black boxes that defines this period, a logic of eclipse rules the day. One can only read around the edges, parsing a medial dimension for insight about the occult body. Nevertheless, this dimension is the *corona* (crown) wherein Technocene sovereignty is most dramatically outlined—the site of struggle, (mis) recognition, and, for the stargazer, symptomatology.

The graphic figures that adorn computer screens, so perfectly termed "icons," stand to be analyzed with a view to the manner in which they figure disciplinary regimens for the self and the world. We have already seen how certain artists find data body portraits disappointing, when used as exemplary icons for people. For them, such portraits are experienced not as windows onto the proverbial soul but as obstructions. To the extent that they are displayed on screens, these portraits can also be described as *screening-off* certain human(e) values in the service of instrumental foci. But the concept of the screen should itself be interrogated. Rather than being merely the "ground" upon which certain symbols are inscribed, computer and smartphone displays are themselves icons that, in addition to promulgating the myth of transparency, enshrine a vision of technology as being safely contained within certain frames, under control, or operating inside limits. Beyond the interior right angles of a given display, however, the situation is quite different. All limits have been surpassed.

It has already been noted that, in the phenomenological sense, certain profound realities only come into being through computation. Yet computation touches everything else too—from face to forest, mineral to micro-organism, mammal to quark. It is everywhere. As a cipher for this principle, Jean Baudrillard's deployment of an image from Jorge Luis Borges comes to mind: a map so large that it eventually covers the whole Earth, becoming a new kind of terrain. Computational mapping and the territory itself have collapsed into something amorphous.[1] The two previous chapters discussed artistic meditations upon an increasingly encrypted or screened-off world; diagnoses concerning a landscape of nested black boxes. The artists discussed in this chapter conjure icons for *agency, metabolism,* or *world-forming power* behind the scenes. Their works allude to the dynamism or generative force within the crypt; to the principle of kinetic *action* taking place beneath the threshold of perception or comprehension; of mysterious *activity* at the occult center. Working at a remove, they figure this activity's disruptive impacts in the visible world, showcasing symptomatic figures that haunt or distort the scenes of life. With such artworks, the affective dimension is colored less by resistance or its impotent cousin, melancholy, than attempts to repress or sublimate *horror.*

Behind-the-scenes operations stalk the lifeworld. Art registers this fact. Ciphers for *obscure institutional power* appear in recent works, as spooks—ghosts, spies, and conspiracies. Otherwise, *obscure computational powers* are represented through figures that stand for generative and recombinatory ferocity. The latter announce the double fate of all beings in the Technocene: first, subjection to the principle of dividuation—disarticulation into component parts. Second, having been so processed, standing as raw materials to be recombined with elements from other sources into novel admixtures. As we shall see, computation and its avant-garde, generative AI, enact a relentless and ever-quickening process of re-form that affects almost every dimension of reality. A class of artworks dramatizes this generative churn, emphasizing a tendency towards spectacular and weird outcomes. They are cryptic icons for algorithmic creativity without perceivable limit, whose powers of *ungrounding* cannot be avoided. They resemble a parade of the undead, of chimeras, and the crypto-zoological. By contrast, though unpalatable, data body portraits commonly pursue proportional relationships to the human subject, expressing a certain banality of evil through their modicum of concern for tracing "human" outlines. It is a protocol that emerging machinic creativity does not repress or possess.

The ciphers in question do not convey the concept of change arriving slowly, or from a great distance. They figure emanation here and now—apparition. Contemporary life is *unheimlich.* Against an intensively disquieting atmosphere, certain artists pursue accommodation with hidden and perhaps irresistible powers through iconicizing acts. Sublimating the feral, some place exemplary chimeras on pedestals. Facing the strange, they endeavor to pursue kinship. Their works announce a syncretist aesthetic—furthermore, a contemporary Surrealism that does not focus on emanations from the individual subconscious, but on the emergent properties of networks, and the dreams of machines.

　　　　　　　　　　　　　　　　　　Poetics of Encryption

Cryptoids

The massive scale of the techno-power network, and its relative unintelligibility, is apt to provoke speculation concerning forces or systems at work behind everyday appearance. With respect to occult centers of institutional power, artists offer tokens (or totems) for such influence—images of spooks. They are inspired by what can only be described as an increasingly creepy distortion of political and economic space by the Internet.

Looking over our historical shoulder, at a work by Trevor Paglen, we see lists of covert CIA programs run by spies—all of them recent. But just like the "non-state actors" targeted by the so-called War on Terror, some of today's political influencers are self-employed. In this context, a 2018 installation by the artist Jonas Staal was presented as a propaganda retrospective for the notorious far-right political operative Steve Bannon—whose covert work with the social-media-influencing group Cambridge Analytica helped to sway the 2016 Brexit referendum and Donald Trump's election to the presidential office of the United States.[2] Featuring the corpus of films written, directed, and produced by Bannon, along with other materials, Staal's curatorial artwork endeavored to uncover the authorial voice or signature of this backroom operator—fleshing him out as a narrative stylist of neo-fascist talking points placed in the mouths of others.

Of course, false identities are a classic attribute of the secret agent. It is strange, however, that one should lie at the heart of a technical system whose very utility consists in the provision of a publicly accessible record.[3] Indeed, a ghost haunts the realm of cryptocurrency: Satoshi Nakamoto, the pseudonymous person or persons who devised the first blockchain database, as part of their decentralized digital currency, Bitcoin—a payment system that first rose to prominence on the dark markets of the encrypted Tor network, where it became a standard mechanism for the anonymous purchase of (sometimes illegal) goods and services. By late 2021, cryptocurrencies had become, in the words of one Bloomberg analyst, "peerless conduits of greed and fear" in the mainstream economy, with a market cap exceeding 1.5 trillion dollars.[4] Despite the attention paid to Bitcoin, the true identity of its inventor has remained unknown.

As Ignota, the artworld re-publishers of the Bitcoin white paper, would relate,

[Nakamoto] developed Bitcoin, authored the Bitcoin white paper, and created and deployed the first Bitcoin implementation.... They also devised the first blockchain database. Satoshi Nakamoto ceased public involvement with Bitcoin at the end of 2010; their last public post was made in 2014 as a rebuttal to claims on the "true" nature of Satoshi's identity. During Bitcoin's peak in December 2017, the Satoshi Nakamoto identity could lay claim to a fortune worth over $19 billion, making Nakamoto possibly the 44th richest person in the world at that time. To this day both the public identity and Bitcoin wallet attached to the identity of Satoshi Nakamoto remain inactive.[5]

Why would an art publisher be interested in publishing Nakamoto at all? The answer is that Nakamoto is an emblematic token for an increasingly encoded world—an icon for the poetics of encryption. Even before Ignota re-published the paper, in a 2014 work titled *Nakamoto (The Proof),* French artists Émilie Brout and Maxime Marion would delve "into the mythology surrounding the blockchain's inventor [while venturing] experimentally into [that system's] infrastructure."[6] The piece comprised a digital scan of a fake passport issued to Nakamoto that the duo commissioned from a forger, who they contacted over the dark web and paid in Bitcoin.[7] The physical document was never delivered but the scanned image—emailed by the forger— was analyzed by the artists, who reconstructed the creator's choices in

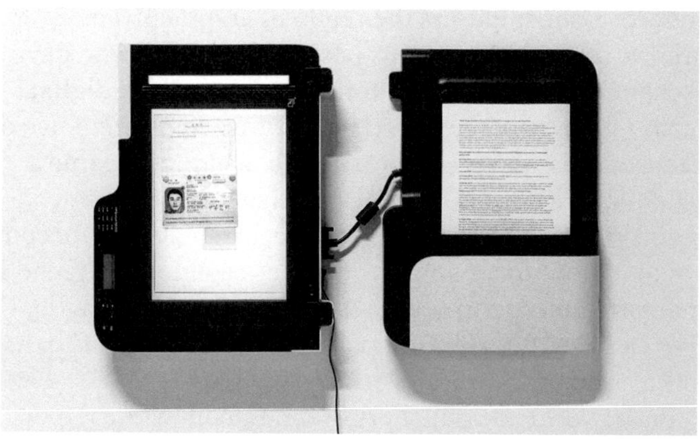

Émilie Brout and Maxime Marion, *Nakamoto (The Proof),* 2014–2018
Pigment printing on backlit paper, scanner HP N6350, LEDs, text on paper, 89.9 × 49.8 × 9.9 cm

Poetics of Encryption

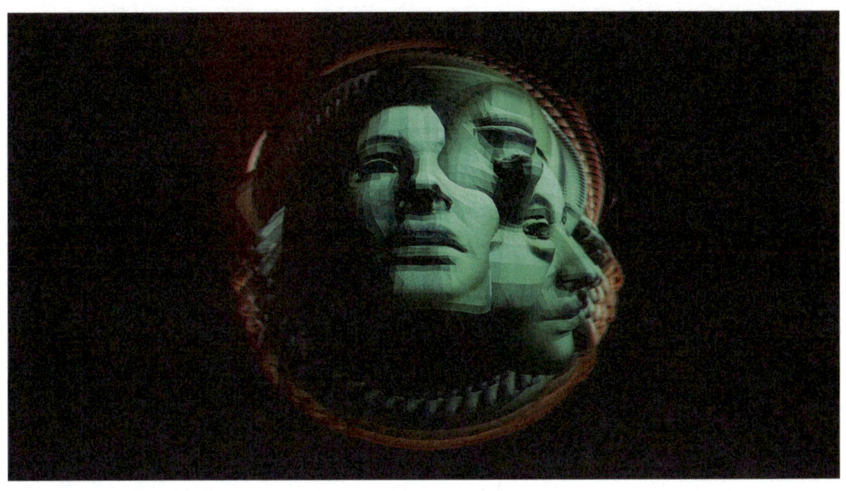

Émilie Brout and Maxime Marion, *Nakamoto (The Myth)*, 2015
HD video, 4:40 min.

a video. Through this project, Brout and Marion explored the Nakamoto identity as a guiding spirit and founding myth for crypto. Their work crystallized broader interest in the construction of "his" allegory: depending on who is asked, Nakamoto amounts to a Jesus-like figure, or some King Arthur.[8] In fact, in the realm of crypto, Nakamoto's own "wallet" is a prominent part of the system's architecture: holding the most bitcoins of any in the network while remaining inactive—save for deposits given by those offering thanks.[9] A perfect "found" icon for the shell game of contemporary financial and libidinal economy; a floating signifier for an empty center of value attending the abandonment of the monetary gold standard.

It is generally accepted that Nakamoto is a false identity. Some believe that no individual lies behind it, but that Bitcoin is controlled by a national government or intelligence agency. Given the sheer amount of money flowing through Bitcoin, and the influence that Nakamoto's anonymous encrypted "wallet" holds for all who trade on the platform—a locked box whose unmoved contents represent a key marker of trust within the system as a whole—is it any wonder that the contemporary cultural scene is awash with conspiracy theories?

Conspiracy theories concern institutional powers behind the scenes. They are also historically associated with times of upheaval. It has long been the case that such theories attempt to pin the blame for complex problems on easy, clearly drawn targets. While Jewish people have been the overt target of some of the most notorious historical examples, many contemporary theories are *crypto-fascist,* deploying ciphers for their hate objects that are often described as "dog whistles"—an auditory metaphor for covert symbolism, announcing the existence of a message that can only be decrypted by those keyed in to the correct frequency. Dogs, of course, can detect sounds that the human ear cannot. In this modus, cartoonish claims (serving as masks) abound. A now classic suggestion is that the world is governed by lizard "Illuminati." Followers of the influential QAnon movement adhere to the view that a cabal of Satan-worshiping pedophile baby eaters runs the world. Common to the anti-Semitic conspiracies of old, the trope of a secret (subhuman, or practically inhuman) "Global Elite," pulling the strings, remains.[10] Like the Nakamoto persona, the real identity of Q—supposedly a high-ranking government whistleblower, whose messages play an important role in driving the narrative—is unknown.

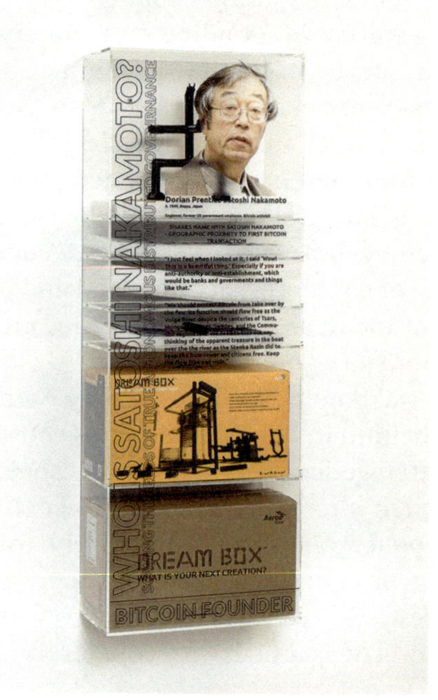

Simon Denny, *Bitcoin/Blockchain Founder Myth "Dreambox" Gamer Custom Case Kit: Dorian Nakamoto*, 2016 UV print on Plexiglas, magic case, parts and packaging, 167 × 62 × 32 cm

While QAnon's links to anti-Semitism are well documented, it is also known as a "big tent conspiracy theory" because it is constantly evolving by adding new features and claims.[11] Notwithstanding the importance of key "influencers" within the conspiracy bubble—chief among them the anonymous person (or persons) posting as Q on the 8kun message board—much of the syncretic work in the "superconspiracy" landscape is crowdsourced: the product of decentralized individual decisions to embellish or interpret the conspiracy's public narrative. These embellishments are, to borrow a term from studies of the new economy, acts of "prosumption."[12]

In fact, there is a tradition of live action role-playing ("LARPing") in this and other conspiracies. The origins of the Illuminati conspiracy can be traced back to the "Letters" page of *Playboy* magazine in the 1960s. What set this historical crucible for conspiracy apart was the role of irony in the creative space. The magazine's "Letters," allowing for pseudonymous authorship, was a site of fun—for propounding strange beliefs or alternative "facts" within a game of role-play. As the successor to print, online message boards allow for wider participation and quicker, more complex developments. They intensify the game, and open up desires to see game-space occupying sites beyond, distorting the reality of extant systems through the stealth entry of alternative ends—the irruption of counter-logic within a given hegemonic field. Certain cynics pursue this course of action for its ludic value, *for the lulz.* On the other side, true believers just go along out of stupidity, imagining that they are really saving the world through attempts to overturn elements of the standing order.

Of course, a dialectic of utility inheres in such phenomena: what may begin as a joke can take on a certain seriousness, depending on how the game is played. The notorious surge in share price for the failing company GameStop, in 2021, as a result of coordinated investment action by members of a Reddit message board, represents a high-water mark in gaming the system. Conversely, the image of a shirtless self-described "Q Shaman" occupying the floor of the United States Senate on January 6, 2021, wearing face paint and a horned Viking-style hat, seemed, especially for many of those on the left, to encapsulate a bad joke latent in the fanaticism of the Capitol insurrection.

Serious play is no new thing. However, in the context of increased online gaming, interest in extended IRL game-space has also grown in contemporary art. This is particularly registered in works concerned with live action role-playing. LARPing, as the practice is colloquially known, generally involves donning homemade costumes including armor and weapons, with which to do battle or otherwise engage friends in a fantasy or sci-fi setting. Works that take on this space sometimes emphasize a tension between unaccountable "childlike" pleasures, and markers for the real that include gore and danger. In this mold, Jon Rafman's video *Sticky Drama* (2015) sees a cast of thirty-five children who are "clad in horrifying appendage-like masks and with bulbous growths upon their faces fight and mutilate each other in a tribalistic manner, all done to a chaotic soundtrack."[13] More concerned with the open-source form of LARPing, and the ways in which it breaks down distinctions between artist and audience, each work by the collective known as Omsk Social Club begins with an open call, asking for players to participate in a specific game. They describe how "participants (or, in art speak, the audience) are then sent emails with their character name, traits and objectives."[14] It is then "up to them to further develop their unique identity."[15] Subsequently, the game "unfolds according to their individual actions."[16] As the artists write, "We aim to induce states that could potentially be fiction or a yet unlived reality for the players.... The game designs examine virtual egos and popular experiences allowing the works to become dematerialized hybrids of modern culture alongside unique personal experiences."[17]

But it is perhaps Ed Fornieles's *Dorm Daze* (2011) that should be taken as one of the earliest examples of artworld LARPing, a work that engaged with social media as a key tool for this practice, and which set the tone for all of the approaches just mentioned. *Dorm Daze* was a performance conducted on a self-contained network within Facebook. Over the course of three months, participating actors inhabited profiles "scalped" from real-life college freshmen from Berkeley, California. Fornieles's stated method was to create a platform that would "self-generate" content. "It was designed so that at the beginning, myself, or anyone else for that matter, would have no idea what it would look like at the end."[18] While following a semi-scripted narrative, directed by Fornieles, actors were encouraged to improvise their interactions. "I looked for groups of existing students at Berkeley with open profiles and then scraped all the information I could.... Images, likes, comments... these became the starting point for the person inhabiting the profile for the duration of the performance."[19] Fornieles termed the production a "Facebook Sitcom," and looked for "American teen stereotypes ... jocks, weirdos, witches, frat boys, sorority girls."[20] The work was, he claimed, "about the way we perform our lives online, but equally, how much of what we perform online slips easily into stereotypes."[21]

Of course, talk of "scraping" or "scalping" people's profiles conveys a degree of creepiness. The latter term even indicates physical violence inflicted on the person to whom the data officially belongs. The idea of a sick puppet show, wherein actors play malign games while wearing the digital skin of others, is not so far from the truth. In Fornieles's sculpture *Aspen Get Away* (2012), a spin-off from the *Dorm Daze* sitcom, a wax arm sits within a pile of wet mud, resting on a tiered shelf made of glass and metal, around which lie numerous photographs and party decorations. Below the shelf, on the floor, a computer monitor displays a live Twitter feed. All of the ensemble's components are associated with one "character" (based on a real person), whose death emerged during the actors' improvisation. According to them, while at a lakeside party in Aspen, Colorado, a young woman took part in an impromptu cruise aboard a speedboat, before drunkenly falling overboard and losing her arm to the boat's propeller. She subsequently lost her life. Disturbingly, while the wax arm in the gallery serves as an evidential prop for this fictional death, the live Twitter feed on the monitor actually belongs to the real person. In this sense, the sculpture-screen serves as an interface between fictional and real lives. This interface is, in terms of aesthetic principles, a kind of spy-mirror—in the sense that only gallery visitors can literally and figuratively look *out* at the real person, beyond the game. The victim, whose identity has been stolen, has no access to their role in the *Dorm Daze* universe; no knowledge of their fictional death on the other side of the black mirror, nor their subsequent undeath in the gallery situation.

In the words of one critic, writing for *i-D Magazine, Dorm Daze* "was not only a work about the network, but made by it; using the infrastructure of social media to comment on that very infrastructure."[22] In this regard, it is important to note Fornieles's use of the term "self-generating." The emergent potential latent within the game's structure and resources is at issue here. To use an agricultural metaphor: the initiator plants and waters the seed of a game, and the soil's active multitude allows it to grow, or take root. "I'm interested in these spiraling forms, which are both heavily crafted and chaotic at the same time," wrote Fornieles; "The group will often produce something far more complex and compelling than the individual ever could."[23] The traffic between the rule of a game, or the guiding hand of its creator/minder, and spontaneous improvisation by players is clearly present in the artist's *Dorm Daze*—just like in the structure of QAnon,

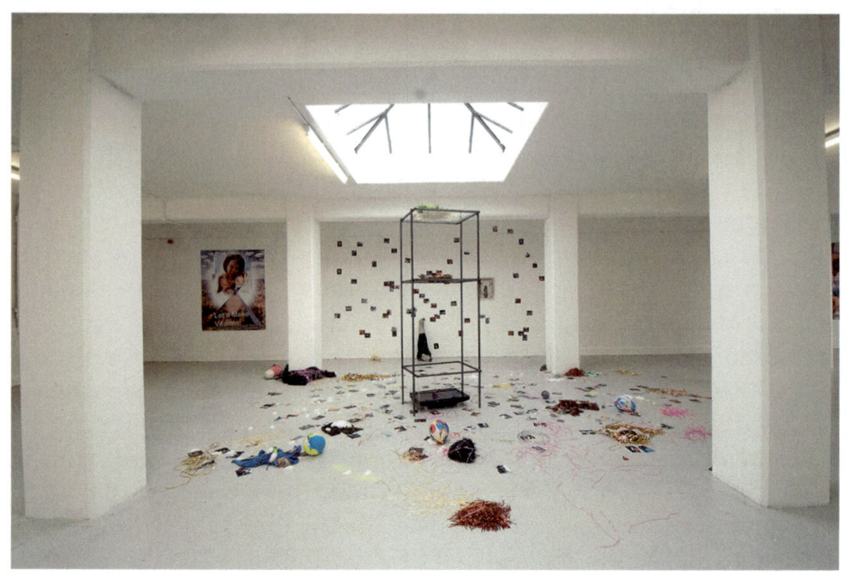

Ed Fornieles, *Aspen Get Away,* 2012
Steel, glass, Twitter feed, computers, *Dorm Daze* photographs

where for a number of years the individual known as Q would seed the
speculative/improvisational medium with cryptic statements (so-called
"Q drops"). In fact, Q would label these statements "breadcrumbs."
In turn, followers of the conspiracy have been known to refer to themselves as "bakers" who assemble crumbs to make "dough" or "bread,"
as they weave together the clues for a better "understanding" of the
narrative.[24] While the stretched metaphor—from cooked crumbs to
ready dough—is somewhat half-baked, the recipe for a certain kind
of decentralized authorship is clear enough. In this light, blurry lines
between fiction and reality in LARPing artworks are of a piece with
broader currents beyond the artworld, where the concept of "Fake News"
names a symptom for the increasing gamification of what constitutes
"truth" or "facts" in both public discourse and street politics.[25]

"Is this the complex analysis of the Rand Corporation? Or is it a
teenager on Instagram who thinks it would be cool if these two labels
were combined? I am interested in those two spheres exchanging
information."[26] At the furthest reaches, as in phenomena like QAnon,
such exchange can be said to culminate in a kind of political ecstasy
where death and desire comingle. However, the artist Joshua Citarella
is talking about narratives concerning possible futures that were

generated through his *Choose Your Future* (2021), an artwork that employs roleplay.[27] In the artist's own words, the project took the following form:

> In 2021, I commissioned a group of artists and Gen Z-memers to write short wiki-style descriptions of improbable futuristic scenarios. To produce these texts, writers were instructed to copy/paste existing Wikipedia entries and to play "mad libs" with the nouns, verbs, and dates. Drawing from political precedents and movements of the past, these short stories recombine history in order to anticipate long tail ideological factions that may emerge in the future.[28]

While the term "mad libs," borrowed from a popular game, conveys a certain juvenile pleasure, Citarella's quick rhetorical shift to West Coast techno-political jargon underlines his concern for gaming's disruptive potential. Reading the setup of *Choose Your Future* against *Dorm Daze,* a clear parallel obtains: rather than LARPing as another individual, whose personal data has been appropriated, Citarella's

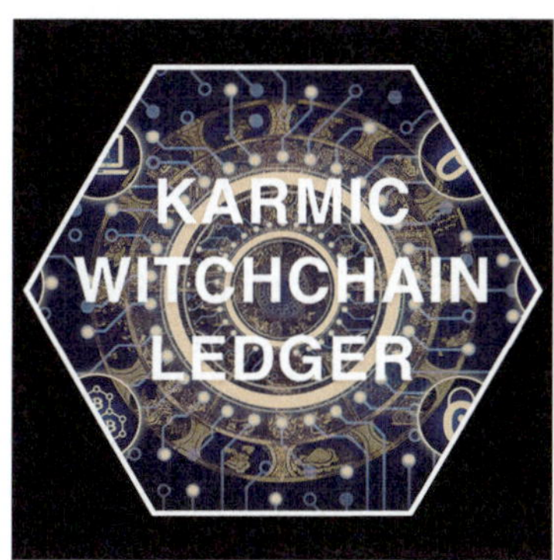

Joshua Citarella, *Choose Your Future
(Karmic Witchchain Ledger),* 2021
Website; SoundCloud audio file,
written by D. Z. Rowan,
read by Mat Dryhurst, 3.18 min.

game involves scalping certain rhetorical formats for quasi-authoritative political and economic discourse, in order to hand them over to actor-trickster groups.

According to Citarella, *Choose Your Future* concerned the "hyperbolic political imaginings of young people, raised on the Internet."[29] On the other hand, in his words, the project mimicked "the process of signal amplification that occurs through social media, when radical takes move from the fringe and into the mainstream."[30] The latter is more interesting in relation to the poetics of encryption, because it concerns the boundary between the inside of a game and its exterior; a focus on the passage from a "radical" signal operating below the threshold of majority perception (e.g. a dog whistle), to its greater detectability and/or uptake. Herewith, an artwork whose aesthetic probes the liminal space of politics—not so much exposing secretly held beliefs, as displaying emergent creative structures and situations handling the *image of politics* or The Political today. In some cases, Citarella's comment seems to suggest, a successful performance within an improvised game-style situation may warp the political space around it.

Unsurprisingly, conspiracy theories feature as both latent and explicit content in the entries dreamt up by Citarella's authors. For instance, an entry on "Gnostic-Bernankianism" would assert that the said belief system—which emerged on a comment thread, with "312 upvotes," and which pursues "the sacred and consistent ascension of The Line"—was "codified as a real system of economic thought by respected public intellectuals such as David Icke."[31] Icke, it should be noted, is a commercially successful conspiracy author whose corpus of more than twenty works concerns an inter-dimensional race of reptilian beings that have hijacked the earth.[32] The *Choose Your Future* entry on a so-called "Karmic Witchchain Ledger" also expresses a paranoiac worldview, while simultaneously picking up on the occult atmosphere surrounding cryptocurrency. As the artist's website outlines,

Decentralized Karmic Accounting is a conspiracy theory that posits the erroneous belief that Witchcoin is "karmic"; that the Witchchain protocol contains intention or occupation sensors installed by the elites for nefarious purposes undisclosed to the general public. Believers in this conspiracy theory say that while normal cryptocurrency adjusts its value according to predetermined formulas, Witchcoin uses the "intention" of users to determine its

Poetics of Encryption

value…. Online rumors suggest that corporate spies use the data gathered on intention surveillance to distribute "bad karma" to users who fail to pay sufficient attention to their client's products. The claim has been dismissed by the Coven of Directors…. Witchcoin conspiracy theories began to circulate after the company published a 2056 report about their users "fully internalized economic value determination system." In 2058, the company was accused of "using mysterious algorithms to detect the intention of a user" on the Witchcoin app. The theories were first posted on anonymous internet message boards, and were among the many conspiracies popularized by Italian-American streaming host Pisan Hiker, in 2059.[33]

Like *Dorm Daze,* Citarella's project plays a double game with prosumption, that "new 'wikinomic' model where businesses put consumers to work."[34] Both activate prosumer platforms (Facebook and Wikipedia, respectively) in order to criticize forms of meaning and identity that these platforms enable—on individual and corporate levels. In Fornieles's case, the apparent topic is "stereotypical" identities; in

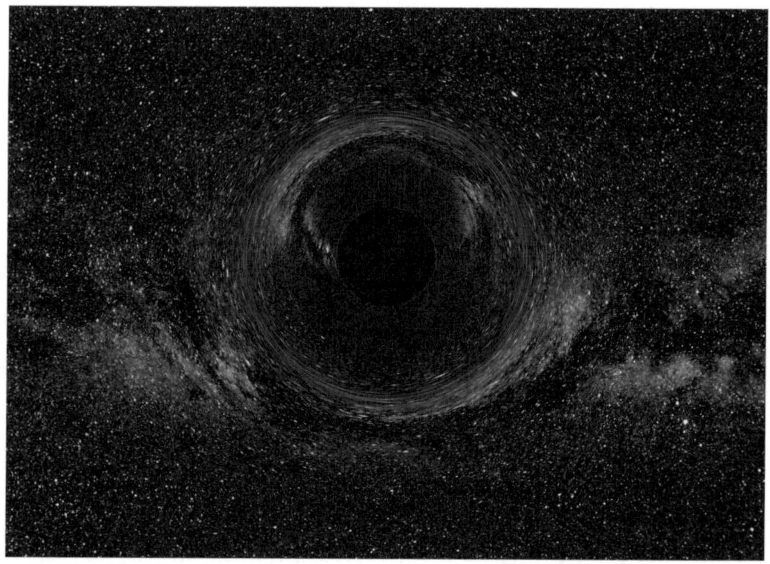

A simulated Black Hole of ten solar masses as seen from a distance of 600km
with the Milky Way in the background (horizontal camera opening angle: 90°)

Citarella's, discursive frames for ideological confabulation. However, on a deeper level, both artists recapitulate the latent power dynamics of prosumption: putting actors and other collaborators "to work" in the generation of their own art. Herein, a question concerning the *what* and *where* of value haunts the artistic scene like a ghost. This specter—emissary from the same plane as Nakamoto, a "dead" college girl, Q, or a Coven of Directors—may even be the question of ethics itself, registering a certain inability to ascribe authorship or clear accountability for the system and its products.

On the artistic plane, the death of the author may not be an issue. And yet, as the victim in *Dorm Daze* seems to indicate, some fictional deaths may need to be answered for. It is not only that the persons scraping and playing with data are hidden, or that they (in a way) parallel the anonymous surveillance systems deployed by governments and corporations. What is more significant is that, in the context of such drama, to the hidden puppet master(s) the individual subject is morally unseen. They appear to be viewed, instead, as a token to be *played* (with detachment), or a *shell* for transaction—for actions that are, effectively, blind to consequences relevant to the appropriated person. In a related vein, players may be ambivalent about the emerging social reality around the game, produced through their recreational traffic with political images. Indeed, the "seriousness" of such gaming is always in play. Performative worship of disorder under the banner of its own icon, Pepe the Frog, even indicates an active nihilism on the part of some memers regarding this issue. Not for nothing is this infamous meme/icon linked with the Egyptian god of obscurity, primordial *darkness,* and chaos, known as "Kek."[35] All told, a lack of ethical interest in consequences beyond the game is a feature of anonymity rather than a bug, and is known to the field of psychology as the "online disinhibition effect."[36]

In the frame of disinhibition, the environmental consequences of blockchain technology are indicative of a contrast between exogenous and endogenous realities. The financial *interior* of the Bitcoin, and other blockchain-enabled applications, bears a parasitical relationship to its exterior. Look, for example, at a work by UBERMORGEN.com titled *Red Coin (Chinese Blood)* (2015), which shows the Bitcoin rigs whirring away in a Chinese warehouse. The redness of the video frame (paralleling the crimson of Evan Roth's *Red Lines*) supposedly relates to blood—lifeforce, of a certain kind. The interior of blockchain may be a utopia of collaboration, but the abject scenario beyond is also relevant. Chief among these is, of course, ecological

Poetics of Encryption

despoliation. The hollowing out of the world beyond, the sucking dry, the rapacious consumption of energy required to run the machines—or, more broadly speaking, the game—has a touch of the vampiric. It is as if the culture of the blockchain, whose most visible self-identity is NFTs, wants to re-make the whole world in its strange image.

Should we be surprised that the alleged founder of QAnon has dabbled in NFTs, having minted images based on screenshots of so-called Q Drops?[37] Much of the NFT landscape represents a value that is invisible with respect to the pictorial. According to the artist and critic Brad Troemel, the value of an NFT is not the art but the network of persons "holding" tokens on the blockchain. Value is, in this sense, a kind of Ponzi scheme—a financial conspiracy. Bored Apes are, in his view, boring in terms of their visible (surface) meaning, but they are dog whistles for something occult, a cartoon screen for the deeper subject: money. Hito Steyerl's comments on art and encryption seem particularly apposite here: "Art is often encrypted to the point of sometimes being undecryptable,... even or especially if there is no meaning whatsoever."[38] But why is art that is empty of "social value" or "message," in Steyerl's estimation, so prominent today? The reason is that such "art" is "a reserve system for dumb, mean and greedy money"; it is a "shell operation that ultimately just shields more empty shells ... bonded warehouses and overdesigned bank vaults inside gilded, gated compounds,"[39] and so on, whose contents are always encrypted. Bored Ape NFTs are a distillation of this principle in digital space. Indeed, the emptiness of the mainstream NFT (as "art") encapsulates the fungibility of meaning under the rule of Fintech. NFT quasi-artworks are visual symptoms for a churn of transactions on the less-visible distributed ledger—transactions that have, within financial game-space, little to do with narratives and meaning beyond trading and ownership. The boredom of the ape is exemplary in registering this ambivalence.

Money, according to the critic Max Haiven, is itself a crypt:

the crypt of the imaginative-cooperative dimensions of labor. Money ... translates our cooperative energies into a solidified (even if still dematerialized) form, which is offered back to us as the means to access the fruits of our cooperation. This was the ultimate meaning of Marx's notion of the commodity fetish, where we are so alienated from the thing we (the proletariat, the cooperating creators) have created that it appears to us not as our own creation but as if endowed with a kind of supernatural value.[40]

With the NFT, the argument is augmented somewhat, because users are effectively alienated from what the servers have created (and maintain) through electronic operations. The creation of a fetish figure (an ape, etc.) is necessary solidification—it puts a face on the faceless. Bored Apes are the pictures on the dollar bill (rather than the number)—but rather than endowing blockchain with a spirit, they represent the ghost of artfulness, haunting the domain of transactions whose humane surplus is ever more reduced.

The idea of a hidden network of actors, haunting people and situations beyond their closed circle, is prevalent in art about the network (as conspiracy) just as much as in online conspiracy theories themselves. More generally, the topic of undeath abounds in art concerning networks, and for good reason.

Corona

As the preceding section indicates, covert human agents often work with technology to achieve their ends. We now turn our attention to *computational powers* operating behind the scenes. These powers are registered in the weirdness of the scenes themselves, which stand to be analyzed as *shadows* cast by the hidden; otherwise, as flares that have emanated from an occult core—shifting shapes and distorted visions playing about the corona. Such images are fascinating as they crystallize some of the dynamism and recombinatory power of computation, as if the sun's thermonuclear fire were captured, some-how, in diamonds mounted on a crown. They are, in a sense, sover-eignty's counterintuitive decoration.

It is common to speak of archives being *dense* with content. The Internet, the greatest archive of all, incorporates an incredible mass of information—and countless links or pathways between its vast holdings. The training-data sets of top AIs are similarly huge. So, too, the amount of neural-net parameters that are created by such training. Engineers sublimate this surplus of signification—nearly every book ever written, every conversation carried out online, and so much more—by means of numerical terms: terabyte, gigabyte, petabyte, exabyte, zettabyte, etc. However, narratives that take in the full "sense" of this mass of meaning are out of the question. In a related vein, pictorial ciphers for data and computational power can only tend in the direction of the surreal: "If you were to store 175 zettabytes [the world's projected amount of data in 2025] on DVDs," as if this idea

                                    Poetics of Encryption

were not insane to begin with, "your stack would be long enough to circle Earth 222 times."[41] But metaphors for scale should not be limited to extension. In fact, the metaphor of density is better at transmitting the *active* power (or dynamism) that attends massive networked data—the way in which it affects the imagination, and warps cultural spacetime.

Imagination is a process and not content *per se.* It is the principle whereby images come into being. As such, imagination is not proprietary to humans. Or, at least, it is not totally under human control. Exploring the metaphor of data density, one might, therefore, speak about how the Internet operates in the manner of a black hole—and the *imagination* that this entails. In such a poetics, the inside of the network-object is figured not so much as a final site—like a cave, or series of sites—to be explored, but rather as a *force,* pulling the surrounding universe into itself. This force moves things, and in the process distorts them. At a certain point, along a passage approaching the deep inside, a threshold is crossed into another dimension—where standard conceptual distinctions, such as inside versus outside, are denatured.

According to the so-called "cosmic censorship conjecture," the center of a black hole cannot be seen from the outside.[42] Its force drags light (and time itself) into its encrypted singularity. However, the region proximate to the event horizon, where the black hole's super-density begins to devour the real, can be observed. Action around the hole forms a visible corona of X-ray light, and high-energy radiation.[43] This perceptible action is the signature of the censored interior. It is a strange vision, however, operating on an X-ray color spectrum. A little deeper along, a further peculiarity applies to objects passing through the event horizon. Stephen Hawking describes a hypothetical astronaut, falling through this threshold, as being "stretched like spaghetti" by the gravitational gradient—the difference in gravitational force from their head to their toe.[44] Beyond this "spaghettification" (a real term in astrophysics), still more distortion: "Along with that, the right side of the body will be pulled to the left, and the left side of the body will be pulled to the right, horizontally compressing the [astronaut]."[45] The figure is also flattened and, to the external observer, frozen—in the manner of a photograph.[46] With regard to its influence on figures still extant in this universe, we may say that black holes effect degrees of travesty and, according to a certain mainstream astrophysical view, *chaos.*[47]

Though "censored," at least one condition of a black hole's singularity has been deduced *a priori:* its interior gravity is so intense that reality (as we know it) breaks down; a scenario that is "no longer part of the regular spacetime and [which] cannot be determined by 'where' or 'when.'"[48] In this condition, almost every kind of identity is scrambled. The artist and writer Jalal Toufic tells a speculative tale concerning the unfortunate astronaut's experience:

> The separation he had to accept inside the supermassive black hole was not only with the universe to the other side of the event horizon, but also with the other travelers on the spaceship, no longer feeling any affinity with them: they presently gave the impression of being, indeed were possibly, ahistorical, unworldly entities that irrupted fully formed.[49]

Rather than pushing the theoretical physics of our critical metaphor into more dubious terrain, let us stop and take stock. What has been described are some principles of *imagination* attending black holes: the distortion of extant figures; intense unpredictability (chaos); the scrambling of what, where, and when; overall strangeness. Such descriptors also apply to the effects of super-dense data troves and massive computation upon the cultural domain: conceptual and visual distortions; spatial and temporal muddles; hybridization without limit; a parade of aliens; and alienation from the once familiar. Toufic's astronaut does not travel alone, but with his lover. In time, she is unrecognizable:

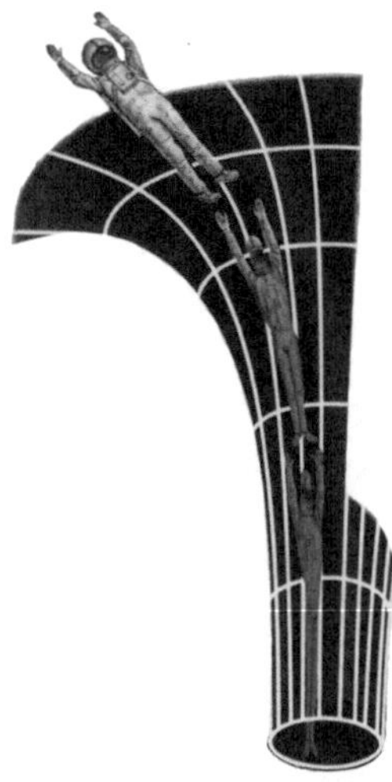

Spaghettification

Poetics of Encryption

Looking at his beloved as they crossed to the other side of the event horizon, he felt that she [was] as alien as a sphinx. I envision the sphinx of Bacon's *Oedipus and the Sphinx after Ingres,* 1983, asking a twenty-first-century Oedipus, now an astronaut, a different riddle at a black hole's event horizon: "What is it that conjointly crosses a gateless gate and doesn't, is two dimensional and three dimensional, and although ostensibly the same totally alien?"[50]

The riddle of how a black hole's polymorphous interior might be experienced firsthand is well put into the mouth of a sphinx, as this classic figure stands for the breakdown of conceptual coherence, and the challenge of making sense of complexity and paradox. But the sphinx's chimerical form is also an apt icon for what obtains about the corona. With the head of a human and a cat's body, it is a plausible sentinel for the effects of digital *imagination*—the warping and disordering of cultural spacetime. Earlier, this principle was termed the "double fate" of most beings in the Technocene. This involves, on the one hand, being subject to the principle of dividuation—disarticulation into component parts—and on the other hand, having been so processed, standing as raw materials to be recombined with elements from other sources into novel hybrids. With its infinite possible permutations, built upon a basic binary of ones and zeros, massive computation effects all manner of hybridizations and disruptions. The contemporary sphinx is a chimera or admixture that serves as a token for this dynamic denaturing, and its endless production of riddles.

In the previous chapter we saw how certain artworks take the literal form of black boxes, while addressing the eponymous cybernetic condition. However, we also saw how not all iconographies of the black box involve the color black, nor the form of a box. As the art of Tilman Hornig showed, transparency can also be used as a visual marker for obscure functionality. In a like manner, sphinxes abound in contemporary art, serving as sentinels for dynamic *computational powers* operating behind the scenes—in fact, altering the scenes of life. Yet, while some chimeras take the literal form of sphinxes, others address the digital production of distortion, disorder, and hybridity through alternative visual markers.

In light of the preceding comments, *Protected: Panorama Cat* (2022) by the Italian artist duo Eva and Franco Mattes is an exemplary totem for a new world in which the strange is a matter of course. The work comprises a taxidermy sculpture of a ginger tabby cat, whose body has been stretched (spaghettified?) to unreal proportions, with the addition of far too many legs. Its form is based on a viral photograph from the genre known as "panorama fails"—a class of glitches and distortions in depicted figures, brought about by the unorthodox use of the panorama function. With the introduction of the panorama feature to smartphones, a flood of surreal mistakes were produced and shared online. A few of these went viral, becoming some of the most viewed images in history. *Protected: Panorama Cat* is a faithful reproduction of one of these photos in three dimensions. Transferring the two-dimensional motif from online space into a sculptural representation, using actual fur, the artists insist on the strange phenomenon's tangible reality. *Protected: Panorama Cat* is a contemporary sphinx, marking a threshold where understanding and nonsense converge—an icon for the digital distortion of both nature and culture, and the new life (undeath?) that this situation entails for everything living today.

Protected: Panorama Cat is not the only artistic sphinx to express a Technocene enigma. There are many more. Further chimeras speak to the power of digital media to deform discourse.[51] In another artwork by Joshua Citarella, a snake with three heads appears on a flag—herald for a strange political hybrid. The flag itself represents

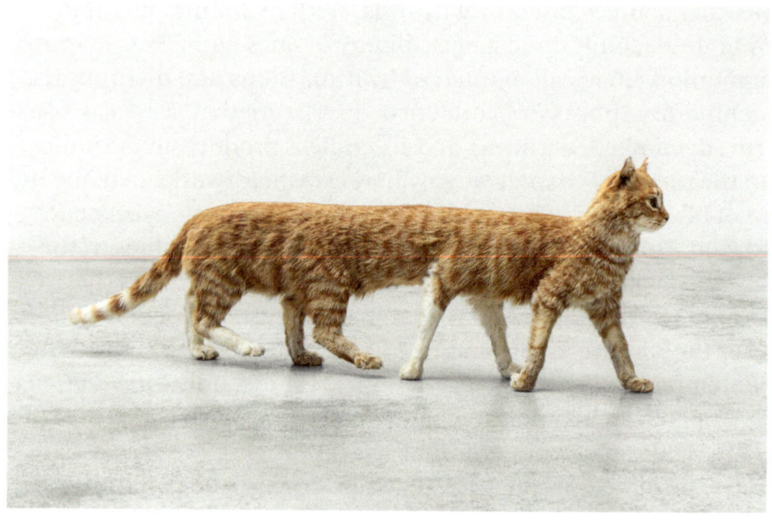

Eva and Franco Mattes, *Panorama Cat,* 2022
Taxidermy cats, polyurethane foam, 96 × 17 × 34 cm

                                    Poetics of Encryption

"Anarcho Collectivist Islamo Minarchism," an ideological riddle if ever there was one, "found" by Joshua Citarella online. Its imagery incorporates a triple-headed Gadsen snake, "representing the unity of individuals, sitting atop a field of collectivist red and minarchist blue." It is just one of many designs gathered from political message boards that feature in the artist's *e-deologies* (2020), an installation comprising thirty-six print-on-demand flags.[52] The title of the project is borrowed from an Internet slang term, which describes the overuse of prefixes and suffixes to create complex ideological labels. According to Citarella, these hyper-specific categories "serve as a gamified form of identity play and niche personal branding in the chaotic landscape of online politics."[53] As he relates, e-deologies are often formalized with a declarative blog-style post and sometimes with the creation of a customized flag. These flags are "usually hung in one's bedroom like a poster of your favorite band or film."[54] Installed in a former sports bar, the exhibition of these flags spoke to the creation of a social situation. "Just as the young radicals of earlier eras might have gathered in pubs and beer halls, today's radical youth convene in the online equivalent and bring with them all the peculiarities of web 2.0 culture."[55]

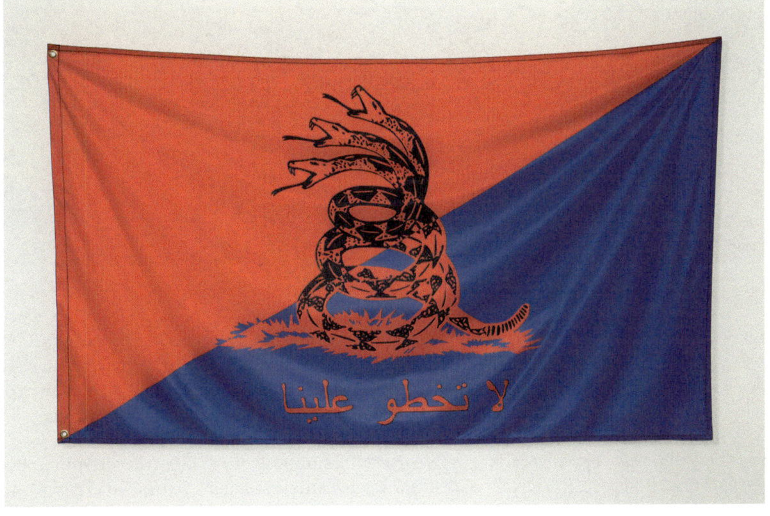

Joshua Citarella, *e-deologies II* (Anarcho Collectivist Islamo Minarchism), 2022
Dye sublimation print on polyester, 152.4×76.2 cm

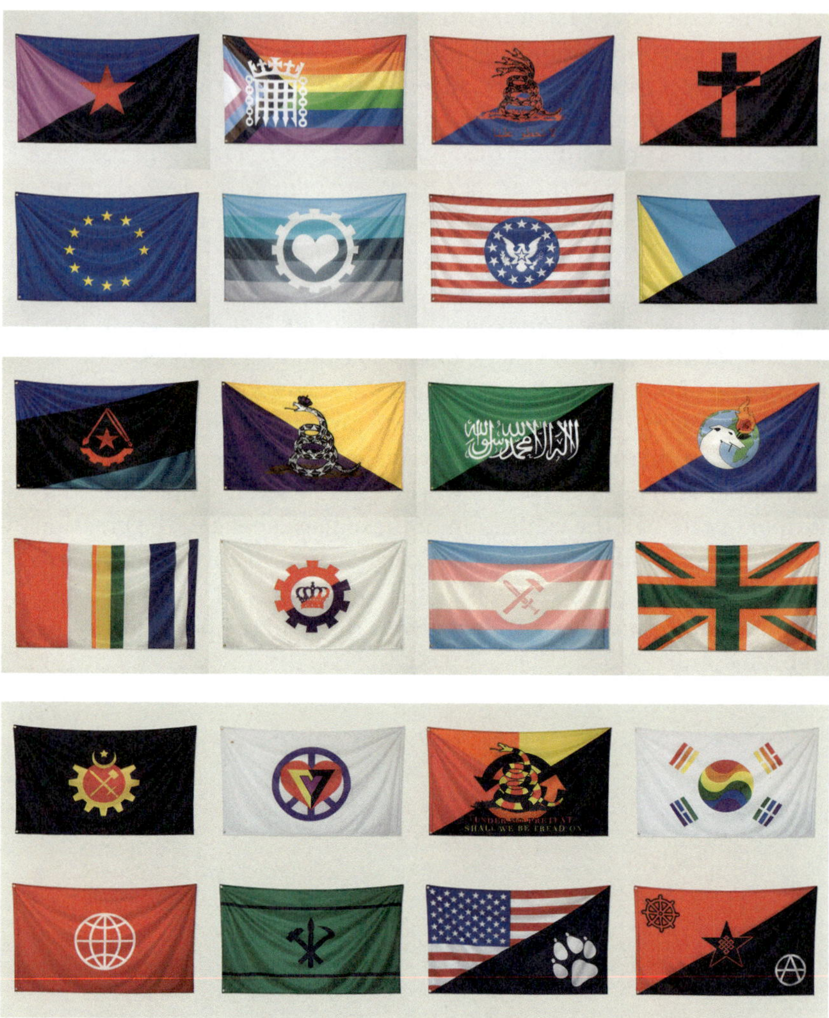

Joshua Citarella, *e-deologies II*, 2022 (1. Queer Transhumanist Anarchism / 2. Progress Pride
Constitutional Monarchy / 3. Anarcho Collectivist Islamo Minarchism / 4. Christian Anarchism /
5. Post-Brexit European Union / 6. Robo Sexual / 7. American Monarchism / 8. Anarcho Capitalist
Individualist Transhumanism), Dye sublimation print on polyester, each 152.4×76.2 cm

Joshua Citarella, *e-deologies*, 2020 (1. Left Egoist Transhumanism / 2. Libertarian Monarchism /
3. Anarcho-Primitivist Caliphatism / 4. Mutual-Transhumanist-Social-Democratic-Distributist-
Georgism / 5. The New European Union / 6. Monarcho-Syndicalism / 7. Trans-Strasserism /
8. United Ireland), Dye sublimation print on polyester, each 152.4×76.2 cm

Joshua Citarella, *e-deologies III*, 2022 (1. Islamo Nazbol / 2. Anarcho-Capitalist Voluntarist
Pacificism / 3. Anarcho-Collectivist Capitalist Mutualism / 4. Trans Korean / 5. Center for Political
Innovation / 6. Primitivist Juche / 7. American K9 Tracker Unit / 8. Buddhist Anarchism)
Dye sublimation print on polyester, each 152.4×76.2 cm

                                                      Poetics of Encryption

The labels and corresponding logos are fascinating: others include "Queer Transhumanist Anarchism"; "Anarcho-Capitalist Individualist Transhumanism"; "Islamo Nazbol"; "Anarcho-Capitalist Voluntarist Pacificism"; "Primitivist Juche"; "Trans Korean"; and "Anarcho-Collectivist Capitalist Mutualism." The last three are especially interesting. In the Primitivist Juche flag, Primitivist green overlays the North Korean flag, representing the will to an isolationist society that rejects both technology and personal freedom. However, not all compound ideologies are so internally consistent. Trans Koreanism registers, in Citarella's telling, the influence of social media personality Oli London. Though White and of British descent, London identifies as South Korean and has undergone multiple plastic surgery procedures to achieve ethnic self-realization. In 2021, his "racial transition" attracted worldwide attention and stirred debate around the validity of transracialism. Later, in 2022, London transitioned genders (before then detransitioning). He now appears on right-wing media outlets as an outspoken detransitioner and a devout Christian. As for the flag of Anarcho-Collectivist Capitalist Mutualism, Citarella offers the following written interpretation:

> *exhales* sometimes the people who make these don't really understand one (or both) of the ideologies. In this case it might be all three. Ancaps and Ancoms will often express support for Mutualism, a political philosophy associated with Pierre-Joseph Proudhon. But you can't have private AND collective ownership. Tbh this guy probably thinks the snake is cool and I hope he reads a book in the near future.[56]

The accretive logic on display in these e-deologies registers the hyperlinked situation of information online: an ethos of interchangeability and conjunction, which is a function of the phenomenology of web browsing. Hyperlinked cultural space is, for the most part, flat with seemingly infinite pathways (transitions) between sites and values. This suggests a lack of privileged vantage points from which to survey a scene. If you want to learn something about climate change, crackpot theories vie with peer-reviewed research on the same plane. Transitions or metamorphoses between one thing and another abound by necessity. The "big tent" conspiracies of Web 2.0 run on similar tracks, building ever more connections into their web of (non) sense-making. Here, instead of self-aware identity play or "niche personal branding," authors are self-described "theorists" whose accounts chart the flatness of the information landscape—both metaphorically and, in the case of Flat Earth conspiracy theorists, *literally*. However, this flatness may be likened to an optical feature of eclipse: the spherical moon being seen as a black disk; likewise, as the flatness of the astronaut, viewed crossing the event horizon. Indeed, accretion is symptomatic of the process or *dynamism* that is the information black hole, pulling one distinct thing after another towards a certain singularity. Yet, while the Internet-archive may swallow up a universe of information, meaning and sense stand to be denatured or flattened as their referents are pulled towards the yawning chasm of datafication.

Human narrative and pictorial frames cannot hope to incorporate everything at once. What makes conspiracy theories so crazy is that they attempt to do so: to keep baby and bathwater; to establish a totalizing narrative that covers *everything*. The dynamic structure of the (visual) meme, however, approaches the same problem through a more circumspect process. Here, accretion and recombination without limit are *not* subordinated to a rhetoric of instantaneous exposure. Unlike conspiracy theories, they embrace their status as riddles—always already somewhat inscrutable and partial, even as they expose a certain problematic or feature of the network-object.

According to Domenico Quaranta, "an internet meme is a piece of content capable of circulating in ever different forms ... that is endlessly customizable to different contexts and messages."[57] Yet memes have a peculiar form: they are experienced as a succession of different moments or iterations—pictorial crystallizations—that only obliquely indicate the totality of their identity as a network object. Each of these moments is self-contained. However, while they may stand alone, exerting a certain fascination, their power emanates from the less-than-visible assemblage that they imply. Of course, a "meme" is not the product of one author or individual decision, but many. And this multifaceted authorship plays out over time. Each image (or iteration) in the meme chain functions in the manner of a photo-graphic snapshot, as a current time-slice of the social network (a combination of people and infrastructure) in operation. As a cumula-tive process, a meme plays out in diachronic succession. As a concep-tual totality, or singularity, the meme is a synchronic multitude that implies the general time of a never-ending present—the network as *all at once*. Here, *Protected: Panorama Cat* provides us with a useful metonym: the many individual legs of the cat (standing, so to speak,

    Poetics of Encryption

for individual images) supporting the intimation of a total body. As contemporary chimeras, however, viral memes have more legs than can feasibly be stitched together, offscreen, in three dimensions.

Leopards in the Temple

"Leopards break into the temple and drink to the dregs what is in the sacrificial pitchers; this is repeated over and over again; finally, it can be calculated in advance, and it becomes part of the ceremony."[58] Kafka's vivid aphorism attunes the mind to the notion of wild intrusion; to the threat that exoteric phenomena pose to order, by draining the cup of consistency. However, when outliers constantly return, is this a case of domesticating them, as the quote seems to suggest? Or, rather, might it amount to a new regime? Perhaps the profusion of sphinxes in contemporary art indicates both.

In turning our attention to such questions and their possible reconciliation in the term "new normal," one looks to art for insight. It is surprising that no critic has made a connection between Kafka's epigram and a work by Paola Pivi titled *One Cup of Cappuccino Then I Go* (2007). This piece involved a live leopard (on loan from a magician) let loose in a gallery containing three thousand cups of coffee. While reimagining the cappuccino as a sacrificial offering is somewhat suggestive (setting up caffeine drinkers as substitute gods), Pivi's work mostly leverages novelty. As it happened, the feline's unlikely, charismatic, and possibly dangerous trespass was limited by predictable health and safety measures—ruling out visitor access until after the animal's departure. A menace in the rear-view mirror, then, glimpsed second-hand, through paw prints and photographs, rendered "ceremonial" or defanged through documentary mediation. What about the artist? Viewed through a lens sensitive to the cooption of institutional critique, her outline is clear: an actor playing the role of cappuccino-drinking leopard—bringing comfortable frisson to the Kunsthalle Basel, "calculated in advance." The photographs even indicate that certain beverages were plastic, their contents solid and, ultimately, unspillable. In this manner, Pivi's work was a play with the aesthetics of complicity wholly symptomatic of its time.[59] As a hedged risk, her leopard was tame. Today, nearly two decades later, the aesthetic of non-human intrusion is more complex.

Domestication is at issue in Kafka's aphorism but, as we have seen, it provokes a further question concerning possible regime change. Or, if not a question *per se,* an imperative: to attend just how different the ceremony becomes after (metaphorical) prowling leopards become part of it. The philosopher Peter Sloterdijk offers his own analysis of the aphorism, casting it as a meditation on "cultural immunologic."[60] For him, it indicates "a process of world literature competing with the rise of the external, the foreign, the fortuitous, and those forces that threaten to burst the sphere."[61] The aim of this process "is to settle every outside, no matter how cruel and unfitting, all demons of the negative and monsters of foreignness, within an expanded inside.... In this sense, order is above all the effect of transference from interior to exterior."[62] For Sloterdijk, certain artworks serve to "process" the emergence of the exoteric within the sanctuary space, domesticating it through acts of reimagination, such that its potential to provoke catastrophic rupture is denied. In line with this perspective, one might say that radical changes to the ceremony are the cost of doing business when a threat is existential. This pragmatic (indeed, syncretist) approach allows both regime change and continuity to adhere simultaneously. Drawing the feral into the cultural frame effects cohabitation with contradiction—*living* with it, however uncomfortable the process.

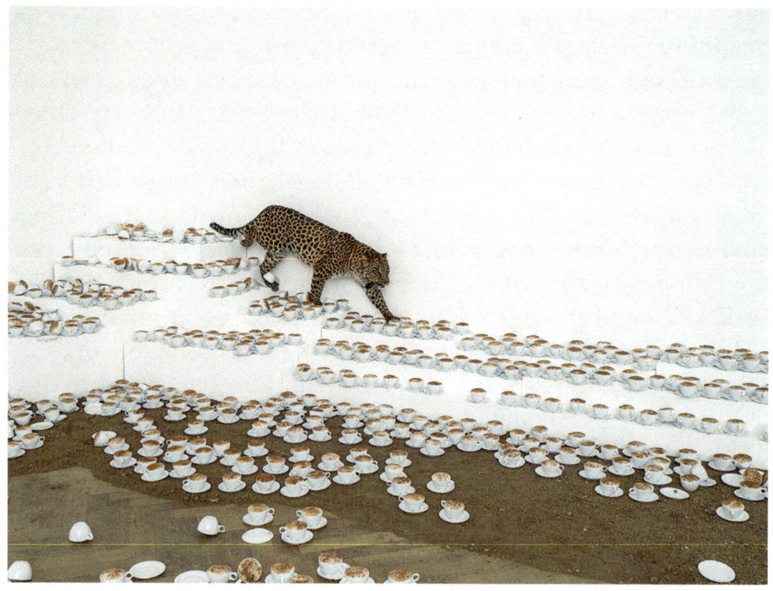

Paola Pivi, *One Cup of Cappuccino Then I Go,* 2007
Photographic print, 160×214 cm

Poetics of Encryption

Moving beyond the somatic language of comfort to aesthetic judgment, one may consider cohabitation with "leopards" a question of sublimating the concept of the unnatural *vis-à-vis* an extant system. In her book *Against Nature,* historian of science Lorraine Daston explains how encounters with the seemingly unnatural provoke distinct emotional responses: horror, terror, and wonder.[63] According to her argument, these emotions monitor violations of different kinds in the assumed natural order, and the intensity with which they are felt reveals how significant this order is for a stable lived experience.[64] Such responses "offer insight into moral intuition."[65] Parsing the monsters of contemporary art, one may observe that the old order is encountered in negative relief—through images calculated to provoke a certain horror or uncanny affect. The monumentality of these images suggests novel ceremonies or "moral intuitions" that revalue the outlier as a kind of totem, metabolizing the shock of the new.

Let us now return to the sphinx (a pseudo big cat) as an exemplary icon for the monstrosity of crossed thresholds. For it appears as such in Marguerite Humeau's work: first, in a series of dramatic sculptures that debuted at Zurich's Haus Konstruktiv in 2017; and also in a piece titled *Riddles* at Berlin's Schinkel Pavilion the same year. These presentations offered a non-archaic visual language for hybridity. Deploying a tension between bio-horror and astringent design, some incorporated security implements such as anti-climb spikes: the sphinx as border-guard system. At Schinkel, through an array of stainless-steel barriers: checkpoint architecture. Elsewhere, a more classic winged cat towered over viewers, conveying otherworldly menace. Through their large scale and slick formal register, these works monumentalize exemplary chimeras as *iconic*—beasts in front of which to prostrate oneself and find a sense of accommodation. Bearing down upon viewers, Humeau's sphinxes seem to demand answers to the riddles that they embody. Otherwise, they appear to indicate that peace must be made with the problem they pose and, following Kafka, that they must be "incorporated into the ceremony."

While the answer to the classical sphinx's riddle was "a man,"[66] the contemporary subject stands to be identified. Humeau's oeuvre indicates that to approach it requires—in the words of Donna Haraway—the aesthetic concept and practice of "sympoiesis": "making-with" non-human others.[67] Throughout her body of work, Humeau stages a digitally enabled recombinatory aesthetic that is not only post-human but post-biological, too, while proposing the emergence of new forms of being and agency. In a series inspired by the sex

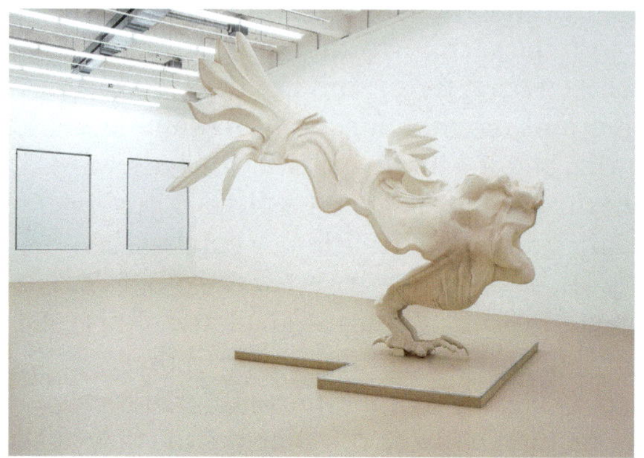

Marguerite Humeau,
*Sphinx Otto Has Absorbed
Humankind,* 2017
Skeleton (steel), artificial
human skin (gel coat, tinted
resin, Carrara marble powder,
fiberglass), skin painted with
anti-human poisonous
pigment made from essence
of plants selected from black
magic recipes, breathing
light, sound, 325 × 600 × 285 cm
Installation view: Zurich Art
Prize, Museum Haus
Konstruktiv, Zurich, 2017

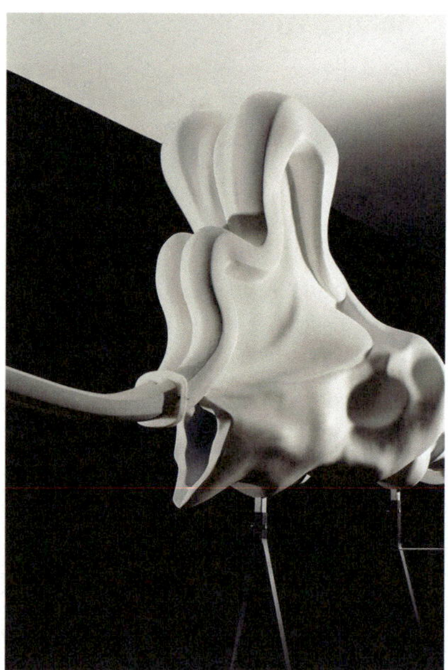

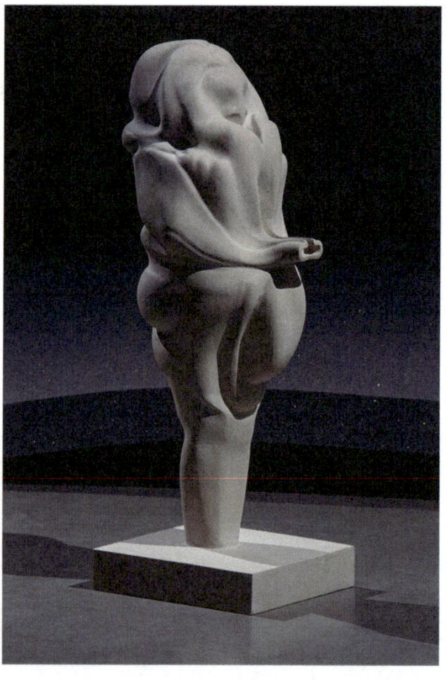

Marguerite Humeau, *Venus of Frasassi,
A 10-year-old female human has ingested
a rabbit's brain,* 2019
Portland limestone, a cappella voice,
86.2 × 28 × 32 cm
Installation view: *Ecstasies,*
Kunstverein in Hamburg, 2019

Marguerite Humeau, *The Opera of Prehistoric
Creatures—Mammoth Imperator,*
-4,5M years ago, 2012
Resonance cavities, larynx with vocal cords,
windpipe, artificial intelligence,
366 × 100 × 530 cm

Poetics of Encryption

organs of plants (once again, scaled up to more-than-human dimen-sions), the prospect of a great flowering of hybridity is offered as
an epic *vanitas.* The artist's floral monoliths express a principle of
fecundity and cross-pollination that is, by implication, not contained
within the walls of any exhibition space (best exemplified by her
gigantic *Rise,* 2021)—nor by "natural" biological code. As with all
introduced species, there is a touch of menace in this cyborg-vegeta-tion. With coiled stamen and tentacle-like curvature, her plants
appear ready to pounce and grab, like carnivorous flowers. Presaging
this vegetal hybridity, Humeau's earlier works splice together histori-cal, biological, and speculative data to imagine crossbreed embryos—
as in *Venus of Frasassi, A 10-year-old female human has ingested a rabbit's
brain* (2019). What is this (and others in her series of embryo-brain
sculptures) if not a pregnant metaphor for unlimited pro-creative
technique, straddling human and artificial intelligence? It is art
for the age of CRISPR, and the real invention of human-animal
chimeras.[68]

Such works stage amalgamation and the topic of crossed thresh-olds as a "live" issue that is impossible to ignore—crystallizing
passages from the "natural" domain of meaning to its other, non-sense, or perhaps even *post-truth;* from human to data bodies and
back; from biological life to alien agency, and more. By extension,
these works also scramble temporal boundaries. Earlier works by
Humeau bring the latter point into focus. While undertaking her
Master's degree in design, the artist managed to gather scans of fossils
belonging to extinct mammals, as well as others from their descen-dent species. By synthesizing the respective data sets she was able to
construct three-dimensional models of sound-producing anatomy.
Using a computer-controlled milling device, she then sculpted these
forms out of silicone, attached them to air compressors, and resur-rected the roars of beasts never-before heard by humans. When
exhibited, the interplay of roars was coordinated by an AI system—a
non-human conductor—into a so-called opera. In staging the crossing
of great distances in time and space, smooth transitions between
animality, digitality, her personal desire, and natural forces, this
project staked out wildly new terrain for contemporary sculpture.
Combining prehistory and science fiction, these works resuscitate the
past and conflate the subterranean and subcutaneous, while updating
the quest genre inherent to the Information Age. All this, before the
term "deepfake" was ever coined. Given the epic sweep of her idea,
it is little wonder Humeau called the series *The Opera of Prehistoric*

Creatures (2012). The title perfectly captures the sense of performance and grandiosity obtaining in her endeavor. Indeed, shortly thereafter, in 2014, she claimed to have resurrected the speaking voice of Cleopatra.[69]

In addition to pointing towards emerging science, Humeau's art can be read as dramatizing the unchecked potency of the autodidact in the Technocene: an updated Victor Frankenstein, able to cobble together eclectic sources and methods to wild effect. We have already seen how conspiracy theories are typified by their attempts to incorporate all contradictions into a unitary carcass. Now that anyone with a computer has access to "information," the ability to splice, and to publish, proliferates outside specialist milieus. In a landscape of mutant-researchers and their monstrous ideas, Humeau's poetics captures or *embodies* the prevailing atmosphere of folly and fascination—a situation in which autodidacts assume the power to resurrect the dead and set their spirits to work in the present, calling forth all manner of Oedipal struggles.[70] In a similar manner to the authors of certain e-deologies, or big tent conspiracy theorists, her art exhibits an interdisciplinarity that borders on indiscipline—as evidenced by the formal eccentricity of her sculptures. And she is not alone.

Qua sympoiesis, Humeau's art is an exemplary performance of hybrid *imagination:* the co-processing (power) of her individual concern and machinic operations. What it offers is the monumental-ization of the chimera, showcasing *any* figure's subjection to the rule of dividuation and recombination. Humeau's totems unsettle visions of a natural order—while proposing that one "stay with the trouble" and effectively co-habit with aliens.[71] This co-habitation is both physical and *imaginative.* But however monstrous her works look, or sound, they do emanate from conscious intention on the artist's part—specifically, *her* vision of finality. Whatever generative process Humeau's digital tools supply, she has the last word concerning when a sculpture is complete. Yet, moving forward, beyond her oeuvre, to certain works by other artists dealing with generative AI, the issue of an untethered, endless, machinic creativity assumes prominence.

Algorithm as Monster

As Humeau's work with prehistoric fossils makes plain, between archival dreaming and cosmic sleep, digitized beings live entirely vigorous, undead lives. For a host of artists bringing AI to bear upon the relics of ancient statuary, this spectral condition is of acute critical import. Their works intimate the prospect of *imagination* beyond sympoiesis by alluding to the absence of human thought in *the dynamic act of computation*. These images of *icons forever being remade* are props that symbolize a ceremony attended only by machines. While designed by artists, they stand for a vector of (re)creation that shoots away from human hands. Indeed, such objects reflect a contemporary "moral intuition" whose content or cult value may be described as *contemplating the end of human(e) aesthetics*—perhaps, even, the intimation of a god-like Artificial General Intelligence (AGI) over the horizon. They do so by showcasing a relentless churn of recombination that, at the very least, destabilizes prospects for art and criticism built upon the Kantian concept of the "finality" of aesthetic judgment.

Whenever disinterred from Italian hillsides, Greek fields, caves, or elsewhere, incomplete Classical statuary has aroused conjecture. The unearthing of the celebrated Laocoön Group in 1506 (missing certain limbs) provoked numerous attempts to "restore" the sculpture to its original composition—through new arms, for instance, affixed in various positions. Today, the additions have been removed but the invitation to speculation remains. Italian artist Davide Quayola's

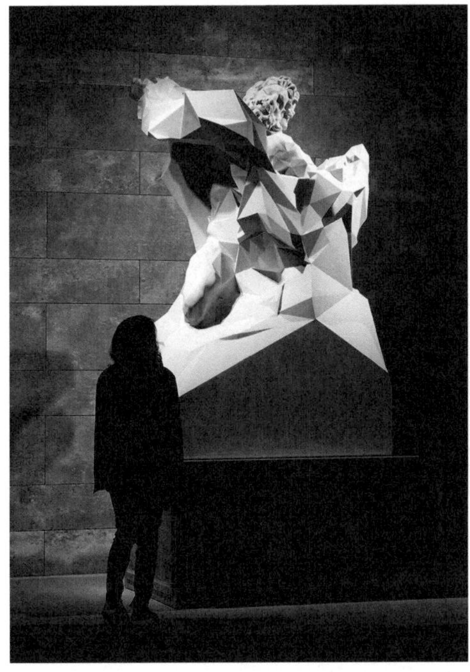

Davide Quayola, *Laocoön* (2016)
Pulverized white marble,
230×123×130 cm

Laocoön series picks up the task of finishing them, deploying the power of virtual and physical tools, including multiple generative adversarial networks (GANs). This strategy has been adopted by other artists working on Classical statuary, including Egor Kraft, whose *Content Aware Studies* (2019) also proposes to complete broken Classical busts and relief sculptures—in the name of "quasi-archeological knowledge production and interpretations of history and culture in the era of ubiquitous computation."[72] While producing three-dimensional models, leading to machine-cut marble sculptures, in which the blanks are filled in, both artists' procedures undercut the notion that a work (of art) may ever be finished.

Indeed, if connoisseurship of pre-modern art once involved interrogating (and policing) distinctions between original and copy, advanced tech renders this task increasingly difficult, while raising other pressing concerns—among them, the prominence of the *version.* In a post-digital landscape, appeals to the "finality" of judgment—established by Immanuel Kant as the basis for any aesthetic claim—are eclipsed by the truly *disinterested* intelligence of the machine, and a surplus of viable endings. Working against any instinct for rest, conclusion, and completeness, the robot keeps working; the versions

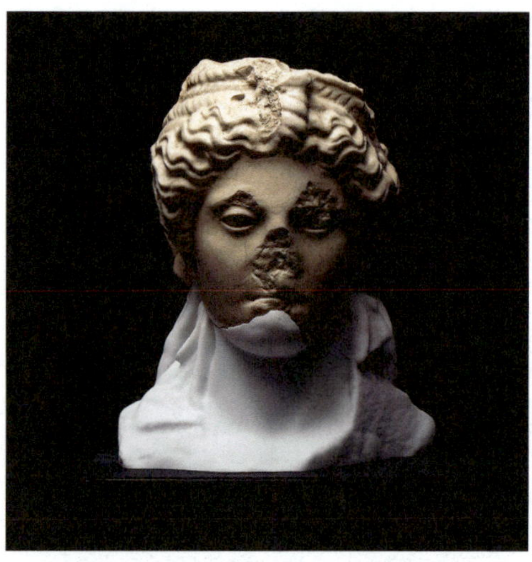

Egor Kraft, *Content Aware Studies,* 2019
Marble, polyamide, machine learning algorithms, custom software, original dataset, multi-channel video installation, dimensions variable

Poetics of Encryption

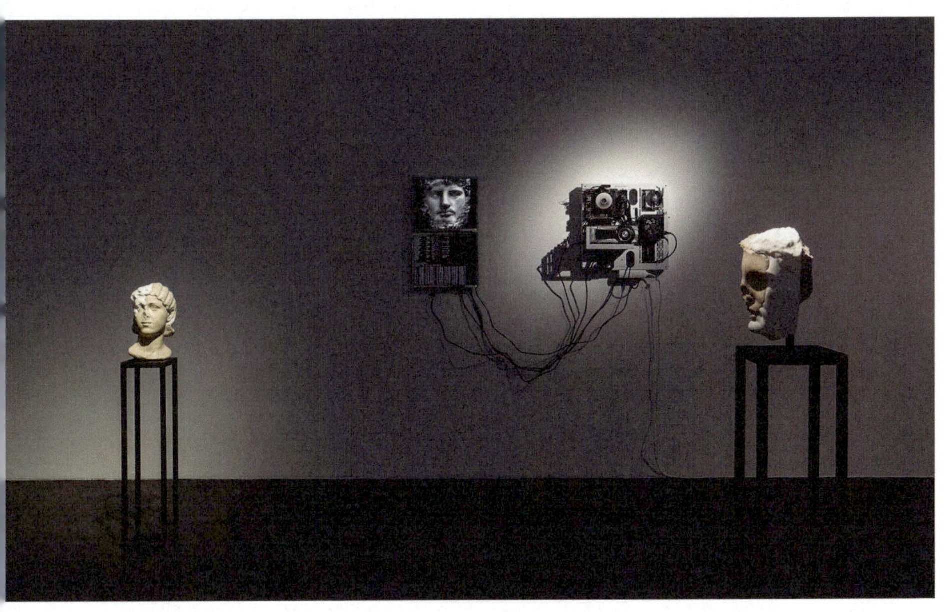

Egor Kraft, *Content Aware Studies,* 2019
Marble, polyamide, machine learning algorithms, custom software,
original dataset, multi-channel video installation, dimensions variable

keep coming. Beyond the locus of "real" time, material, or energy, the virtual threshold of an artwork stretches into the distance, moving towards the computational event horizon, whereupon its objecthood distorts or approaches a kind of quantum superposition; being both here *and* not here; then *and* now. Both Quayola's *Laocoön* series and Kraft's *Content Aware Studies* explore this expanded (spaghettified) form of objecthood, showcasing only a few of the almost infinite number of "complete" sculptural options for the missing figural elements—archeological findings from a manifold of (digital) future-pasts. Today, these works suggest, what once appeared finished or unavailable—whether through the passage of time, or even death—has been rendered provisional: specifically, subject to further (re)computation. While *Panorama Cat* has eight legs, the new Laocoön has unlimited possible arms in time.

Yet, while such works express a Technocene temporality that scrambles past and present, they—counterintuitively—appear to propose a number of "rules" or algorithms implicit in the source artwork's composition. At first, these found "rules" seem to indicate that something about the original guides or directs the production of a new version. This is, however, only a partial perspective, and one that conceals the extent to which machine vision casts a veil over the item in question, so that supplementary projections can play out on its surface. *Iconographies* (2016), another suite of works by Quayola, makes this clear. The series comprises various large-format digital photographic prints featuring mosaic-like forms in rich colors—ostensibly, the result of an AI mapping or tracing latent geometric figures *within* the compositions of Renaissance master paintings. Did the historical authors of such works imagine things this way? Even if they did, they left behind no vector diagrams like the ones that make up *Iconographies.* And, if earlier critics might have identified the principle of a serpentine line within a colorful scene, the machine sees much more—a network of triangles implicit in Peter Paul Rubens's *The Tiger Hunt* (1615–16), for instance. Thus, what the bots behind *Iconographies* see undercuts both the historical artist *and* the historical reception of their work. They picture something else. Here, human viewers are not looking at a painting by other means: they are looking into an abyss.

According to Virgil, Laocoön was a priest who was killed for nearly exposing the warriors hidden inside the legendary Trojan Horse. His ill-advised investigation—tapping the sculpture's body with his spear—called forth the wrath of the gods, who sent a serpent to dispose of him and (for good measure) his sons. It is interesting to

Poetics of Encryption

consider Laocoön's fate in light of his trespass: daring to entertain the possibility that, behind a seemingly inanimate figure, hidden, intelligent machinations are at work. Artists like Quayola and Kraft place the algorithm in the position of Laocoön, testing the sculptures in question with a view to unlocking their secrets and possibilities. Unlike the priest, the computer can never know too much, as its way of knowing—what Kraft calls "knowledge production," or what we have termed its *imagination*—is a dynamic force that cannot be captured in a single image. It must consume ever more, and while doing so, create ever more images.

As should be clear, digitizing a historical art object allows for its reanimation. All the things that an ancient sculpture could be— the possible limbs that it might have; the way it might sustain the projection of a geometric plane in a certain direction, beginning here and ending there—are (historically) *unsaid.* Does saying (demonstrating) them reanimate the original, so that *more* of it is revealed, in some way? In such cases, has a bot discovered a previously encrypted aesthetic rule? In fact, the opposite is the case. What is on view, or *crystallized* in marble, is the algorithm as an actor that may keep expressing itself indefinitely. It creates sculpture after sculpture; one painting after another (temporally speaking). In considering the above, there is a striking gulf that separates Laocoön's work of interpretation (and its stakes) from that of a computer, operating on found sculptures. The algorithm cannot be punished, in any meaningful sense, for its action. Perhaps it is only when the critic *can* be put to death that their enterprise becomes meaningful. Death carries the clearest sense of "finality," after all. In viewing generative art there is no last word. Perhaps a key marker of the Technocene is that, in this period, we must increasingly speak of the *undeath of the author* or critic. Indeed, if Barthes' death of the author concept outlined how a text's ultimate meaning lies not with the author, but readers, then generative art may even suggest the "death of the reader"— with respect to the relevance of human interpretations whatsoever.

In today's culture wars, a proliferation of bots crowds the scene, creating content and "fixing" things. Having disturbed the priests of high culture, they continue working, crawling over and through the ruined fragments of a civilization that seems at once near to us and yet so very far away. While highlighting the vitality of the generative mechanism, Quayola and Kraft point towards our own passing— labor-erasure by computers, or inscription within technical systems that extract and reconfigure the interior of culture without any emotion or concern for meaning. Their work engages with high-water marks in humanism, antiquity, and expression, only to subject them to radical formal alteration. The bass notes in this iconographic chord are prelapsarian, one suspects, in order to set up the ultimate incommensurability of the higher ones. So what is emerging or gestating behind the mask? A leopard's reordering of the temple that is (human) cultural space, on its own terms; a vision or mode of influence that will continue to develop over time, regardless of whether or not we make good sense of its progress.

Theophanies of AI

What happens to the content of the archive, and wider cultural space, when tethers are further loosened? For *Babylonian Vision* (2020), Nora Al-Badri set a GAN to work on images of ancient objects. Its training data comprised ten thousand photographs of archeological items, gathered from five of the world's largest museum collections of Mesopotamian, Neo-Sumerian, and Assyrian art. Her bot then *imagined* two hundred new objects: archeological deepfakes.[73] The items,

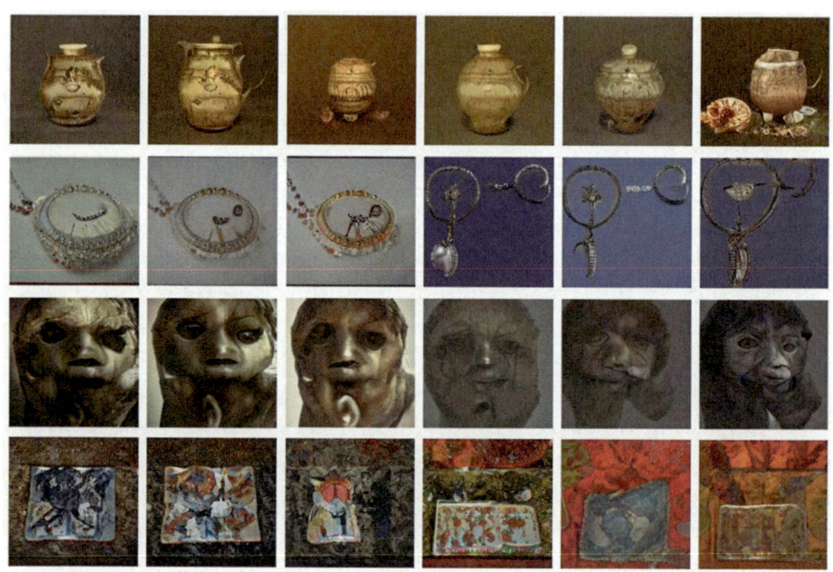

Nora Al-Badri, *Babylonian Vision*, 2020
GAN video

                                        Poetics of Encryption

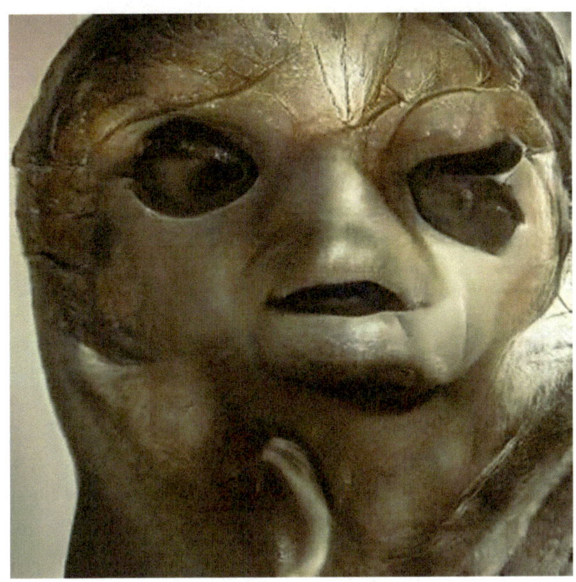

Nora Al-Badri, *Babylonian Vision,* 2020
GAN video

displayed in a video slideshow, look "dream-like, with misshapen vessels, vaguely human-shaped statues, and incomplete pieces of jewelry."[74] And yet, though warped, these "neuronal ancestral sculptures"—as Al-Badri terms them—eerily track the visual feel of the source material.

While compiling the training data, Al-Badri sought permission from each museum. Only two had APIs that allowed for easy and clear use of their photographic holdings. "The other three either charged or had onerous rules to get [at the volume of data] needed."[75] One stated that she would have to request individual clearance for each photo required.[76] Undeterred, Al-Badri worked around the rights restriction, performing a *jailbreak*—collecting images through web crawling, and scraping.[77] Because training data is never discernible in a GAN's algorithm, her method benefitted from legal deniability—of the same kind exploited by corporate machine-learning projects.[78] As Al-Badri relates, "the largest collections in the world ... cannot prove that I used their datasets to train the system. In many instances, the black box aspect of AI can be a problem but in some cases, it can also be liberating."[79]

Al-Badri frames her project in terms of decolonization, stating that the array of new images expresses "technoheritage" as "a way of practicing resistance: taking back and re-possessing cultural data and its built-in narratives."[80] In an open letter to museums—published for my *Open Secret* project at KW Institute for Contemporary Art—she rails against the museum sector's proprietary attitude towards digitization, which, she claims, "has engendered a notion that certain museums may become *Datenkraken,* hoarding datasets relating to holdings (whose physical monopoly they already possess). The practice leads to moments ... where I am [legally] compelled to mention the British Museum [*sic*] when I digitally publish or re-mix an artefact from Iraq."[81] Rejecting claims to universality put forward by Western museums, which she understands as colonial hubris, Al-Badri proposes the post-national fecundity of her technoheritage concept: "For me, technoheritage looks towards another scenario of the future. Rather than preserving information, it can contribute with new material."[82] She continues: "Data can be stateless.... Citizens of the world cannot yet overcome national citizenship; I wonder whether data can be our avant-garde in that struggle.... The virality and the afterlife of (cultural) data has real beauty and power.... Let the data dance!"[83]

Rhetoric aside, the analogue being of ancient sculptures is, of course, resolutely unique. In apparent reverence for this originality, Western museums pursue an active *care-for* method that parallels mummification. If such museums once liberated the funerary object from its grave, they did so only to re-entomb it within a display case and conservation system. Yet, as Al-Badri asserts, the release of these objects' digital doubles (their scans, or photo documentation) into the world effectively frees and reanimates them, so that they may continue to "dance" through intercourse with AI. While reclaiming the past (from museum storerooms or password-protected digital archives), her new objects supposedly enable a radical cultural proposition: "The abstraction of the [GAN's] output allows us to contemplate the images and their language," she states, "as a form of visual memory not limited to the input objects—a memory that transcends them, and which is able to generate new memory objects."[84] There is potential, thus, for "an *archive of infinite abundance.* Through GANs, one generates new materialities, which rise to the surface as *the affective qualities of the original in a post-original form.*"[85]

This vision of infinite abundance contrasts with concerns about a relentless churn of alternative facts. And yet, in Al-Badri's own words, a "post-truth" concept may have some decolonial affordances—specifically, a vision of inheriting memory (heritage) from technology. In fact, the link between truth and memory is as old as written records. As discussed in chapter one of this book, the mythic river of forgetfulness has a name—Lethe. And the negation of this name comprises the word "truth" in the culture from which the concept springs: *alētheia* (not to forget; *to remember*). Bearing this in mind, one is able to dig deeper into Al-Badri's technoheritage concept, understanding it as a hybrid between lived human memory, the material memory of archeology/ sculpture, and the silicon memory of computer chips. It is a memory chimera—a Mesopotamian sphinx for today. By extension, each of her ancestral neuronal sculptures stands for a captured instant of *imagination* (a process or movement); for the dynamic interplay between these three memory components, rendered as a procession of unbelievable bodies—part vase, part idol, part clay tablet, and more, without end.

A post-truth memory culture is, according to Al-Badri, "a mood without a frame, recalling the infinite"[86]—something that, she suggests, engages a principle of Mesopotamian aesthetics. She quotes Iraqi Assyriologist Zainab Bahrani's remarks on this sensibility while proposing that such words could also plausibly apply to the GAN:

> The images I present are often infinite in their compositional form and conception. They resist the frame and are often depicted as segments taken out of the potentiality of an endless composition that can be repeated in an endless series of mirrorings, pulling the image into a vertiginous *mise en abîme*.... For Mesopotamia, the place from which we have the earliest textual and archaeological evidence about concepts of the image and aesthetics, I make the case that images had a diachronic presence; they were seen as objects that transcend time and that carry or embody traces of time itself.[87]

The suggested correspondence is highly provocative, as it pushes our own survey further towards the conclusion that a new esoteric religious sensibility, built around mysterious traffic between human and black box machine, is emerging today. And it further helps us define the temporal import of the term "Technocene" itself: as a moment in history wherein the chimerical conjunction of human and non-human memory systems begets cultural oscillation between amnesia and total recall, and an *imagination* that swings between *in-sight* and *ex-it* from all that is familiar.

As we have just seen, to symbolize the encrypted resolution of such tensions, artists pursue an indirect approach—highlighting the partiality of material perspective, and the momentary character of the crystallization, while offering a parade of chimeras. These monsters monumentalize the unsolved riddle that is *black box culture,* and its visual formulation—through paradoxical images that serve the same apotropaic function as the sphinx in the ancient world: warding off harm or evil influences by making them, *per* Sloterdijk, part of the ceremony. One may observe that this strategy appears congruent with a particular branch of medieval metaphysics, focusing on mankind's indirect relation to God or ultimate reality—namely, fifteenth-century theologian Nicholas of Cusa's 1440 doctrine "On Learned Ignorance," which was heir to the "way of denial" inaugurated by Pseudo-Dionysius the Areopagite and his ninth-century acolyte John Scotus Eriugena. Both were forms of negative theology. Negative, because the intellectual project proceeded from the idea that God—as ultimate reality—escapes human knowledge. As Cusa had it, we can only "know that we do not know God."[88] God, as infinite—or "maximum"—cannot be "measured" by human conceptions, or completely contained by a description or predicate.

It would take a few centuries before Ludwig Wittgenstein would offer the analytic prescription appropriate to this condition: "whereof one cannot speak thereof one must be silent."[89] The medieval mind was more speculative—literally, at times, obsessed with squaring the circle. The theologian Clyde Lee Miller, in his Stanford Encyclopedia of Philosophy entry on Cusa, offers a wry characterization of this propensity: "As so often in Christian thinking, this sort of apophatic preamble does not prevent Cusanus from spending a whole book proposing how we might comprehend the incomprehensible God 'incomprehensibly.'"[90] Indeed, through a series of "geometrical" exercises which are supposed to condition the reader to hold antithetical or opposing concepts in mind, Cusa stakes a path towards thinking the unlimited deity. One such figure in this (ultimately mystical) intellectual system is the proposition that *God is a sphere whose center is everywhere and whose circumference is nowhere.*[91] On reflection, the sphinxes of contemporary art—and especially the notion of neuronal ancestral sculptures—are not so far away from such exercises.

Following the "apophatic" conception of nature as ultimately unknowable, Cusa emphasized that "each being, in its emergence and its essence, was a singular and contingent manifestation of divine plenitude, a unique theophany."[92] With the artworks discussed in this

Poetics of Encryption

chapter, I have proposed something similar: that they are icons standing for a certain theophany. Not of God *per se,* but for the principle of the imagination of the network in operation, even if the operations of that network are, at the deepest level, inaccessible and unknowable.

Dark Times

The politics of access and exclusion from engineered systems is becoming ever more fraught. Under the circumstances, recent art speaks to secured domains—even without access to proprietary algorithms or secret data troves. Addressing the buried, hidden, or inaccessible dimensions of tech—activating concepts that have to do with an occult *interior*—is a precondition for discussing the human condition in the Technocene, wherein subject formation plays out in relation to encrypted sites. A statement by Martin Heidegger is germane to this choreography: "Being-alone is [merely] a deficient mode of Being-with."[1] Exclusion from encrypted space can nevertheless function in the same way that a plaster mold does, delivering a negative impression of the inaccessible facet. While by definition pointing to the lost positive, this impression may yet be high-fidelity and full of meaning. Living with a "known unknown" is still being-with, after all.

A *poetics of encryption* strives to make the inaccessible virtually present, while running on an old system.[2] Although "analogue" media are of a different order to the digital, possibly suggesting their unsuitability for the critical task at hand, art has long addressed the unknown, and things that belong to other worlds. A tradition of apophatic theology (and irony) stands as a powerful training schema for postures taken in relation to a landscape of black boxes. No matter how secure the encrypted space, an approach may be ventured along the *via negativa:* by speaking about the impossible challenge of calling *it* by its true name; picturing travesty instead of perfection; and, most importantly, supplying an abundance of images for embodied relations to the obscure interior.

The *via negativa* characterizes much contemporary art. Its uptake indicates faith on the part of artists, holding on to a human picture, irreducible to some data set, within surveillance capitalism's dispiriting landscape.[3] It is an *analogue culture of the digital,* diametrically opposed to *digital analogues of culture* (such as novels written by AI). This art thinks in *ana-logic*—the only free translation system for those who do not write code. It speaks through analogy—the people's tongue. As such, it expresses an ideology of freely distributed intellectual and linguistic competence, in a world otherwise marked by viciously unequal access to information. Nevertheless, it is an open question whether this ideology, and its iconographic manifestation (in certain works of art), serves as an effective counterbalance to the profusion of black boxes in everyday life.

What is clear, however, is that this approach exhibits a tendency to reimagine (and up) the stakes of the graphical user interface (GUI).

Commonly experienced as visual icons on computer and phone screens that purport to be part of a "desktop," including file folders and a trash bin (items seemingly *of* this world), a GUI is a sur-face whereupon analogues of the digital *sous*-face are drawn. It is the liminal zone where reality, fantasy, and power come together. Bearing this in mind, much new art registers a growing understanding that the mediating mask(s) of tech do not end with the screen's edge; they are prevalent everywhere else too, occupying an expanded field without limit, and have become the ideological AstroTurf upon which any politics must walk. Against extant simulations of ground, the *poetics of encryption* proposes a substitution: a patchwork of mediating figures (artworks) that stand as an alternative, complex, open-source GUI for the world at large.

From the ancient myth of Orpheus and Eurydice, through to the gods of Egypt and Mesopotamia, via Albrecht Dürer's esoterism, and an emerging aesthetics of recombination, anachronism is never far from attempts to describe encryption through iconic or narrative frames. By employing the prism of an embodied imaginary, such attempts release spirits older than computation: an ecstasy of images, gushing forth from the hidden place that is cultural memory, other-wise repressed by the ahistoricity of binary code. By reflecting on them, it is clear how Technocene subjects rediscover esoterism, and a mythic tone traversing life and death. Marshaling heady visions of interiority, the *poetics of encryption* toggles between enlightened concern and occult dreaming.

Notes

* Paolo Lucentini, ed., *Liber viginti quattuor philosophorum* (Milan, 1999).

Dark Arts [pp. 6–10]

1 Gaston Bachelard, *Earth and Reveries of Repose: An Essay on Images of Interiority,* trans. Mary McAllester Jones (Dallas, 2011), p. 2.

2 Gaston Bachelard, *Air and Dreams: An Essay on the Imagination of Movement,* trans. Edith R. Farrell and C. Frederick Farrell (Dallas, 1988), p. 1.

3 Ibid., p. 2.

4 This entry point concerns "how ciphers are designed to obscure information to some and not to others, how decisions are made about who can be privy to the secrets they obscure, and who can gain access to the technologies of encryption in the first place." Sarah Myers West, "Cryptographic Imaginaries and the Networked Public," *Internet Policy Review: Journal on Internet Regulation* 7, no. 2 (May 2018), https://policyreview.info/articles/analysis/cryptographic-imaginaries-and-networked-public (accessed January 9, 2023).

5 Ibid.

6 Ibid.

Black Site [pp. 12–51]

1 William Shakespeare, *The Works of Shakespeare: The Tragedy of Hamlet* (London, 1899), p. 107.

2 See Benjamin Bratton, *The Stack: On Software and Sovereignty* (Cambridge, MA, 2016).

3 See Ashlee Vance, "The Future of Space Is Bigger Than Jeff Bezos, Richard Branson, or Elon Musk," Bloomberg (website), July 16, 2021, https://www.bloomberg.com/news/articles/2021-07-16/billionaire-space-race-between-bezos-branson-and-musk-is-just-the-beginning (accessed November 6, 2022).

4 Anchorage was a distinctly gendered phenomenon, a fact worth bearing in mind as we consider other prosthetic enclosures. Anchoresses outnumbered anchorites from the twelfth to sixteenth centuries: there were around three times as many women as men in the thirteenth century. See Ann K. Warren, *Anchorites and their Patrons in Medieval England* (Berkeley, 1985), p. 20. The average anchorite's cell was approximately twelve feet square; see Mary Wellesley, "The Life of the Anchoresse," The British Library (website), March 13, 2018, https://www.bl.uk/medieval-literature/articles/the-life-of-the-anchoress#footnote1 (accessed November 6, 2022).

5 Ibid.

6 There is no hard historical connection between the two. However, their respective architectural scenarios—both enclosed in tiny spaces—share a suggestive parallel through the importance of the aperture. Moreover, there is a clear similarity between the Greek *anachoreo* (to withdraw), the basis for anchorite, and the Japanese term, which means "pulling inward, being confined." See Edd Gent, "The Plight of Japan's Modern Hermits," BBC News (website), January 29, 2019, https://www.bbc.com/future/article/20190129-the-plight-of-japans-modern-hermits (accessed July 1, 2022).

7 The name *hikikomori* is used interchangeably for both the social phenomenon and the individual recluse.

8 Franz Kafka, quoted in Gaston Bachelard, *Earth and Reveries of Repose: An Essay on Images of Interiority,* trans. Mary McAllester Jones (Dallas, 2011), p. 11.

9 Bachelard 2011 (see note 8).

10 An argument for the necessity of hierarchical struggle among humans, through appeal to the neurochemistry of lobsters, is infamously advanced in the hit self-help book by Jordan B. Peterson, *12 Rules for Life: An Antidote to Chaos* (New York, 2018), p. 28.

11 See David Lethbridge, "Sartre's Crabs," *Sartre Studies International* 21, no. 1 (2015): 75–89.

12 An important work, yet its reception was somewhat overshadowed by Rafman's more popular series of screenshots from Google Street View, developed as large C-print photographs titled *Nine Eyes of Google Street View,* as well as published on blogs, as PDFs, and in books.

13 "Continuing the early Greek conception of Orpheus as the revealer of mysteries, the possessor of keys to the underworld, artists who seek to learn the inner truths of things and to penetrate the secrets of nature and the cosmos, the mysteries of life, often

142

look to Orpheus as a guide." See Judith E. Bernstock, *Under the Spell of Orpheus: The Persistence of a Myth in Twentieth-Century Art* (Carbondale, 1991), p. xxiv.

14 See Virgil, *Aeneid,* trans. Frederick Ahl and Elaine Fantham, vol. 6, no. 2, notes 703–51 (Oxford, 2007), for the image of Lethe in mythic action. Additionally, a useful intellectual summary of the figure appears in Ahl's note 705: "*river Lethe:* Virgil's version of Plato's 'River of Indifference' yields a pun on Latin *letum,* 'death.' In Greek *lēthē* means 'forgetfulness.' In the Myth of Er [which features in Plato's *Republic*], souls about to enter bodies drink of the River of Indifference, whose waters induce forgetfulness (*lēthē*). Er does not drink, so he is not subject to *lēthē.* In Greek, the prefix 'a-' forms a negative, as it can in English: *a*moral, *a*sexual. *Alēthēs,* the adjective translated into English as 'true,' was taken by Plato to mean 'non-forgetful,' and its noun, alētheia ('truth'), to mean 'non-forgetfulness,'" p. 373.

15 The term "world picture" appears in Hito Steyerl's key work *How Not to Be Seen: A Fucking Didactic Educational .MOV File* (2013). In this work, one of the proposed strategies for chosen disappearance is to evade the camera's resolution. While Steyerl clearly references satellite photographic surveillance, the term itself first emerges in a lecture by Martin Heidegger. See Martin Heidegger, "The Age of the World Picture," in *Off the Beaten Track,* trans. Julian Young and Kenneth Haynes (Cambridge, 2002), pp. 57–72.

16 "In 1946, an alliance was formed between five Anglophone countries and their security agencies: the US (NSA), the UK (GCHQ), Australia (ASD), Canada (CSEC) and New Zealand (GCSB) comprising of a series of bilateral agreements on surveillance and intelligence-sharing. Though these arrangements are commonly referred to as the United Kingdom–United States Communication Intelligence Act (UKUSA) agreement, the documents underpinning the Five Eyes alliance are numerous, intricate, and secret. Pursuant to these arrangements, each of the Five Eyes states conducts interception, collection, acquisition, analysis and decryption activities, sharing all intelligence information obtained with the others by default....

Intelligence-sharing agreements have now expanded beyond the Five Eyes to include other states: 9 Eyes: the Five Eyes, with the addition of Denmark, France, the Netherlands and Norway; 14 Eyes: the 9 Eyes, with the addition of Germany, Belgium, Italy, Spain and Sweden; 41 Eyes: all of the above, with the addition of the allied coalition in Afghanistan." See "Five Eyes," Privacy International (website), https://privacyinternational.org/learn/five-eyes (accessed November 10, 2022).

17 Such projects follow the iconoclastic tradition of Hans Haacke, whose attention to the economic framework of one particular museum would martyr the muses, skewering their moral domicile in a tracing of financial flows. See Hans Haacke's exhibition *Shapolsky et al. Manhattan Real Estate Holdings, A Real-Time Social System, as of May 1, 1971,* Solomon R. Guggenheim Museum, New York, 1971.

18 In the video, Wakeling visits the points where the eponymous cable surfaces, at Fire Island, New York; the southwest tip of England; the coast of the Netherlands; and a German island off the Danish border. The video is a narrative log of people and places encountered in the course of research, interspersed with facts about transatlantic communications. Attention oscillates between the inhuman scale of global communications and the trivial details of Wakeling's passage as an individual trying to comprehend it, approximating the underground, off-limits flow of information on foot and by train.

19 So many *puncta,* in the sense given by Roland Barthes to the *punctum*—conveying a meaning to the viewer without invoking the symbolic system offered by Google's interface.

20 See André Spicer, "Amazon's 'worker cage' has been dropped, but its staff are not free," *The Guardian,* September 14, 2018, https://www.theguardian.com/commentisfree/2018/sep/14/amazon-worker-cage-staff (accessed November 10, 2022).

21 Simon Denny represented New Zealand at the 56th Venice Biennale in 2015.

22 As observed by the critic Brian Droitcour in the e-book, Brian Droitcour, ed., *Field Visits for Chelsea Manning* (March 17, 2016).

23 Ibid.

24 Ibid.

25 In New York, England, the Netherlands, and Germany.

26 See "Landscape series," on the artist's website: http://www.evanroth.com/~/works/landscapes/#hemisphere=east&strand=113 (accessed November 10, 2022).

27 Arrayed on a gallery wall, Roth's red landscapes flicker across a mass of variously sized screens, suggestive of a mutant command and control center—with Ethernet cables spilling onto the floor, out of the room, and into the walls. As such, the viewer is presented with a series of windows onto the world, all opened at once like so many browser tabs. Leaning on the trope of the panopticon, this dramaturgy directs any question of morality towards the viewer. For these are not just windows. In light of Roth's sketch of just how they operate, in laser beam, it would appear that the Internet screen does not just get looked at: it touches the things that it mediates; it handles scenes and landscapes.

28 Pressing our allegory once more: According to the classic myth, Orpheus, disregarding the demand that he not look back over his shoulder, cannot help but turn towards Eurydice. Rather than accepting her presence, as they ascend in the direction of an exit from the house of Hades, he feels compelled to look. That look might as well symbolize the original sin of visual mediation or technical sensing: the anthropo-*seen* landscape is Eurydice condemned—the environmental scene according to technologically augmented Anthropos. It is the vision that steals and kills.

29 Jussi Parikka, *A Geology of Media* (Minneapolis, 2015).

30 See Nadim Samman and Boris Ondreička, eds., *Rare Earth* (Berlin, 2015).

31 See the artists' website: https://www.cohenvanbalen.com/work/h-alcutaau (accessed November 10, 2022).

32 Ibid.

33 Another work, *Inlands* (2016), is an abstract pictorial rendition of open mines in the Democratic Republic of Congo, rendered in elements excavated from that soil—produced by electroplating gold, copper, tin, and nickel onto bronze sheets.

34 See the artist's website: https://marymattingly.com/html/MATTINGLYElements.html (accessed November 10, 2022).

35 Jussi Parikka, *The Anthrobscene* (Minneapolis, 2014).

36 See Anthrodendum/S.Minds, @savageminds, Twitter, https://twitter.com/savageminds/status/542226785107054593 (accessed January 12, 2015).

37 So-called financial market "bubbles," and in old-fashioned magna opera of philosophy, such as Peter Sloterdijk's *Bubbles: Spheres I: Microspherology,* trans. Wieland Hoban (Los Angeles, 2011). In this initial volume of his 2,500-page work, Sloterdijk, a self-described "student of the air," reimagines the history of Western metaphysics as beginning with the discovery of self (bubble) before moving on to the exploration of world (globe) and the poetics of plurality (foam).

38 A portion of the economy that exchanges intangible services and products, including software, databases, and intellectual property. There are at least two key features of the weightless economy. First, products have a high initial cost to develop, but a very low cost to reproduce and distribute. Second, products can be distributed infinitely. These two factors mean that the weightless economy can be among the fastest growing and most profitable sectors of business. See Jason Fernando, "Weightless Economy," *Investopedia,* September 30, 2022, http://www.investopedia.com/terms/w/weightless-economy.asp (accessed November 10, 2022).

39 As accounts such as Bratton's demonstrate, power truly moves through the latter.

40 Which is at the heart of a many-layered machine.

41 One wherein the avant-garde figure of the "artist-engineer" first proposed by Aleksandr Rodchenko might, following its Stalinist travesty, be rehabilitated.

42 Geopolitical theories by two figures from opposing ends of the ideological spectrum dovetail in implying that Fuller's book was less a manual than a prolegomena.

43 Parag Khanna, *Connectography: Mapping the Future of Global Civilization* (New

York, 2016), pp. xvi–xvii. He continues: "The true map of the world should feature not just states but megacities, highways, pipelines, Internet cables, and other symbols of our emerging global network civilization."

44 Our own subjective enrollment in this is less as citizens of a *polis* or as *homo economicus* within a market, but rather as users of a platform. As I see it, the work of geopolitical theory is to develop a proper history, typology, and program for such platforms. See Benjamin H. Bratton, "The Black Stack," *e-flux* 53 (March 2014), https://www.e-flux.com/journal/53/59883/the-black-stack/ (accessed November 10, 2022).

 45 Khanna 2016 (see note 43), p. 15.
 46 Bratton 2016 (see note 2), p. xviii.
 47 Ibid., pp. 4, xviii.
 48 Ibid., pp. 3–4.
 49 Ibid., p. 4.
 50 Bratton 2014 (see note 44).

51 From attention to the geology of media in the art of Revital Cohen and Tuur Van Balen, to the mapping of transatlantic cables in the productions of Trevor Paglen and Lance Wakeling; from the labor conditions at Google scanning facilities, in a project by Andrew Norman Wilson, to Simon Denny's physicalization of the PowerPoint ideology of the PRISM surveillance enterprise.

52 See "Project: *The Atmosphere, A Guide* (2013/16)," on the artist's website: http://tomorrowmorning.net/atmosphere (accessed November 11, 2022).

 53 Ibid.
 54 Ibid.
 55 Ibid.

56 See Samman and Ondreička 2015 (see note 30).

57 "A new form of extractivism defines life in the twenty-first century. It is one that reaches into the furthest corners of the biosphere and the deepest layers of human cognitive and affective being: The stack that underpins contemporary technological systems goes well beyond the multi-layered 'technical stack' of data modeling, hardware, servers, and networks. Today's full stack reaches into capital, labor, and nature, while demanding an enormous amount from each." See Vladan Joler, *New Extractivism,* video, 17:33 min., 2020, https://extractivism.

online/ (accessed November 10, 2022).

58 The Yerevan Biennale was curated by Eva and Franco Mattes. The video version was commissioned by the author for an online exhibition titled *Open Secret,* hosted by KW Institute for Contemporary Art, Berlin, in 2021.

59 Vladan Joler, "New Extractivism," 2020, https://extractivism.online/ (accessed November 10, 2022).

 60 Ibid.
 61 Ibid.
 62 Ibid.

63 "This self-centered personal space is filled with images and meanings selected by algorithms partly with respect to its affective and cognitive reactions. The user is in a specific closed circle, communicating with oneself in a particular form of self-stimulation and exposed to a constant flow of spectacle. Therefore, this cave or prison cell is a place of pleasure from which, as in Plato's cave, the prisoner does not even have the will to come out. In this assemblage of allegories, millions of caves or prison cells form the unique and invisible panopticon structure." Part of Joler's footnote to the section addressing the "Platopticon." It should be noted that the title brings the concept of Plato's cave together with the figure of the Panopticon, first proposed by the Enlightenment philosopher Jeremy Bentham: a prison wherein inmates might be under supervision at any given moment (though without their being able to verify this)—a condition that was supposed, in theory, to inculcate better behavior. See Joler 2020 (see note 59).

 64 Ibid.
 65 Ibid.
 66 Ibid.

67 "If we consider the labyrinth in connection with the cave, coiled around it and ending finally with it, then in the complex thus formed the cave is at the innermost central point, which corresponds perfectly with the idea of the spiritual centre, and which agrees equally well with the equivalent symbolism of the heart.... When the same cave is the place of both initiatic death and of 'second birth,' it must be considered as giving access not only to subterranean or 'infernal regions,' but also to supra-terrestrial domains. This again corresponds to the notion of the central point, which is, both macrocosmically as well as microcosmically, the point of communication with all the high and lower states." René Guénon, *Fundamental Symbols: The Universal Language of Sacred Science,* trans. Alvin Moore Jr. (Cambridge, 1995), p. 144.

68 Joler 2020 (see note 59).

69 Critical Art Ensemble, *Flesh Machine: Cyborgs, Designer Babies, and New Eugenic Consciousness* (New York, 1998), p. 146.

70 Joler 2020 (see note 59).

71 Bratton 2014 (see note 44).

72 Ibid.

73 He quotes Federico Campagna: "The crumbling of subjectivity under Technic is accompanied by the emergence of a new existential figure: the abstract general entity (AGE)." Federico Campagna, *Technic and Magic: The Reconstruction of Reality* (London, 2018), quoted in Joler 2020 (see note 59).

74 Beyond a purely material frame, it can be observed that "jurisdictional" accommodates the soft specificities of site identified by Miwon Kwon, i.e. "cultural debates, a theoretical concept ... a historical condition, even particular formations of desire." See Miwon Kwon, "One Place after Another: Notes on Site Specificity," *October* 80 (Spring 1997), p. 93. Indeed, today's authorial vector may incorporate acts of renovation, rescoring, renegotiation, and even re-desiring, in its (sovereign) operations. For more, see Nadim Samman, "Errant Curating," *On Curating* 50 (June 2021), pp. 100–110.

75 Samman 2021 (see note 74). Alternatively, see Dehlia Hannah, ed., *A Year Without a Winter* (New York, 2018).

76 See note 14.

77 That is, provided adequate preparations have been made in life.

78 See Joscelyn Godwin, *Arktos: The Polar Myth in Science, Symbolism, and Nazi Survival* (Grand Rapids, MI, 1993), p. 165.

79 According to his contemporary, Poliziano, Ficino's "lyre,... far more successful than the lyre of Thracian Orpheus, has brought back from the underworld what is, if I am not mistaken, the true Eurydice, that is Platonic wisdom with its broad judgment." Cited in John Warden, "Orpheus and Ficino," in *Orpheus:*

The Metamorphoses of a Myth (Toronto, 1982), p. 86. It can also be noted that Ficino translated ancient Orphic hymns from Greek into Latin in 1462, and based his Neoplatonic theology and musical cosmology on the persona of Orpheus. See Judith E. Bernstock, *Under the Spell of Orpheus: The Persistence of a Myth in Twentieth-Century Art* (Carbondale, 1991), p. xii.

80 Godwin 1993 (see note 78), p. 165.

81 Wilfred Mellers, *The Masks of Orpheus: Seven Stages in the Story of European Music* (Manchester, 1987), p. 4.

82 Ibid.

83 See "blue pill," *Cambridge Dictionary,* https://dictionary.cambridge.org/dictionary/english/blue-pill (accessed April 19, 2020). Also see Eli Pariser, *The Filter Bubble: What the Internet is Hiding from You* (New York, 2011).

84 I note that the word "grotesque" means "of the grotto," its colloquial sense of ugliness issuing from this subterranean reference.

85 Plato, *The Republic* (Oxford, 1973), 514a–520a; emphasis mine.

86 See "troll," *Britannica,* https://www.britannica.com/topic/troll (accessed April 7, 2020).

87 See Justin Cheng et al., "Anyone Can Become a Troll: Causes of Trolling Behavior in Online Discussions," CSCW '17: Proceedings of the 2017 ACM Conference on Computer-Supported Cooperative Work and Social Computing (New York, 2017), pp. 1217–30.

88 Sylvia Jaki et al., "Online hatred of women in the Incels.me forum: Linguistic analysis and automatic detection," *Journal of Language Aggression and Conflict* 7, no. 2 (November 2019): 240–68.

89 Stevie Smith, "Not Waving but Drowning" (1957), https://poets.org/poem/not-waving-drowning (accessed April 9, 2020).

90 See "Gaming Bed," https://www.bauhutte.jp/product/gaming-bed (accessed April 10, 2020).

91 The exhibition referenced is *Orogenesis,* curated by Nadim Samman and Michele Iodicci, July 17–September 23, 2019. See Juliana Cerqueira Leite, *Orogenesis* (London, 2019).

92 See "National Aeronautics and Space Administration," NASA (website), last

146

modified August 27, 2020, https://msis.jsc.
nasa.gov (accessed April 19, 2020).

93 Byung Chul-Han, *In the Swarm: Digital
Prospects* (Cambridge, MA, 2017) p. 32.

94 It is a vision in stark contrast to
the interpretation of Paleolithic hand prints:
"The undulating surface of the caves was
not a canvas but a thin membrane between
the artist and the spiritual underworld.
The hand prints in this way are not symbols
but the remains of a ritual in which sprayed
pigment, and not paint as we think of it,
sealed the hand into the wall—the hand
becoming invisible against the rock surface,
penetrating into the underworld." See
Charles Stankievech, *Archaeopsychic
Archipelago: A Speculative Map for the
Drowned World,* exh. cat. Toronto Biennial
of Art (Toronto, 2020); cf. Lucy Steeds,
"Georges Bataille: Unhinging Prehistory,
Unbecoming Humanity," in Mihnea
Mircan and Vincent W. J. van Gerven Oei,
eds., *Allegory of the Cave Painting* (Milan,
2015).

95 I quote from Byung Chul-Han's
counter-argument to Flusser, put forward
in Chul-Han 2017 (see note 93), p. 32.

96 Michel Serres, *Statues: The Second Book
of Foundations,* trans. Randolph Burks
(London, 2015), p. 4.

97 Ibid.

98 To Chul-Han's undeath.

99 For the link between "incel" culture
and neo-fascist violence, see Mark
Townsend, "Experts Fear Rising Global
'Incel' Culture Could Provoke Terrorism,"
The Guardian, October 30, 2022, https://
www.theguardian.com/society/2022/oct/
30/global-incel-culture-terrorism-
misogyny-violent-action-forums
(accessed November 12, 2022).

100 I am indebted to Charles Stankievech
for pointing out the link between Serres's
Challenger and the car involved in the hate
crime. See "Charlottesville car attack,"
Wikipedia, last modified November 3, 2022,
https://en.wikipedia.org/wiki/Charlottes-
ville_car_attack#Biography (accessed
April 19, 2020).

101 Titled *The retrospective view of the
pathway, (pathways),* 1990–2016. For the quote,
see "Roger Hiorns," *Wikipedia,* last modified
April 7, 2022, https://en.wikipedia.org/wiki/
Roger_Hiorns (accessed April 19, 2020).

102 Tom McCarthy, "Adventures of the
Black Box," draft article manuscript, 2021.

103 Ibid.

104 Ibid.

105 As part of the exhibition *Eclipse: Art
in a Dark Age.* Emanating from within it, a
looped voice-recording was transmitted over
a two-kilometer radius by FM radio.

106 Tom McCarthy, "Adventures of the
Black Box," *London Review of Books* 43, no. 22
(November 18, 2021), https://www.lrb.co.uk/
the-paper/v43/n22/tom-mccarthy/adventures-
of-the-black-box (accessed February 10,
2023).

107 McCarthy, 2021 (see note 102).

Black Box [pp. 52–95]

1 See "Occult Blood," *Oxford Reference,*
https://www.oxfordreference.com/
view/10.1093/oi/authority.20110803100244463
(accessed January 9, 2023).

2 The specific sense of the Latin *occultare*
(secrete), which is frequentative of *occulere*
(conceal), is the relevant point. This
definition usefully outlines two orders of
relation to presence. The first is pheno-
menal, the second, microphenomenal.

3 Shoshanna Zuboff, *The Age of Surveillance Capitalism: The Fight for a Human
Future at the New Frontier of Power* (London,
2019), p. 8; emphasis mine.

4 With respect to paranoia, film fans will
recall that the plot of *2001: A Space Odyssey*
revolves around a supercomputer named
HAL, who attempts to wipe out all the
humans onboard a spaceship, having
classified them a threat to its mission.

5 "The cave and tower walls are constructed of multiple opaque layers and built
mostly by ghost work or invisible labor. The
bricks of this structure are made of black
boxes, closed code and hardware, glued
together with the invisible network
infrastructure. They are covered with layers of
corporate secrets, patents and copyrights."
Vladan Joler, "New Extractivism. Assemblage
of concepts and allegories," in Sara Buraya
Boned and Ida Hiršenfelder, eds., *Degrowth
and Progress* (Ljubljana et al., 2021), p. 63.

6 In fact, more detailed measurements
only disclose further indeterminacy in
subatomic domains. See Werner

Heisenberg's uncertainty principle: the celebrated statement establishing that the position and the velocity of a particle, such as a photon or electron, cannot both be measured exactly, at the same time, even in theory. Ordinary experience provides no clue to this principle, because the uncertainties implied for ordinary objects are too small to be observed. "Only for the exceedingly small masses of atoms and subatomic particles does the product of the uncertainties become significant." See "Uncertainty Principle," *Britannica,* last modified September 21, 2022, https://www.britannica.com/science/uncertainty-principle (accessed October 4, 2022).

7 These can be referred to as "hyperobjects."

8 At the time of writing, DeepMind is Google/Alphabet Inc.'s most powerful AI. MassiveText includes various sources including MassiveWeb (a compilation of web pages), C4 (Common Crawl text), Wikipedia, GitHub, books, and news articles. See "Massive Text," https://paperswithcode.com/dataset/massivetext (accessed October 27, 2022), and Alberto Romero, "DeepMind Is Now the Undisputed Leader in Language AI with Gopher," December 14, 2021, https://towardsdatascience.com/deepmind-is-now-the-undisputed-leader-in-language-ai-with-gopher-28ob-79363106011f (accessed October 27, 2022).

9 According to UNESCO, knowledge societies are about capabilities to identify, produce, process, transform, disseminate, and use information to build and apply knowledge for human development. See "Knowledge Society," UNESCO—International Bureau of Education (website), http://www.ibe.unesco.org/en/glossary-curriculum-terminology/k/knowledge-society (accessed October 27, 2022).

10 Alienation obtains when their inscrutability is identified and then accepted as the cost of doing business—not least because, when agency and social space (tangible life goods) are premised upon traffic with its mysterious functionality, questions of trust and deception loom.

11 In the manner of Vladan Joler, we may even claim that encryption is experienced in the manner of a fractal.

12 Its cursed doppelganger is, as we shall read, the data body.

13 Brian Massumi, *Parables for the Virtual: Movement, Affect, Sensation* (Durham, NC, 2002), p. 45.

14 See Andrew Butterfield et al., eds., *Oxford Dictionary of Computer Science* (Oxford, 2016), p. 52.

15 Indeed, "The test for the correctness of the pattern created is viability, not truth…. The pattern discerned is a consequence of the interaction of the observer and the Black Box, as described by the observer. The Black Box and the observer act together to constitute a (new) whole." See Ranulph Glanville, "Darkening the Black Box," *blogs.gwu.edu* (blog), June 2017, https://cpb-us-e1.wpmucdn.com/blogs.gwu.edu/dist/d/257/files/2017/06/Darkening-the-Black-Box-20ua224.pdf (accessed October 27, 2022).

16 The media list for Nicolai's *anti* reads "lightweight structure, sound module, theremin module, transducer, amplifier, light-absorbent black paint," and the work's dimensions are 255×255×300 cm. See the artist's website: http://www.carstennicolai.de/?c=works&w=anti (accessed March 25, 2020).

17 Ibid.

18 Ibid.

19 Philip L. Sohm, "Dürer's 'Melencolia I': The Limits of Knowledge," *Studies in the History of Art* 9 (1980): 13–32.

20 Raymond Klibansky et al., *Saturn and Melancholy: Studies in the History of Natural Philosophy, Religion, and Art* (Montreal and Kingston, ON, 2019), p. 345.

21 At the very least, the sequence of subjectivities exists at the moment of interface—even if they dissolve into shadow later.

22 The fetish of secrecy. Marx's comments on the commodity make perfect sense here: a commodity "is a vexed and complicated thing, abounding in metaphysical subtleties and theological niceties." Karl Marx, *Capital: A Critique of Political Economy,* vol. 1, ed. Friedrich Engels, trans. Samuel Moore and Edward Aveling (New York, 1936 [1867]), p. 81.

23 See Paul Fiegelfeld and John Durham Peters, "Not Apollo but Vulcan is the God of Cyberspace," in Nadim Samman and Boris Ondreička, eds., *Rare Earth* (Berlin, 2015), pp. 92–99.

24 I Corinthians 13:12. The relation between Saint Paul's dark mirror and Plato's cave is noted in René Guénon, *Fundamental Symbols: The Universal Language of Sacred Science,* trans. Alvin Moore Jr. (Cambridge, 1995), p. 155.

25 See "Robot," on the artist's website: https://www.susannahertrich.com/work/robot/ (accessed October 27, 2022).

26 Ibid.

27 Bruno Latour, *Pandora's Hope: Essays on the Reality of Science Studies* (Cambridge, MA, and London, 1999), p. 304.

28 See Garnet Hertz, "Art After New Media: Exploring Black Boxes, Tactics, and Archaeologies," in *Leonardo Electronic Almanac* 17, no. 2 (January 2012): 205, https://leoalmanac.org/wp-content/uploads/2012/04/LEAVol17No2-Hertz.pdf (accessed February 10, 2023).

29 Ibid.

30 Slavoj Žižek, "Edward Snowden, Chelsea Manning and Julian Assange: our new heroes," *The Guardian,* September 3, 2013, https://www.theguardian.com/commentisfree/2013/sep/03/snowden-manning-assange-new-heroes (accessed October 27, 2022), quoted in Susan Kozel, "Performing Encryption," in Martina Leeker et al., eds., *Performing the Digital: Performance Studies and Performances in Digital Cultures* (Bielefeld, 2016), pp. 126–27.

31 Ibid.

32 Joler's source reference for this concept is Mary L. Gray and Siddharth Suri, *Ghost Work: How to Stop Silicon Valley from Building a New Global Underclass* (Boston and New York, 2019).

33 For those inclined to this sort of sensitivity, Apple also profaned through the rhetorical gesture of un-*veiling.*

34 Thus, appreciation must go to Trevor Paglen's work with boxes. Straddling the black box as a recording device (or vampire's coffin), and the cipher for *obscure agency,* his photographs of the NSA headquarters picture an information black site (to those who are being recorded by it).

35 See "Beny Wagner: Invisible Measure," Import Projects (website), http://import-projects.org/invisible-measure.html (accessed October 4, 2022).

36 Ibid.

37 Ibid.

38 See Paul Scheerbart, "Vanquishing vermin," in *Glass Architecture,* trans. James Palmes, in Dennis Sharp, ed., *Glass Architecture, by Paul Scheerbart; and Alpine Architecture, by Bruno Taut* (New York, 1972), p. 54.

39 See "Research," Transparency International (website), https://www.transparency.org/en/research (accessed October 27, 2022).

40 "Its value for poor countries in which corruption is a huge challenge is uncertain." Tina Søreide, "Is It Wrong to Rank? A Critical Assessment of Corruption Indices." CMI Working Paper WP 2006, Chr. Michelsen Institute, Bergen, 2006, p. 12. https://www.cmi.no/publications/file/2120-is-it-wrong-to-rank.pdf (accessed October 27, 2022).

41 Tilman Hornig, quoted in Yusuke Shono and Sosuke Masukawa, "Tacit Sculpture: Tilman Hornig," trans. Mina Kato, *Massage Magazine* (June 2015), https://themassage.jp/en/archives/600 (accessed October 27, 2022).

42 The transparent "skin" of both sculptures was actually made of cellulose acetate, a novel material at the time.

43 See "History," Deutsches Hygiene-Museum (website), https://www.dhmd.de/en/about-us/the-museum/history (accessed October 27, 2022). While known, initially, as the *Gläserne Frau,* the object was made of a celluloid-like material related to Cellophane and derived from acetylcellulose (but without celluloid's flammability), known as "Cellon."

44 Jeffrey T. Schnapp, "Crystalline Bodies: Fragments of a Cultural History of Glass," *West 86th: A Journal of Decorative Arts, Design History, and Material Culture* 20, no. 2 (Fall–Winter, 2013): 173–94.

45 Joler 2021 (see note 5).

46 See the exhibition text for Tilman Hornig by Johannes Thumfart, "The Diaphane: On Materiality and Immateriality of the Computer Screen," www.tilman-hornig.info, 2014, http://tilmanhornig.info/projects/589.html (accessed October 27, 2022).

47 According to Moore's Law, the capacity of microchips doubles every eighteen months.

48 Simanto Saha et al., "Progress in Brain Computer Interface: Challenges and

Opportunities," *Frontiers in Systems Neuroscience* 15 (February 25, 2021), https://www.frontiersin.org/articles/10.3389/fnsys.2021.578875/full (accessed October 27, 2022).

49 Thumfart 2014 (see note 46).

50 "The hopes for a bodiless information-economy turned out to be ideology in the Marxist sense, i.e. a 'reversal of reality.'" Ibid.

51 "Phiz (noun): A face or facial expression." See "Phiz," *Collins Dictionary,* https://www.collinsdictionary.com/dictionary/english/phiz (accessed August 28, 2020).

52 Philosopher Byung-Chul Han has written about the relationship between counting and accounts.

53 See Critical Art Ensemble, "Appendix: Utopian Promises—Net Realities*," in *Flesh Machine: Cyborgs, Designer Babies, and New Eugenic Consciousness* (New York, 1998), p. 146.

54 "By the time war erupted in 1939, I.B.M. technology—primarily punch cards and the Hollerith machines that tabulated them—was widely in use by the Germans in the military, the SS, the railways and other key institutions." See Gabriel Schoenfeld, "The Punch Card Conspiracy," *The New York Times,* March 18, 2001, https://archive.nytimes.com/www.nytimes.com/books/01/03/18/reviews/010318.18schoent.html (accessed October 27, 2022).

55 See "On Computer Vision," on the artist's website: https://ahprojects.com/on-computer-vision/ (accessed October 27, 2022); emphasis mine.

56 See "Classification.01 (2017)," https://mimionuoha.com/classification01 (accessed October 27, 2022).

57 Juan Manuel Durán and Karin Rolanda Jongsma, "Who is Afraid of Black Box Algorithms? On the Epistemological and Ethical Basis of Trust in Medical AI," *Journal of Medical Ethics* 47 (2021): 329–35.

58 Ibid.

59 Leo Kelion, "Google tackles the black box problem with Explainable AI," BBC News (website), November 24, 2019, https://www.bbc.com/news/technology-50506431 (accessed October 27, 2022).

60 Franz Fanon, *Black Skin, White Masks* (London, 1986), p. 231.

61 "Knowing that the techniques used for facial analysis are also used for pedestrian tracking, I wondered what would happen if self-driving cars couldn't detect people of colour? Furthermore, I learned that companies like HireVue use facial analysis technology to inform hiring decisions. What if the system was unfamiliar with faces like mine and prevented qualified persons from gaining employment? In fact, Amazon scrapped an internal AI hiring tool that displayed gender bias. The tool was trained on ten years of hiring data and categorically gave a low rank to any application that included the term 'women' or listed certain women-only colleges." See "Joy Buolamwini: Examining Racial and Gender Bias in Facial Analysis Software," *artsandculture.google.com,* 2019, https://artsandculture.google.com/story/joy-buolamwini-examining-racial-and-gender-bias-in-facial-analysis-software-barbican-centre/BQWBaNKAVWQP-Jg?hl=en (accessed October 27, 2022).

62 "In the case of AI sorting through job applications, finding the words that lead to discrimination is fairly straightforward. However, when AI is analysing faces, it can be much harder to determine which attributes could lead to harmful discrimination." Ibid.

63 This statistic is quoted according to the investigative journalism organization, ProPublica. The software was called the "Correctional Offender Management Profiling for Alternative Sanctions" ("COMPAS"). See Stephen Buranyi, "Rise of the racist robots—how AI is learning all our worst impulses," *The Guardian,* August 8, 2017, https://www.theguardian.com/inequality/2017/aug/08/rise-of-the-racist-robots-how-ai-is-learning-all-our-worst-impulses (accessed October 27, 2022).

64 "If you're not careful, you risk automating the exact same biases these programs are supposed to eliminate," Kristian Lum, quoted in Buranyi 2017 (see note 63). Also see Maurice Chammah, "Policing the Future," The Marshall Project (website), March 2, 2018, https://www.themarshallproject.org/2016/02/03/policing-the-future?ref=hp-2-111#.UyhBLnmlj (accessed October 27, 2022).

65 Ranulph Glanville, "Inside every white box there are two black boxes trying to get

out," *Behavioral Science: Journal of the Society of General Systems Research* 27, no. 1 (January 1982): 1–11, https://doi.org/10.1002/bs.3830270102 (accessed October 27, 2022).

66 This is according to their official biography. "Depending on where you are and on your past search history, googling them could yield their page or a Wikipedia list of American artists, that is to say, a list dominated by white men. Artist, who came of age as the internet did, evades the low-grade surveillance technology of the search engine by using it against itself." See Tiana Reid, "American Artist Shows How Tech Trains Us to See the World as Cops Do," *Art in America,* November 13, 2019, https://www.artnews.com/art-in-america/aia-reviews/american-artist-queens-museum-predictive-policing-60221/ (accessed October 27, 2022).

67 Ibid.

68 See Julie Hoangmy Ho, "Slowing Down to See Black and Blue," *The New York Times,* October 24, 2019, https://www.nytimes.com/2019/10/23/arts/design/american-artist-my-blue-window.html (accessed October 27, 2022).

69 Part of a broader project to draw attention to horrible outcomes delivered by AI models trained on problematic data.

70 One of the most widely used training sets in machine learning research and development.

71 See Kate Crawford and Trevor Paglen, "Excavating AI: The Politics of Images in Machine Learning Training Sets," https://excavating.ai/ (accessed October 27, 2022).

72 Ibid.

73 Ibid.

74 See Cristina Ruiz, "Leading online database to remove 600,000 images after art project reveals its racist bias," *The Art Newspaper,* September 23, 2019, https://www.theartnewspaper.com/2019/09/23/leading-online-database-to-remove-600000-images-after-art-project-reveals-its-racist-bias (accessed October 27, 2022).

75 As described by Alli Shultes, reporting for the BBC, Mechanical Turk "pays workers around the world pennies to perform small, monotonous tasks." See Alli Shultes, "'Racist' AI art warns against bad training data," BBC News (website), September 17, 2019, https://www.bbc.com/news/technology-49726652 (accessed October 27, 2022).

76 Ibid.

77 See the website *Ghost Work,* https:/www.ghostwork.org (accessed October 27, 2022).

78 The ghost in the machine—a worker reduced to a troll.

79 Ruiz 2019 (see note 74).

80 "Toxic degeneration" is now taken as a given in natural language processing (NLP) systems pre-trained on large web corpora. In light of the many human ghosts refracted through the model, the diagnostic language of engineering is not without its own problems: strictly speaking, the AI generates text. The term "degenerate," applied to the generation of unwanted text, is therefore a metaphor—and one with uncomfortable historical resonances. It seems that on both sides of the interface, people are dehumanized. See Samuel Gehman et al., "Real Toxicity Prompts: Evaluating Neural Toxic Degeneration in Language Models." Paper delivered as part of EMNLP 2020: The 2020 Conference on Empirical Methods in Natural Language Processing, online, November 16–20, 2020. https://aclanthology.org/2020.findings-emnlp.301.pdf (accessed October 27, 2022).

81 Simple convolutional neural nets are already as capable of detecting melanoma (malignant skin changes) as experts are. However, skin color information is crucial to this process.

82 Joy Buolamwini and Timnit Gebru, "Gender Shades: Intersectional Accuracy Disparities in Commercial Gender Classification," *Proceedings of Machine Learning Research* 81: Conference on Fairness, Accountability and Transparency (2018): 77–91. https://proceedings.mlr.press/v81/buolamwini18a/buolamwini18a.pdf (accessed October 27, 2022).

83 Harvey 2021 (see note 55).

84 Glanville 2017 (see note 15); emphasis mine.

85 Susan Kozel, "Performing Encryption," in Leeker 2016 (see note 30), p. 118.

86 Ibid.

87 See Hito Steyerl, *How Not to Be Seen: A Fucking Didactic Educational .MOV File* (2013), https://www.artforum.com/video/hito-steyerl-how-not-to-be-seen-a-fucking-didactic-educational-mov-file-2013-51651 (accessed October 27, 2022).

88 See "Trevor Paglen and Jacob Appelbaum: *Autonomy Cube*," e-flux Announcements (website), October 20, 2015, https://www.e-flux.com/announcements/2916/trevor-paglen-and-jacob-appelbaumautono-my-cube/ (accessed October 27, 2022).

89 See "Autonomy Cube," on the artist's website: https://paglen.studio/2020/04/09/autonomy-cube/ (accessed October 27, 2022).

90 An IP address is a unique identifier that tells websites and services exactly who you are online. Concealing and spoofing one's IP address is the cornerstone of private browsing.

91 See "CV Dazzle," on the artist's website: https://ahprojects.com/cvdazzle (accessed October 27, 2022).

92 A popular (at the time of development) and open-source face detector, the "CV" standing for computer vision.

93 Speculating on the evolution of this strategy, Harvey suggests that newer forms of the CV dazzle "could target other algorithms, such as deep convolutional neural networks," for instance, "but would require finding vulnerabilities in these algorithms." (See note 91).

94 *HyperFace* development began in 2013 and was first presented at 33c3 in Hamburg, Germany, on December 30, 2016.

95 Inspired by the lack of multidimensional representations of Black women in technology, the 2017 Sundance Film Festival display proposed a speculative "Afrocentric countersurveillance aesthetic"—offering fashion and cosmetic products, VR experiences, and neurocognitive impact research. The project's core technology was an audio-visual VR experience powered by Unreal Engine 4 game engine software, wherein visitors found themselves within a reimagined Black hair salon, inhabiting a Black woman's body, parsing a possible future of pioneering Black brain research and neuromodulation through the culturally specific ritual of hair care. See the website *Hyphen Labs:* http://www.hyphen-labs.com/nsaf.html (accessed October 27, 2022).

96 They were subsequently employed in public interventions and performances.

97 See Michal Kosinski and Yilun Wang, "Deep neural networks are more accurate than humans at detecting sexual orientation from facial images," *Journal of Personality and Social Psychology* 114, no. 2 (February 2018): 246–57.

98 See "Facial Weaponization Suite," on the artist's website: https://zachblas.info/works/facial-weaponization-suite/ (accessed October 27, 2022).

99 Ibid.

100 For a direct proposal of the machine's distortion of the human, instantiating a "fascist sibling" to the classical visage, it is worth recalling Jon Rafman's series of busts *New Age Demanded* (2013), whose warped faces would appear in the 2014 remake of *RoboCop,* a film about the brutal technical pursuit of law and order.

101 William Blake, "The Letters of William Blake," *Wikisource,* last modified August 30, 2018, https://en.wikisource.org/wiki/Page:The_letters_of_William_Blake_(1906).djvu/175 (accessed October 27, 2022).

102 See Jacques Derrida, "*Fors:* The Anglish Words of Nicholas Abraham and Maria Torok," trans. Barbara Johnson, in Nicholas Abraham and Maria Torok, *The Wolf Man's Magic Word: A Cryptonymy,* trans. Nicholas Rand (Minneapolis and London, 1986), pp. xi–xlviii.

103 Max Haiven, "The Crypt of Art, the Decryption of Money, the Encrypted Common and the Problem with Cryptocurrencies," in Inte Gloerich et al., eds., *Money Lab Reader 2: Overcoming the Hype* (Amsterdam, 2018), p. 130.

104 Ibid.

105 Ibid; emphasis mine.

106 See Nadim Samman, "Errant Curating," *On Curating* 50 (June 2021), pp. 100–110; see also Dehlia Hannah, ed., *A Year Without a Winter* (New York, 2018).

107 Gareth Harris, "Treasure of Lima: A Buried Exhibition—Absurdity or Great Art Adventure?," *Financial Times,* June 13, 2014, https://www.ft.com/content/68c125c6-ed76-11e3-8a1e-00144feabdc0 (accessed October 27, 2022).

108 Eventually, the project would be re-exhibited IRL, *under the table.*

109 Haiven 2018 (see note 103), p. 130; see also Harris 2014 (see note 107).

110 Perhaps this aesthetic even registers the new "right to be forgotten," enshrined in

EU law under the General Protection Data Regulation (GDPR) of 2016. See "Everything you need to know about the 'Right to be forgotten,'" GDPR.EU (website), https://gdpr.eu/right-to-be-forgotten/ (accessed October 27, 2022).

111 Thumfart 2014 (see note 46).

112 Ibid.

113 Ibid.

114 It is well known that contemporary electronic devices are intentionally built to be discarded, their obsolescence clearly planned. See Hertz 2012 (see note 28), p. 176.

Black Hole [pp. 96–137]

1 Anthropocene geography is in-line. See my comments in chapter one on Evan Roth's project *Red Lines*.

2 Staal's stated aim was "to present a vision of the effects of the visual and ideological architecture of the alt-right to a broader audience in order to open spaces and opportunities for critique and resistance." See "Steve Bannon: A Propaganda Retrospective. An exhibition project by Jonas Staal," Het Nieuwe Instituut (website), https://steve-bannon-propaganda-retrospective.hetnieuweinstituut.nl/ (accessed December 6, 2022).

3 The so-called "distributed ledger" of blockchain—a digital system for recording the transaction of assets in which the transactions and their details are recorded in multiple places at the same time. Unlike traditional databases, distributed ledgers have no central datastore or administration functionality.

4 Akshay Chinchalkar, "Crypto Barrels Toward 2022 After Adding $1.5 Trillion in Value," Bloomberg (website), December 20, 2021, https://www.bloomberg.com/news/articles/2021-12-20/cryptocurrencies-and-bitcoin-btc-2021-year-in-charts (accessed December 6, 2022).

5 "The White Paper," Ignota (website), https://ignota.org/products/the-white-paper (accessed December 10, 2022).

6 Domenico Quaranta, *Surfing with Satoshi: Art, Blockchain and NFTs* (Milan, 2022), p. 196.

7 Ibid.

8 For Jesus, see Tobias Huber, "The Prophecy of Satoshi Nakamoto: Bitcoin as Religion," *Bitcoin Magazine,* October 19, 2021, https://bitcoinmagazine.com/culture/bitcoin-as-religion-cult-satoshi (accessed December 7, 2022). For King Arthur, see Sandra Faustino, Inês Faria, and Rafael Marques, "The myths and legends of king Satoshi and the knights of blockchain," *Journal of Cultural Economy* 15, no. 1 (2022): 67–80.

9 Kai Sedgwick, "People Keep Sending Satoshi Nakamoto Bitcoin," Bitcoin.com (website), December 24, 2017, https://news.bitcoin.com/people-keep-sending-satoshi-nakamoto-bitcoin/ (accessed December 7, 2022).

10 "A strong sinew of antisemitism runs through QAnon, with George Soros and the Rothschild family identified as key 'puppet masters' of the conspiracy." David Lawerence and Simone Rafael, "Antisemitism in the Digital Age: Superconspiracies—QAnon and the New World Order," Bell Tower News (website), November 5, 2021, https://www.belltower.news/antisemitism-in-the-digital-age-superconspiracies-qanon-and-the-new-world-order-123567/ (accessed December 7, 2022).

11 Kevin Roose, "What Is QAnon, the Viral Pro-Trump Conspiracy Theory?" *The New York Times,* September 3, 2021, https://www.nytimes.com/article/what-is-qanon.html (accessed January 9, 2023).

12 "Prosumption involves both production and consumption rather than focusing on either one (production) or the other (consumption). While prosumption has always been preeminent, a series of recent social changes, especially those associated with the internet and Web 2.0 (briefly, the user-generated web, e.g. Facebook, YouTube, Twitter), have given it even greater centrality." The phenomenon is "part of a new 'wikinomic' model." George Ritzer and Nathan Jurgenson, "Production, Consumption, Prosumption: The Nature of Capitalism in the Age of the Digital 'Prosumer,'" *Journal of Consumer Culture* 10, no. 1 (March 2010): 13–36.

13 Andrew Nunes, "LARPing Meets Slime-Covered Bedrooms in London, *Vice,* October 14, 2015, https://www.vice.com/en/article/kbnpjz/larping-meets-slime-covered-bedrooms-in-london (accessed December 28, 2022).

14 Ibid.

15 Emily McDermott, "Omsk Social Club Interview," *Arts of the Working Class,* November 18, 2019, https://artsoftheworking-class.org/text/omsk-social-club (accessed January 9, 2023).

16 Ibid.

17 Omsk Social Club, quoted in ibid.

18 Felix Petty, "performing ourselves: revisiting dorm daze with ed fornieles," *i-D,* March 23, 2016, https://i-d.vice.com/en/article/ywvkw5/performing-ourselves-revisiting-dorm-daze-with-ed-fornieles (accessed December 9, 2022).

19 Ibid.

20 Ibid.

21 Ibid.

22 Ibid.

23 Ibid.

24 Mattathias Schwartz, "A Trail of 'Bread Crumbs,' Leading Conspiracy Theorists Into the Wilderness," *The New York Times,* September 11, 2018, https://www.nytimes.com/2018/09/11/magazine/a-trail-of-bread-crumbs-leading-conspiracy-theorists-into-the-wilderness.html (accessed December 10, 2022).

25 Most fully exhibited in the notorious January 6th Capitol insurrection.

26 See "Choose Your Future," on the artist's website: http://joshuacitarella.com/chooseyourfuture/ (accessed December 10, 2022).

27 Ibid.

28 Joshua Citarella, "My Political Journey: G," *Arts of the Working Class,* January 3, 2022, https://artsoftheworkingclass.org/text/my-political-journey-g (accessed December 10, 2022).

29 Ibid.

30 Ibid.

31 Artist's website (see note 26).

32 Icke has proved himself to be an anti-Semite whose endorsement of the *Protocols of the Elders of Zion* led to him being dropped by mainstream publishers.

33 Artist's website (see note 26).

34 Ritzer and Jurgenson 2010 (see note 13), p. 17.

35 According to the Southern Poverty Law Center, Kek, a banner figure for the alt-right, "dwells in that murky area … between satire, irony, mockery, and serious ideology." The god Kek is "a bringer of chaos and darkness, which [happens] to fit perfectly with the alt-right's self-image as being primarily devoted to destroying the existing world order." See David Neiwert, "What the Kek: Explaining the Alt-Right 'Deity' Behind Their 'Meme Magic,'" Southern Poverty Law Centre (website), May 9, 2017, https://www.splcenter.org/hatewatch/2017/05/08/what-kek-explaining-alt-right-deity-behind-their-meme-magic (accessed December 10, 2022).

36 See John Suler, "The Online Disinhibition Effect," *International Journal of Applied Psychoanalytic Studies* 2, no. 2 (June 2005): 184–88.

37 David Gilbert, "QAnon Is Selling NFTs Now," *Vice,* September 21, 2021, https://www.vice.com/en/article/qj8qgq/qanon-ron-watkins-selling-nfts (accessed December 10, 2022).

38 Hito Steyerl, "If You Don't Have Bread, Eat Art!: Contemporary Art and Derivative Fascisms," *e-flux* 76 (October 2016), https://www.e-flux.com/journal/76/69732/if-you-don-t-have-bread-eat-art-contemporary-art-and-derivative-fascisms/ (accessed December 10, 2022).

39 Ibid.

40 Max Haiven, "The Crypt of Art, the Decryption of Money, the Encrypted Common and the Problem with Crypto-currencies," in Inte Gloerich et al., eds., *Money Lab Reader 2: Overcoming the Hype* (Amsterdam, 2018), p. 129.

41 Bernard Marr, "How Much Data Is There In the World?" Bernard Marr & Co. (website), https://bernardmarr.com/how-much-data-is-there-in-the-world/ (accessed December 10, 2021).

42 This holds that, "generically, every singularity that forms as a result of [star] collapse is hidden from view behind an event horizon…. The singularity is always cut off from the external universe." Pankaj S. Joshi and Ramesh Narayan, "Black Hole Paradoxes," *Journal of Physics: Conference Series* 759 (2016), https://iopscience.iop.org/article/10.1088/1742-6596/759/1/012060 (accessed December 9, 2022).

43 The latter results from friction created by materials moving at incredible speed. See "Black hole Markarian 335 has major flare," *Astronomy Now,* October 28, 2015, https://

astronomynow.com/2015/10/28/black-hole-markarian335-has-major-flare/ (accessed December 10, 2022).

44 Stephen Hawking, *A Brief History of Time* (New York, 1988), p. 256.

45 Andrew Fraknoi, David Morrison, and Sidney C. Wolff, *Astronomy* (Houston, 2018), p. 878. Available online, https://assets.openstax.org/oscms-prodcms/media/documents/Astronomy-OP_zItt6LJ.pdf (accessed December 10, 2022).

46 Steyerl 2016 (see note 38).

47 See Luca Bombelli and Esteban Calzetta, "Chaos around a black hole," *Classical and Quantum Gravity* 9, no. 12 (December 1992), https://iopscience.iop.org/article/10.1088/0264-9381/9/12/004 (accessed December 10, 2022).

48 John Earman, *Bangs, Crunches, Whimpers, and Shrieks: Singularities and Acausalities in Relativistic Spacetimes* (Oxford, 1995), pp. 28–31.

49 Jalal Toufic, "A Hitherto Unrecognized Apocalyptic Photographer: The Universe," *e-flux* 55 (May 2014), https://www.e-flux.com/journal/55/60318/a-hitherto-unrecognized-apocalyptic-photographer-the-universe/ (accessed December 10, 2022).

50 Ibid.

51 I recall the X-ray spectrum at the black hole's corona—"colors" that cannot be seen with the naked eye, as their particular range within the electromagnetic spectrum does not fall within the 400 to 700 nanometers that are visible to humans.

52 First shown at the FiDi Arsenale in February 2020, an exhibition staged in a condemned sports bar in downtown Manhattan, curated by Bika Rebek, Matt Shaw, and Collin Clarke.

53 As stated on the artist's Instagram. See "joshuacitarella," Instagram, last modified November 8, 2022, https://www.instagram.com/p/CktO2QIL563 (accessed December 10, 2022).

54 Ibid.

55 Ibid.

56 Ibid.

57 Quaranta 2022 (see note 6), p. 205.

58 Franz Kafka's *Zürau Aphorisms,* number 20, quoted in Peter Sloterdijk, *Bubbles: Spheres I: Microspherology,* trans. Wieland Hoban (Los Angeles, 2011), p. 55. There are various translations available; others substitute the word "ritual" for "ceremony."

59 Arriving at the apex of a steamy art market whose bubbles would pop just one year later, after the presentation of Damien Hirst's taxidermy *The Golden Calf* (2009) at Sotheby's in London, as part of the sale *Beautiful Inside My Head Forever,* on the same night as the collapse of Lehman Brothers on September 16, 2008.

60 Sloterdijk 2011 (see note 58), p. 56.

61 Ibid.

62 Ibid.

63 Lorraine Daston, *Against Nature* (Cambridge, MA, 2019), p. 33.

64 "Specialized and gripping emotional responses to perceived disorders." Ibid., pp. 41–42.

65 One need not buy into Daston's tripartite taxonomy of the passions to find her argument interesting—to the extent that she claims that the formal characteristics of the response indicate the nature concept in play. This is less a case of spotting fake cappuccinos than understanding leopards of varying spots.

66 In Sophocles's play *Oedipus the King,* the riddle "What creature walks on four legs in the morning, two legs at noon, and three in the evening?" is answered by Oedipus, who says, "a man." This maps the human lifecycle: in the morning of life (childhood), the infant crawls on all fours; in the afternoon of life (adulthood), the human being walks upright on two legs; in the evening of life (elderhood), the senior citizen walks with help from a cane.

67 Donna Haraway, *Staying with the Trouble: Making Kin in the Chthulucene* (Durham, NC, 2016), p. 59.

68 CRISPR is a powerful digital tool for editing genomes. See "CRISPR," *New Scientist,* https://www.newscientist.com/definition/what-is-crispr/ (accessed December 22, 2022). See also Desiree Schneider, "The five: chimeras created by science," *The Guardian,* August 11, 2019, https://www.theguardian.com/technology/2019/aug/11/the-five-chimeras-human-monkey-hybrid-genetic (accessed December 22, 2022).

69 In a work titled *Cleopatra—That Goddess* (2014).

70 The reading of Mary Shelley's *Frankenstein* through the Freudian lens of the Oedipus complex is well known. Let us also note that the sphinx poses its riddle to none other than Oedipus in the classic myth.

71 *Staying with the Trouble* is the title of Donna Haraway's book, in which the concept of "sympoiesis" is outlined (see note 67).

72 See "Egor Kraft: Content Aware Studies," ZKM | Center for Art and Media (website), https://zkm.de/en/content-aware-studies (accessed December 10, 2022).

73 See the artist's website: https://www.nora-al-badri.de/works-index (accessed December 28, 2022).

74 Jackie Snow, "These historical artefacts are totally faked," *Wired,* October 24, 2021, https://www.wired.co.uk/article/fake-artefacts-ai (accessed December 28, 2022).

75 Ibid. These two were the Metropolitan Museum of Art in New York, and the Cleveland Museum of Art.

76 Ibid.

77 In tech, jailbreaking "allows [a] device owner to gain full access to the root of the operating system,… freeing users from the 'jail' of limitations." See "What is Jailbreaking—Definition and Explanation," Kaspersky (website), https://www.kaspersky.com/resource-center/definitions/what-is-jailbreaking (accessed December 28, 2022).

78 Yangzi Li, "Does Black-Box Machine Learning Shift the US Fair Use Doctrine?" *Journal of Intellectual Property Law & Practice* 16, no. 11 (2021), https://ssrn.com/abstract=3998805 (accessed January 9, 2023).

79 See Régine Debatty, "Using AI to Question the Power Structures of Western Museums. Interview with Nora Al-Badri," *We Make Money Not Art* (blog), January 20, 2021, https://we-make-money-not-art.com/using-ai-to-question-the-power-structures-of-western-museums-interview-with-nora-al-badri (accessed December 10, 2022).

80 Nora Al-Badri, "Technoheritage. Proposed by Nora Al-Badri," *Open Secret KW,* 2021, https://opensecret.kw-berlin.de/glossary/#letter-T (accessed December 28, 2022).

81 Nora Al-Badri, "The Post-Truth Museum," *Open Secret KW,* August 16, 2021, https://opensecret.kw-berlin.de/essays/the-post-truth-museum (accessed December 28, 2022).

82 Al-Badri 2021 (see note 80).

83 Al-Badri August 16, 2021 (see note 81).

84 Ibid.

85 Ibid.

86 Ibid.

87 Zainab Bahrani, *The Infinite Image: Art, Time and the Aesthetic Dimension in Antiquity* (London, 2014), quoted in ibid.

88 See Joshua Ramey, *The Hermetic Deleuze* (Durham, NC, and London, 2012), p. 33.

89 Ludwig Wittgenstein, *Tractatus Logico-Philosophicus,* trans. C. K. Ogden (London and New York, 1922), p. 23.

90 Clyde Lee Miller, "Cusanus, Nicolaus [Nicolas of Cusa]," *Stanford Encyclopedia of Philosophy* (Winter 2021 edition), http://plato.stanford.edu/entries/cusanus/ (accessed December 10, 2022).

91 Borrowing the concept, it seems, from the fourth-century *Liber XXIV philosophorum,* wherein twenty-four definitions of God are set forth, one of which is "an infinite sphere, whose center is everywhere and whose circumference is nowhere."

92 Ramey 2012 (see note 88), p. 33.

Dark Times [pp. 138–40]

1 Martin Heidegger, *Being and Time,* trans. John Macquarrie and Edward Robinson (Oxford, 1962), p. 157.

2 In 1998 the philosopher Peter Sloterdijk remarked that "current writings about virtual space are just in time to participate in the 2,400-year anniversary of the virtual"—whose origin he identified as the Platonic exposition of the world of ideas. The claim cannot be so quickly dismissed. Peter Sloterdijk, *Bubbles: Spheres I: Microspherology,* trans. Wieland Hoban (Los Angeles, 2011), pp. 66–67.

3 Operating "through unprecedented asymmetries in knowledge," surveillance capitalism pursues a "future [wherein] we are exiles from our own behavior, denied access to or control over knowledge derived from its dispossession." Indeed, its operations are, according to Shoshanna Zuboff, "designed to be unknowable to us." Shoshanna Zuboff, *The Age of Surveillance Capitalism: The Fight for a Human Future at the New Frontier of Power* (New York, 2019), p. 16.

Image Credits

Cover image
Erick Beltrán

p. 11 Photo: William Anders
Courtesy NASA

Black Site [pp. 12–51]

p. 13 © 2000–2023 BE-S Co., Ltd.
pp. 17–18 Courtesy the artist and
Sprüth Magers
p. 21 Courtesy the artist
p. 21 Photo: Joshua Citarella
Courtesy Carroll/Fletcher
p. 26 Courtesy the artist
pp. 28–29 Courtesy the artists
p. 30 Courtesy the artist
p. 33 Courtesy the artist
p. 36 Courtesy the artist
p. 38 Courtesy Metahaven and MIT Press
p. 42 Courtesy the artist
p. 44 © 2000–2023 BE-S Co., Ltd.
p. 46 Courtesy the artist
p. 47 Photo: Brennan Gilmore
p. 49 © Roger Hiorns
Courtesy the artist; Luhring Augustine,
New York; Corvi-Mora, London; Marc Foxx
Gallery, Los Angeles; and Annet Gelink
Gallery, Amsterdam
p. 51 Photo: Jesse Hunniford/MONA
Courtesy Rachofsky Collection Dallas

Black Box [pp. 52–95]

p. 57 Photo: Uwe Walter
Courtesy the artist
p. 61 3D Animations: Iñigo Bilbao /
Filming: Nicolas Torres Correia
Courtesy the artist
p. 65 Courtesy the artist
p. 66 Courtesy the artist
p. 68 Photo: Steve McFarland (Creative
Commons)
p. 68 Photo: Ed Uthman (Creative Commons)
p. 72 Courtesy the artist
pp. 74–75 Photos: Deutsches Hygiene-
Museum Dresden (Creative Commons)
p. 77 Courtesy the artist
p. 80 © Trevor Paglen
Courtesy the artist; Altman Siegel,
San Francisco; and Pace Gallery

p. 82 Courtesy the artist; Andrew Kreps
Gallery, New York; and Esther Schipper,
Berlin/Paris/Seoul
p. 83 Photo: Timo Ohler
Courtesy Trevor Paglen/Jacob Appelbaum;
Metro Pictures, New York; Altman Siegel,
San Francisco
p. 85 Photos: © Adam Harvey
Courtesy the artist
p. 86 Photo: © Hyphen-Labs and
Adam Harvey / hyphen-labs.com
Courtesy the artist and Hyphen-Labs
p. 89 Photo: Chris O'Leary
Courtesy the artist
p. 91 Photos: Julian Charrière, 2014
pp. 93–94 Photos: Melania Dalle Grave
and Agnese Bedini for DSL Studio
Courtesy the artists

Black Hole [pp. 96–137]

pp. 100–101 Courtesy the artists and 22,48 m²
© Aurélien Mole
p. 102 Photo: Nick Ash
Courtesy the artist and Petzel Gallery,
New York
p. 106 Courtesy the artist
p. 107 Courtesy the artist
p. 109 Image: Ute Kraus, 2005; background
image of the Milky Way: Axel Mellinger
(Creative Commons)
p. 114 Courtesy NASA
p. 116 Photo: Melania Dalle Grave for
DSL Studio
Courtesy the artists
p. 117 Courtesy the artist
p. 118 Courtesy the artist
p. 122 Photo: Hugo Glendinning
Courtesy Kunsthalle Basel,
Massimo De Carlo, Perrotin
p. 124 Photos: Julia Andreone and
Stuart Bailes
Courtesy the artist and C L E A R I N G,
New York/Brussels
p. 127 Courtesy the artist
p. 128 Courtesy the artist and
Alexander Levy
p. 129 Courtesy the artist
pp. 132–33 Courtesy the artist

Thanks

Dehlia Hannah, Krist Gruijthuijsen,
Louisa Elderton, Lena Kiessler,
Charles Stankievech, Ala Roushan,
Daniel Barber, Ed Davenport,
Bill Roberts, Julian Charrière,
Leon Kruijswijk, Sofie Krogh
Christensen, Tom McCarthy,
Simon Denny, Christiane Paul,
Trevor Paglen, KW team,
Benita von Maltzahn, Anja Kress,
my family, and all the artists.

Colophon

Author
Nadim Samman

Managing editor
Louisa Elderton

Project management
Fabian Reichel

Copyediting
Bill Roberts

Graphic design
Neil Holt

Typeface
Arnhem

Production
Thomas Lemaître

Reproductions
DLG Graphic, Paris

Printing
Livonia Print, Riga

Paper
Munken Print White Vol. 1.5,
90 g/m²

© 2023 Hatje Cantz Verlag, Berlin,
and the author
© 2023 for the reproduced
works by Nora Al-Badri, Jason
Appelbaum, Tuur van Balen,
Amy Balkin, Zach Blas, Émilie
Brout, Juliana Cerqueira Leite,
Joshua Citarella, Revital Cohen,
Kate Crawford, Simon Denny,
Ed Fornieles, Adam Harvey,
Susanna Hertrich, Marguerite
Humeau, Vladan Joler, Egor Kraft,
Félix Luque Sánchez, Maxime
Marion, Eva and Franco Mattes,
Mary Mattingly, Mimi Ọnụọha,
Trevor Paglen, Davide Quayola,
Jon Rafman, Evan Roth, Charles
Stankievech, and Britta Thie:
the artists

© 2023 for the reproduced works
by Julian Charrière, Roger Hiorns,
Tilman Hornig, Carsten Nicolai,
and Hito Steyerl: VG Bild-Kunst,
Bonn, and the artists

Published by
Hatje Cantz Verlag GmbH
Mommsenstraße 27
10629 Berlin
www.hatjecantz.com
A Ganske Publishing Group
Company

ISBN 978-3-7757-5265-7 (Print)

ISBN 978-3-7757-5267-1 (ePub)

Printed in Latvia

Co-produced with KW Institute
for Contemporary Art

KW Institute for Contemporary
Art is supported by the
Senate Department
for Culture and Europe

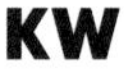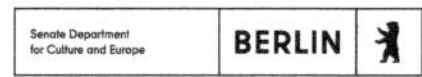